NUMBER 13

New American Review

A Touchstone Book
Published by
Simon and Schuster

Distributed in UK and British Commonwealth
by Secker & Warburg

NEW AMERICAN REVIEW
Editor: Theodore Solotaroff
Managing Editor: Rhoma Paul
Poetry Editor: Richard Howard
Associate Editors: Daniel Moses, Alix Nelson
Assistant to the Editor: Carole Cook

Production Associates: Frank Metz (art), Helen Barrow (design),
Suzanne Frisbie, Susan Edwards, Tom Kieran, Ruth Randall

Cover design by Lawrence Ratzkin

A Touchstone Book
Published by Simon and Schuster
Rockefeller Center, 630 Fifth Avenue
New York, New York 10020

Distributed throughout the United Kingdom, the British
Commonwealth (excluding Canada) and Europe by
Martin Secker & Warburg Limited.

FIRST PRINTING

SBN 671-21111-0 Touchstone paperback edition
Library of Congress Catalog Card Number: 67-27377
Manufactured in the United States of America

The editors invite submissions. Manuscripts will
not be returned unless accompanied
by stamped self-addressed envelope.

Contents

Editor's Notes

THE FIRST THING to say about *NAR 13* is that it introduces the unusual talent of James McCourt.

His story, "Mawrdew Czgowchwz," came to us out of the blue—unsolicited, unagented, unexpected. One day last winter a typical-looking young writer in jeans, bandanna, and beard stopped by and dropped off his manuscript with the modest hope that it might find a home at *NAR,* and if not, that we would make sure there was enough postage on the envelope to return it to him in England. A few weeks went by, then one afternoon I came upon the story, read a few paragraphs, and went into the state of excitement that editors share with fishermen and lovers. It was not only that James McCourt was so gifted, that his tale of this ultimate diva and the New York opera scene of the late 40's was all wit and magic and assurance—"dazzling," as the narrator would say—or that a sophisticated writer of fiction could have such love for his subject, take so much delight in the objects of his imagination.

All of that was on my mind; but what especially moved me was the idea of McCourt—unpublished, unknown, but already so far along, so accomplished and purposeful and distinctive. And he was far from being alone. Work of this quality and freshness had been coming our way for a good while now and, often enough, "over the transom." I felt that a fine new range of possibilities was being spoken for by this abundance. There was already some sense of that in poetry, but it was true now of prose as well, even as the bitching and groaning about the state of fiction ran its usual inattentive course.

Some of these possibilities are borne out in the rest of *NAR 13*: an issue devoted, as it were, to the overflow of talent and new tendencies that, in our view, mark the present literary scene. We have included about ten more writers than we normally do, to make the issue as richly diverse and indicative as possible. We have also scrapped the usual distinction between fiction and essay since the character of much of the prose that appears here belies that distinction, indeed deliberately erases it.

If literary prose shows new energy and scope, it is partly because writers have been releasing it from the leashes of narrative and exposition respectively and letting it run free. Indeed, the very notion of genres seems to be less and less significant in any of the arts. The imagination of alternatives, which is perhaps the central feature of culture today, opens the way for its own modes of dramatization and speculation, for free forms and mixed forms that enable the alternatives to emerge, the potency and multivalence of common experience in an unhinged age to be given their due.

These are abstract propositions, but I believe they quickly fill with content once one begins to read his way through *NAR 13*. Even where the narrative framework seems fairly clear and conventional—as in the contributions by Borges, García Márquez, and Joyce Carol Oates —isn't it true that the purpose of the fable in each case is not so much to tell what can be told but rather to speculate about a dimension of existence that eludes the narration? On the other hand, the pieces by Chatain and Rivera, which might seem to be more or less standard memoirs, are decidedly not, according to their respective authors, to be read as factual, but are rather records of an imagination at play with its memories. In the contributions of Leonard Michaels and Grace Paley, the issues of writing fiction become a paradigm of the complexity of experience and vice versa, while what is imagined and what is not become inextricably mingled. John Haag's "Atlantis on $5.00 a Day" is an extended set of metaphors that turns a small, private chapter of recent social history into an appropriate fable. Gilbert Sorrentino's delicious

(*continued on page 249*)

Mawrdew Czgowchwz

James McCourt

THERE WAS a time (time out of mind) in the eternal progress of "diva-dienst," at that suspensory pause in its career just prior to the advent of what was to be known as "Mawrdolatry," when the cult of Morgana Neri flourished in the hothouse ambience of the Crossroads Cafe, in the shadow of the old *Times* building, across Broadway from the very hotel (a ghostly renovated ruin) where Caruso had sojourned in the great days, whose palmy lobby, once ormolu and velvet, had been transformed into a vast drugstore, and in Caruso's suite a chiropodist had been installed. There at the Crossroads Cafe, November after November (for Neri was a dead-center Scorpio), the great world's concerns were blithely ignored, controverted by endless, ponderous rituals. The rolling electric *Times* sign might proclaim in its career the end of the modern world; *I Neriani,* unbothered, would rant on over the latest Neri triumph at the house, on record, in Paramus, at the Stadium. Neri's opinions on everything and everyone in music were recited by initiates in antiphon over tables littered with clippings, reviews, vile coffee, and majestically autographed glossies of the diva, in black-and-white and in sepia (none of a later vintage than the last year before the war). Neri was considered ageless; her voice deemed eternal. The elders, who could actually speak of the Neri *début,* were revered as prior saints. Tapes of Neri's broadcast performances passed like transcripts of the Orphic mysteries from fool to fool. For many years Neri's record ings outsold those of her every rival at Macy's, at the Disco phile, on Mulberry Street and Mott. With a degree of justification the partisan critic Francobolli could speak of the "seemingly endless Neri Era."

It ended. Time told on Neri, whence the "Neriad" took a turn for the tragic, thought better of the route, and devolved into near-farce. A contretemps absolute in its severity beset *I Neriani*. The walls fell from the fantasy temple of Morgana L'Ultima. Mawrdew Czgowchwz had come to town. Mawrdew Czgowchwz became the diva of the moment and the moment went on. She gave a new meaning to "presence," becoming, as Halcyon Paranoy decreed, "of the moment its life, its persona emblematica, itself." She wedded music to mimicry to create "musicry." She was the definitive diva; she still is.

TIME MAY BE SAID to waste and to lose and to kill; all the rest is precious. One saw truth, heard it in key perhaps three times in one perfect week, then perhaps (like as not) not again for the entire season. One relished, one hoarded the grand moments as the hints of a promise that would leave no "next" in its wake, whence there would be sufficient remembrance. Meanwhile one waited on lines. . . .

Her picture was on every front page that week just prior to the vernal equinox, the full moon, and the earliest Easter there could be. The *Times* allowed the whole of column seven, under a studio photograph of her as Octavian bearing the silver rose:

NEW YORK, March 17—The celebrated "falcon-contralto" Mawrdew Czgowchwz landed last night at midnight from Rome at International Airport to be met by a crowd of some three thousand persons. Miss Czgowchwz arrived here a scant day prior to her first appearance of the season, tonight at the Metropolitan.

Miss Czgowchwz's public feud with the management was settled amicably last weekend in the wake of a hunger strike in which several thousand of her admirers had participated, and which resulted in a two-week sit-down demonstration in front of the opera house on Broadway and 39th Street. Placards proclaimed the strikers' intention to sit out the season unfed. (Miss Czgowchwz acknowledged this tribute last week by singing Mahler's "Kindertotenlieder" from the steps of the Palais Chaillot in Paris.) A settlement has now been reached and Miss Czgowchwz has decreed that "all is forgiven."

In addition the diva has made the startling announcement that she now feels ready to move into a new vocal category, that of the dramatic soprano "d'agilità." In a daring artistic move Miss Czgowchwz will appear tonight for the first time in her career as Violetta in Verdi's *La Traviata*. The performance is completely sold out. Standing room was sold yesterday to five hundred persons out of the thousands who had remained on the sidewalk in weakened condition after their hunger strike. The performance is to be broadcast on the opera network. Last minute negotiations for a telecast are being held through the night.

Continued on Page 73, Column 1

Miss Czgowchwz does not intend however to forsake the realms of the mezzo-soprano repertoire in which she has won triumphant notices in every capital of the Free World. The diva has coined a new category for herself, which she calls the "oltrano." Explaining the move in her press conference at the airport early this morning, she announced: "I am in my fortieth year. I will this year sing forty roles, three times each, here and there." The roles are:

Violetta, in "La Traviata"; Desdemona, in "Otello"; Leonora, in "Il Trovatore"; Azucena, in the same opera; Lady Macbeth, in "Macbeth"; Mistress Quickly, in "Falstaff"; Amneris, in "Aïda"; The Princess of Eboli, in "Don Carlo"; "Norma," the title role; Elvira, in "I Puritani"; Donna Elvira, in "Don Giovanni"; Donna Anna, in the same opera; the Countess in "Le Nozze di Figaro"; Astrafiammante, the Queen of the Night, in "Die Zauberflöte"; Gluck's "Orfeo," the title role; Poppea in "L'Incoronazione di Poppea"; the Marschallin, in "Der Rosenkavalier"; Octavian, the title role in the same opera; "Elektra" and "Salome," the title roles; The Dyer's Wife (Die Färberin), in "Die Frau Ohne Schatten"; Sieglinde, in "Die Walküre"; Brünnhilde, in the same music drama; Elisabeth, in "Tannhäuser"; "Manon" and "Thaïs," the title roles; "Louise," the title role; Dalila, in "Samson et Dalila"; "Carmen," the title role; Cassandra, in "Didon et Aeneas"; Didon, in the same opera (in the same performance); Oberon, in Britten's "A Midsummer Night's Dream"; "Turandot," the title role; Minnie, in "La Fanciulla del West"; Cio-Cio-San, in "Madama Butterfly"; Marie, in Berg's "Wozzeck";

Jocasta, in Stravinsky's "Oedipus Rex"; Emilia Marti, in Janacek's "The Makropoulos Secret"; Leonore, in "Fidelio"; and La Mère Supérieure in Poulenc's "Dialogues des Carmelites."

Miss Czgowchwz currently claims a working range of three octaves and a third, from C below middle C to E-natural in alt, and frankly admits to having three register breaks and four "voices." "One for each season of the year," she explains, "like the air."

Mawrdew Czgowchwz was given police escort to the Plaza Hotel while many of the crowd at the airport marched back. Some went barefoot. At the hotel a mob filled the lobby while the singer was further interviewed and photographed by the press. Early this morning the crowd was dispersed and most of the demonstrators retired to Central Park or sat on the grandstands put up for today's St. Patrick's Day Parade.

Miss Czgowchwz is to be carried from the Plaza to the opera house at noon today in an elaborate sedan chair especially constructed for the occasion by the prominent furniture designer and "decoupagiste" Gaia della Gueza, a close friend of Miss Czgowchwz. A party of cafe society and theater celebrities is expected to join stars of the musical world for lunch at Louis Sherry's restaurant in the opera house, at which time Mawrdew Czgowchwz, oltrano, will discuss her plans in more detail.

Before retiring, Miss Czgowchwz appeared at the window of her tower suite to sing Schubert's "An Die Musik," accompanied by Dame Sybil Farewell-Tarnysh, the renowned British keyboard virtuoso. Her final words were, "Yes, it is good to be back."

That was Czgowchwz, her story, history. But out of it the Czgowchwz people forged differences. They dealt in genres, discovering that tragedy lay in the quotidian depiction of anything (anything gorgeous); that comedy conversely swelled to bursting, in proud dimensions. All the rest, the reportage, was waste.

IT HAD all begun at and in a certain place and time, as Paranoy was to demonstrate in *The Czgowchwz Moment*. But waiting for Czgowchwz was quite outside history; it was the Thirty-fourth day of the thirteenth month, in the fifth season. In the seasons they were to remember, to chronicle the each and every time that she, herself, *stessa*, would mount the boards, made up from assorted paint pots at a table mirror ringed in merciless bulbs ablaze, and heap upon music a variety of disguises, none of which could ever hope to equal or to obscure what she was in her immutable self. So many times Czgowchwz, or Czgowchwz to this or that root or power, was still Czgowchwz, as is the number one; and Czgowchwz over Czgowchwz, like Czgowchwz in an endless hall of electric Czgowchwz mirrors, was but Czgowchwz.

In the late summer of 1947 Ralph had returned from a loft party on lower Seventh Avenue, fed up. Flipping on the predawn FM airwaves, he picked up a transcription of the Midsummer Night Prague Festival Gala. A scant hour later he came ranting through the heat to the front door of a particular brownstone kibbutz on St. Marks Place, under the dogstar, carrying a tape in both hands as if it were alive. He was smoking two cigarettes. None inside had been prepared for the sublime, all being together in bed. It *had* to be heard, he told them all. Gin-milk cocktails and coffee were made while Ralph went on declaring, nearly pleading, which seemed hardly necessary. He had only the last part of it, but it *had* to be heard. (Ralph was and remains the truest of devotees, keeping a recorder plugged into a radio receiver day and night, day in, day out, until the end of time just in case and on the off-chance that anything diverting should fly in from anywhere on earth, and if beyond. . . .) At that moment in time a certain seven first heard together the art and voice of Mawrdew Czgowchwz. What *could* they say?

It was Amneris' Judgment Scene, sung in what one of the seven thought of at the time as "perfect something— vaguely Slavic," with B's to singe the gums and chest tone, as Ralph put it, "for days." Dawn shrieked in through slits in louvered wood shutters as the tape was played a second time. The Gems Spa emporium on Second Avenue was raided for cigarettes a short time later and the tape was played a third time. When Ralph left, at noon, the pact had been drawn up, sealed in tears, and taped: FIND MAWRDEW GORGEOUS!!! (Despairing of ever knowing her name, which the dozey announcer had spelled, but not dared attempt pronouncing, they called her "Gorgeous" and let it go for the time. Time has not changed it.)

They played that first tape at parties for months and got letters off to every management on Fifty-seventh Street, to the Metropolitan, to the Festivals, begging for more (in fraught yet tempered phrases after the fashion of the forties). That same first morning they had composed the first Czgowchwz fan letter, in every language they knew, and had sent it off to Prague.

It happened slowly, but it happened. She sang in Russia, at Omsk in September, at Minsk and Vitebsk in October and November, and in December at Nunidjy-Novograd in what had once been a smallish winter palace. The seven had their reply for the New Year, a letter which hangs framed on Ralph's wall, written in the Cyrillic alphabet, and signed

In early 1948 despair threatened. There was no Czgowchwz news for months. Her seven American friends, all of whom had photostatic copies of the letter nailed to their walls, languished in the cold and uninspired ambience of a late forties New York season. No other person in Gotham seemed to have heard the predawn August broadcast.

IT WAS QUITE SOON thereafter that history took over for a time, cruelly, efficiently, with few stylish flourishes. On the tenth of March, 1948, a person of eminence was thrown or fell from a window in Prague. Prague itself fell directly thereafter. Czgowchwz reacted. The flawless gesture of her crash-landing at dawn on Bastille Day 1948 on the Champs Elysées, after a precarious solo flight in a single engine prewar flying machine was no more to be believed, nor less great art, than her first appearance at the Opéra (the Salle Garnier), singing Amneris in French. It took the rest of the summer to fetch her to America. The Secret Seven met her at the pier at Hoboken, together with the managers, many and various; they took control at the start, teaching her English. (Ignorant as she was at the time of her *true* origin, she seemed to be *remembering*, although in almost anguished reluctance. She spoke English in just three weeks, albeit persisting in her Eastern European intonation. It was thought uncanny, but no more.)

The career blazed. The Carnegie Hall recital, where she sang the *Erwartung* in fully open chest, in tone, tore the lid off. She debuted at the Metropolitan the next week as Amneris, singing it in Czech, on a whim. Luigi Francobolli, in one of the now defunct dailies, proclaimed the next day, with characteristic gush, that "a voice of the size, sweep, impact, and delineation of a flaming angel, projected with the pathos, premonition, and despair of a dying swan was encountered by your correspondent last evening in a debut to sear the mind, obliviating comparisons." Thompson proclaimed himself speechless, and went on gorgeously for three columns. Certain hags in the late afternoon had reservations. On Saturday, Kolnishwasser said: "One could hardly object to her singing it in Czech with capework of such pointed brilliance; a contralto with every difference." (K's summation was of course absolutely sibylline in its prescience . . .)

Those first years began: The Czgowchwz Era. Neri commenced to frazzle; lines were drawn. It was given out that a frantic contralto could never presume to dethrone Neri, "La Serena" (an idle prediction). Czgowchwz went to London, Rome, Bayreuth, Berlin, Milan, Barcelona, Lisbon, Buenos Aires, San Francisco, Chicago, Stockholm, Naples, Venice, Paris, Boston, and returned. Ralph went along; everything she did is on Ralph's tapes. They wept who did, to realize they belonged to someone like Czgowchwz. They saw her in New York on Sundays for tea, sherry, and the rest.

THE FORTIES · ended; the opera house came under new management. A certain presence (it shall be nameless) intervened in glowering dyspeptic manner, to direct and otherwise disrupt the affairs of operatic state. Neri kowtowed, cow that she was; Czgowchwz, mulish, stood her ground, as graciously as she might. Yet eventually the impasse devolved. They fired Czgowchwz by a wire to

Rome where she was in secret recording sessions on a new disc.

The hunger strike began at once, in late February of the year of the Czgowchwz Return. Ralph lost forty pounds. Others ate saltines, matzohs, drank distilled water. The rest boozed, guzzled, and moaned. Carmen stood her ground as always, and Arpenik the Wise and Kind persevered; she kept the best Armenian restaurant in New York going along although she herself would not touch so much as a dollop of ekmek. Gaia della Gueza's being socially prominent and the Countess Madge O'Meaghre Gautier's sudden spontaneous endorsement of the "*causa* Czgowchwz" started a riot of talk as each would arrive by night in mink and sable wraps to sit with the others, munching occasional grapes. Sympathy arrived in headline tributes from the notables about Gotham. Dolores, dead now, was publicly appalled outright, for three weeks, daily, although ignorant of the issues.

On the Tuesday of the strike's second week Ralph received a package on the line; it was postmarked Paris. Opening the box in tremolo, he discovered a loaf of nut bread, a note in the wrappings reading: "*Mangele, bimbo, ti prego!*—M," and the first inscribed studio demo of CZGOWCHWZ SINGS SOPRANO. He passed out. The remaining Secret Seven carted him on the BMT down to St. Marks Place where was heard in New York the first Czgowchwz E-natural *in alt*. The entire record was Czgowchwz, unmistakably, but Czgowchwz in a new register. The voice had thinned to a spearhead shaft on the top; it had opened like the portals of doom at the bottom. It had breaks, or creases, never before heard in any voice. Yet what endured was somehow more *essential* Czgowchwz. "Quintessential Czgowchwz!" Alice screamed. "Definitive in its own right," Paranoy insisted in the April *Opera*. Ralph, revived, lamented: "She wobbles in thirds!" Dixie, defiantly opposed to the transformation that first day, moaned: "She sounds like an Electrolux; the tops are like steel wool!" Others gagged on saltines, and a new era was upon the world, for the better or for doom. . . .

The Secret Seven rode out to International Airport with the nameless fiend who sat mute as stone the way out and the way back. He carried the contract which must yet be signed before the *Traviata* could be sung. On the way back, the Seven nibbled a second nut loaf Czgowchwz had had baked in Paris. She had altered mysteriously. They stood beside her as she flung jonquils down to the assembly, and recorded the "An Die Musik" on Ralph's portable machine. (The jonquils, relics now, came from Max Schling's.) It was gorgeous, as gestures go.

The Secret Seven and the Countess Madge were to have a box. The Countess had had the same one, number seven, for every Czgowchwz performance. The Secret Seven normally stood for other performances, staying faithful to the line, keeping in touch with rumor, its labyrinthine progress toward the inner chamber known variously as "the truth" and "absolute fiction." On occasion one or another of them would drop into the wings or claque for Dalila Rigatoni, or descend into the pit of hell backstage and "super," helping out in small ways. The Countess took a fancy to this last diversion, and she and Alice became the two whores in the window at Lillas Pastia's in every Czgowchwz *Carmen*. The Countess managed to get a coarse horse-laugh in during the "Chanson Bohème" on a broadcast. It's all on Ralph's tapes.

THE MARCH 17th afternoon was chilly. The Irish swept endlessly up Fifth Avenue as if replenished hourly by fresh shiploads of immigrants. The odd-thousand Czgowchwz lot were gathered around the "Czgowchwz fountain" singing a cacophonous mélange of separate favorite aria snatches against the chill wind off the river. The Secret Seven, less Ralph, huddled in a hansom on the far side of Central Park South. Distracted fans with shrieky tendencies encircled the barouche, begging at once for confirmation and denial of hosts of rumors, all of them mutually exclusive, but many too close to certain waters of truth to be answered with anything but knowing sideways glances. Ralph arrived, majestically, the crowd instinctively parting before him, falling this way and that. He climbed into the carriage with customary unbothered aplomb. He directed the driver to circuit the Park, and then proceed to Chez Gautier, leaving the fans to rant as the coach rattled off westward, overfull. All entrances to the hotel were covered against the threat of vulgar display on the part of *I Neriani*.

Gaia della Gueza's chair, *"La sedia Czgowchwz,"* was set in the Palm Court. It was of ormolu, teak, and enamel flame under a canopy of aureate silk. A host of intimates sat on divans and banquets taking ritual tea in Moravian crystal goblets. This elegant horde nibbled salmon and charlotte Russe awaiting the lady of the day who arrived at noon in winter white linen and sheared beaver, her hair plaited in twists, fringes, guiches, and bangs, all titian flame and fabulously wrought.

Racks of spring lamb were turning over Sherry's coals while pots of sour cream and quantities of pilaf sat chilling and steaming respectively. Casks of Sherry's sherry were tapped as the early uglies staggered in to lunch on the Guild. Meanwhile stuffed derma and pastrami washed down with Cel-Ray tonic and seltzer sustained the waiting standees at the long tables of the cafeteria across the street from the old dingy Brewery on Broadway.

Czgowchwz mounted her chair; the selected bearers took their positions. Many fans careened through the revolving doors, revolving again and frantically spilling out and down the smart cold whitewashed steps of the biggest cathouse in Gotham. The Irish straggled on, oblivious. Czgowchwz was carried to the Met in G-G's chair.

Giddy multitudes stormed Bill's Bar to watch the press conference Czgowchwz had scheduled after lunch for three o'clock on the sidewalk with the standees. Only the anticipation of her next great contrivance mattered; the sole virtue was attendance. Feeling was running high among the outlandish who had arrived from fastnesses everywhere, by turnpike, railroad, air, sea, canal, and on foot to storm the heavy doors and stand guard on the fire escapes hanging over the Yankee Renaissance facades on Thirty-ninth and Fortieth streets, Broadway and Seventh Avenue. The Executive Office was barricaded day and night. Police lines—composed entirely of Mott and Mulberry Street Italian rookies humming this or that Verdi-Bellini-Puccini-Ponchielli-Mascagni-Leoncavallo-dalla Piccola tune, glad to a man to be relieved of the Fifth Avenue detail—stood their silent watch and ward in a gay trapezoidal cordon. Protest did not occur.

In the Executive Office the gray eminence, the spider of the Escorial come again, squatted immobile, touching no food, splenetic, belching malodorously, breaking ill winds. Beneath the window the fans jeered encamped while the muted strains of "Ein Heldenleben" beat against the office panes and rebounding, froze into paranoid anguish within. All outdoors were intent on cramming Czgowchwz in, on storing memories of her against the day of wrath. Time howled at the gates in the guise of a near cyclone from Hoboken; the gates held. Paranoy, in the *Czgowchwz Daily Newsletter* declared: "Magody, lysody, hilarody, simody, travesty, mimicry, and mad chicane scatter broadcast on the pavement as Czgowchwz goes before the eyes and ears of the world in fabulous Pathé urgency."

The Secret Seven were on edge. Drinking mulled mead and neat Irish whiskey at the Countess Madge's druidic hearthside, they witnessed the inwrought splendor of the Czgowchwz curbside interview. Ralph, careening elliptically about the oval parlor, ranted: "I can't believe her! I can't be—lieeve her! . . . So I won't." Thrust roughly into an overstuffed *fauteuil,* he lapsed into stunned cataleptic attitudes, gazing in a wildly "nineties" fashion into the blazing turf, listening absently to the frankly sexual moan of the March wind in the tall hollow chimney. That same wind had all but blown Czgowchwz out of her baroque sedan at Forty-second Street outside the Crossroads Cafe. She stood now center-screen, flamboyant in disarray, her hair fallen out in spiral cascades now blowing over her face like something out of the last reel of *A Stolen Life.* Closing the interview, summing up, hinting at the future, all the while she welcomed destiny's career in front of untold numbers through the magical agency of video. Silence blew whispers into forsaken hollow corners all over Gotham as she, in piquant, radiant French, mused: *"Je suis encore tout étourdie. Dans cette carosse d'une vie, c'est mon premier voyage!"* The cameras withdrew; the screens all over town went dark or refocused to pick up the last wan brigades of reeling Irish on Fifth

Avenue. Ralph, overheated, overcome, fell about murmuring, "Could she be?"

It became a question of taste, of what to eschew, of how rare to distill, of a taxing if delicious *épluchage*. In the preserving of certains, day by day, meticulous, fanatic care was of the essence. The Countess Madge O'Meaghre Gautier said it well: "As the pearl is achieved through the stimulus of finely comminuted particles of silicone and is destined to be worn about the soignée necks of some of the better carcasses in town, we take Czgowchwz out of the thrall of time and cultivate a legend." Czgowchwz was all in all, and all the while, a person to be preserved.

A weary odd-thousand maundered in the weirdish twilight outside the opera house after the Czgowchwz interview. Most were ticket holders and/or habitués—hangers-on—used to nothing but waiting, who could not go anywhere else. Yet they lacked that perfection of unity, atonement. They wrangled; they split into factions; they dished. They demonstrated the truth of what Czgowchwz herself had said (in English) watching them one afternoon during her first season: "Two tents don't make a camp; at least not any two tents." They carried on.

The Irish had retired to Yorkville's several cellar watering holes. Alice, feeling in her fertile soul that it had turned suddenly fine and mild (a mirage), rushed the season in singular fashion. As Czgowchwz was carried back to the Plaza in the wake of the St. Patrick's Day Parade, she, Alice, fled the Countess', sped into Max Schling's to buy more baskets of jonquils, and danced in the vanguard of the procession singing the whole of *"Printemps qui commence"* several times through and finishing off with snatches of the Flower Duet and *"Alla stagion' di fior . . ."* Mad others had cleaned out several Woolworths' stocks of orange crepe paper streamers and were covering the length of the green line up Fifth Avenue to the Plaza in this, the emblematic Czgowchwz color. At Fiftieth Street the Scarlet Eminence, doting casually on acolytes in the lessening glow of later afternoon vespers, wondered at the profane fuss outdoors. Workers proffered guttersnipe sagacities here and there as the curious procession went its way unmolested (and untelevised).

At the Ansonia, Neri was in the throes of taking a lesson from the Principessa Oriana Incantevole, the ancient of days, known to be stone deaf since the bombing of Rome. Together they went on with their Marchesi nonetheless. The sun began to set behind Hoboken. At five Czgowchwz went to her bath in mixed spirits, thinking seriously for the first time in her life about Isolde and how to attack The Curse.

AT SEVEN O'CLOCK the floodlights went on outside the Plaza, the opera house, and the Roxy all at once. As hookers hit the big town, Carmen and Annamae were interviewed by CBS, NBC, and ABC as the first ones on line. There were moments in the interim when expectation dealt such austere fatigue that one felt incapable of continuing, and might have crept off to the Roxy were it not for the actual grace of commitment. A coherence was managed *ensemble* for television. At 7:03 Czgowchwz appeared again on the steps of the Plaza and proceeded with the reassembled Secret Seven and a caravan of thirty hansom cabs down Central Park South, down Seventh Avenue and Broadway, past the Roxy throngs and into the glare of the Rialto. Hookers wondered; the mounted police spoke ill. The horde at Fortieth Street went fairly berserk. The minion from the "Talk of the Town" fell into a sewer, which misfortune affected only slightly his exquisite account of the demonstration in the Easter issue. Czgowchwz was safely escorted to her dressing room. She slipped into a black lace Louis Philippe number, was shackled in rubies and coruscée baguettes, meanwhile vocalizing in ascending whirly spirals while a few of the far-gone ticketless beat their heads against the brick wall beneath the window.

Meanwhile, up at Sherry's, they were pouring in. Neri arrived with the Principessa Oriana Incantevole and Rinuccia Bagatelli, that likable drudge whose bovine dispassion and languid tempi were as famous among her detractors as was the rather opulent and even timbre of her instrument among her many immigrant votaries. Neri was grimly, wickedly *"noblesse oblige,"* sipping astringent scarlet Camparis and signing autographs for lame geriatrics, pillars of Society and Culture. In a noisy corner Leah

Lafin and Moe Mohr, twin stars in the bestseller bookworld, were discussing and signing stray copies of, respectively, *The Last Word* and *Having Had*. Dolly Farouche and members of the Broadway circuit were being raucous together on the stairs. Banquo Canolli, Alzira Toscanova, and Zaguina Milanese, with assorted attendants, and Maisie Halloran were at a long table. Margo Channing Sampson and her Bill were obvious. Movie stars, concert stars, opera stars, fallen stars sparkled on and off. "There were," as Paranoy reported, "moments of stillness, and moments of near sin." The standees above and below rattled, enmeshed. The Secret Seven and the Countess Madge moved quietly into their box. At three minutes past eight the lights went down. Many luckless stragglers stumbled outrageously to their seats through thickets of righteous disapproval.

THE OVERTURE rose tier by tier through layers of numb silence. Chiave was in best form. When at

the curtain flew up revealing Mawrdew Czgowchwz downstage center, in profile, flicking open in a stroke a thrillingly outsize fan depicting Paris laying an orange at the feet of Helen, there were twelve minutes of sustained hysteria. She broke the tableau only once. At the nine-minute mark she turned full-face in a flash, raising her eyes to the top tiers. Confetti and flowers rained on the stage. The Alfredo, Turiddu Stameglio, entered jauntily from the wings stage right, picked a single camellia from the dozens at her feet, and placed it, stunningly, in her hair. She beamed delight. There was some fainting, but it was controlled. Members of the chorus, magnetized by instant triumph, concerted lustily. The diva began to sing.

Singular departures from house rules occurred; older, wiser, original gestures reasserted the traditions let go by the boards. The *"Brindisi"-"Libiamo"* was repeated twice. (Had Czgowchwz herself not spoken that same afternoon of Violetta's curious obsessive compulsion for putting off indefinitely the success of moment after moment?) Here she was then, Violetta-Camille, returning to the first flush of the occasion in elliptical vortices. Stameglio was in the perfect bloom of lyric tenor youth. One could see through one's relentless spyglass that Czgowchwz was under great strain; the camellia in her hair had begun to go brown as she fell into the bagnoire divan at *"Oh, qual pallor!"* Her hand mirror caught flickers of spotlight, reflecting eerily through the auditorium. A few thousand eyes hung shut in torpid ecstasy only to fly open again in violent longing. A dead hush fell gratefully during Stameglio's impeccable rendering of the *"Un dì felice . . ."* "The actuality of salty tears did nothing to impair the perfect tonality and ardor of this exemplary artist's plea" (Paranoy, in a reminiscence review of the recording of the performance which appeared underground some weeks later). At long last Mawrdew Czgowchwz was alone on that vast stage facing the unknown in *the* artistic crisis of her career (to date), the tormented finale to Act I of *La Traviata*. Rose Rebus, mezzo, beloved of millions, a household word, was heard to whisper nervously to her companion in the Grand Tier: "Mary, if she brings this off, I'm Galli-Curci!"

At the words *"È strano . . ."* the Countess Madge O'Meaghre Gautier fainted sideways into Ralph's lap. Ralph slapped her face and held on to his glasses. Flowers began to fall again, continuing through the scene, but Czgowchwz mused relentlessly, weaving enchantment.

Bolting from the sofa, silencing the delirious applause at the end of the *"Ah, fors'è lui,"* she let out two *"follie!"* that were "louder and wider than anything heard in Italian opera since Emmy Destinn" (Paranoy, next day in a broadside proclamation distributed everywhere). Shock waves hammered the listening throng. The Principessa

Oriana Incantevole *heard* and fell to her knees in the Neri box raving of miracle cures. The three *gioire's* were each of them bigger than anyone's *ho-yo-to-ho's*. Disbelief, suspended, choked itself and dissolved. Passionate credence swept the audience like a revival conversion. In the Guild Row of the Grand Tier an association director, fattened on production kickbacks, died in his seat unnoticed. Backstage Stameglio had first to be held down then revived for his cue.

The *"Sempre libera"* began; it built. The voice grew; the sides of it fell off, the bottom opened (like the portals of doom), and Czgowchwz soared in flames to B-naturals full-voice. There were involuntary screams, shock upon shock, fresh denials from every tier, but Czgowchwz sped *forza-allegretto*, waltzing in circles until there was to be seen but a single swirl of jet lace pinwheeling in dervish vortices, sustaining a wobble as wide as the proscenium arch. She tore off the baguettes and flung them to the floor like a wanton hysteric at the final *gioir*. There was laughter, a febrile, ghostly cascade of it: the echo of Stameglio's sobbing *"croce e delizia"* from the wings. The final measures were upon her; the penultimate optional E-flat hung fire. She rose higher and wider by turns. The voice seared, shooting out of the whirling smoke of her consumptive waltz. *"Il mio pensier . . . il mio pensier . . . ah . . . ah . . . ah!"* For an instant there was no sound; then something unheard since the creation—a Czgowchwz fortissimo A-natural above high C the color of the core of the sun. Mawrdew Czgowchwz ripped the camellia from her hair which then cascaded over her face like a flaming veil, threw the Baccarat bell goblet against the wall, and collapsed. The gold drapes fell.

She appeared for one solo call during which she knelt amid screams for one half hour while many in the audience were removed to the sidewalks and fell about the pavements. Mawrdew Czgowchwz wept.

THE PERFORMANCE redid history. The *"Dite alla giovine"* seemed to come from a voice within the voice; the *"Amami Alfredo"* from a voice without. The arrival Chez Flora in Act III sent altogether venereal waves of gasping through

the theater as the diva swept down the staircase in vermilion
and jet brocade with awesome mantillas. The *"Alfredo,
Alfredo, di questo cuore . . ."* was so *dolce-piano* that
Stameglio, unrestrained, fell at the Czgowchwz feet and
had to be dragged from the scene. The reading of the
letter in Act IV betrayed in its reverie a Garbo quality
no other actress but Edwige Feuillère has ever shown.

At Violetta's last phrase: *"Rinasce . . . m'agita,"* Neri
was seen running up the aisle in tears, destroyed (having
crawled down to the standing stalls in a daze for the
final scenes). Ralph was running down the same aisle and
nearly broke Neri's leg in the collision. Bagatelli, dethroned,
dissolved. There was universal ecstasy. The performance
ended at midnight. Applause went on in tidal waves for
an hour, reaching a furious peak when they tried to ring
down the asbestos at half-past-twelve. A flock of white
doves was released from the Family Circle. The house
lights stayed on; the electricians mutinied. Czgowchwz
was brought back from her dressing room wearing a
chintz masterpiece by Framboise. The management was
forced to announce that the opera house would remain
open for as long a time as the audience wished to stay.
Relay cameras were rolled in and many of the stars were
interviewed in the lobbies in a you-are-there marathon
which canceled the small hours' showings of *The Great
Lie, Deception,* and *Humoresque* on the box. Czgowchwz
ordered cases of champagne and baskets of blini, fruit,
and cheese. A party was set up onstage in the first-act set.
The musicians stayed on to play waltzes, and later, swing
numbers and torpid third-stream jazz. Czgowchwz, having
changed into a little black dress, danced with everybody.
Art and life were fused. . . .

GRAY DAWN LIGHT, that torment of sleeping soaks, broke
on the horizon as scheduled on that morning after of
mornings after. The Irish pitched and turned one upon
another all over town, like groups of weary sots docking
at Dublin after a night, any night, on the Irish Sea.
In the star dressing room at the opera house, Mawrdew
Czgowchwz, hastily repairing her face in make-do fashion,
glanced out the window to see the first faint shadows on

the sidewalk. They were mopping up at Bill's across the street. On her dressing table lay the predawn edition of the *Times* with an ecstatic front-page review of three acts of her performance. Musing on the relentless, instant processing of gesture into report, she gathered herself to herself and, taking a nosegay of morning glories from a box among the dozens in the room, walked dreamily to the stage. Ordering the huge scenery doors in the Seventh Avenue back wall of the theater opened, she turned to the enchanted throng. The first complete silence since just before midnight fell on the auditorium as the draft swept in. Singing *"L'alba separe della luc'è l'ombra"* with Sybil at the piano, she announced the evening ended. Then, shrouded in chinchilla, she walked without further ceremony out the great wide gap in the opera house wall, and up Seventh Avenue through the all-but-deserted Rialto alone, followed at a distance by her retainers, like a star.

The Arc Inside and Out

A. R. Ammons

I f, whittler and dumper, gross carver
into the shadiest curvings, I took branch
and meat from the stalk of life, threw

away the monies of the treasured
treasurable mind, cleaved memory free
of the instant, if I got right down

shucking off periphery after periphery
to the glassy vague gray parabolas
and swoops of unnailable perception,

would I begin to improve the purity,
would I essentialize out the distilled
form, the glitter-stone that whether

the world comes or goes clicks gleams
and chinks of truth self-making, never
to be shuttered, the face-brilliant core

stone: or if I, amasser, heap shoveler,
depth pumper, took in all springs and
oceans, paramoecia and moons, massive

buttes and summit slants, rooted trunks
and leafages, anthologies of wise words,
schemata, all grasses (including the

tidal *Spartinas*, marginal, salty
broadsweeps) would I finally come on a
suasion, large, fully-informed, restful

scape, turning back in on itself, its
periphery enclosing our system with
its bright dot and allowing in nonparlant

quantities at the edge void, void, and
void, would I then feel plenitude
brought to center and extent, a sweet

easing away of all edge, evil, and surprise:
these two ways to dream! dreaming them's
the bumfuzzlement—the impoverished

diamond, the heterogeneous abundance
starved into oneness: ultimately, either
way, which is our peace, the little

arc-line appears, inside which is nothing,
outside which is nothing—however big,
nothing beyond: however small, nothing

within: neither way to go's to stay, stay
here, the apple an apple with its own hue
or streak, the drink of water, the drink,

the falling into sleep, restfully ever the
falling into sleep, dream, dream, and
every morning the sun comes, the sun.

Down in the Village: A Discourse on Hip

OR,

WATCH OUT FOR THE CYNOSURE

Milton Klonsky

> Our age demands something more: it de-
> mands, if not lofty then at least loud-voiced
> pathos, if not speculation then surely results,
> if not truth then conviction, if not honesty
> then at least affidavits to that effect, if not
> emotion then incessant talk about it. It there-
> fore mints quite a different species of privi-
> leged faces.
>
> —S. Kierkegaard, *The Concept of Irony*

HE MUST HAVE SEEN ME coming a half a block away
at the same time I spotted him, a ? stooped over an !, in
the alcove of a combination Health Food & Head Shop on
8th St. where he had set himself up for the night. No doubt
a panhandler, I figured, but even for the Village *what a
panhandler*. His tall and wiry frame was bent over
what seemed, at first, a kind of pilgrim's staff but was
really, I saw as I came closer, an old mopstick, with a
VOTE FOR BELLA ABZUG shopping bag crammed with his
orts and scraps and other personal garbage at his feet,
which of course were bare, scabbed, and encrusted with
funk, and though it was mid-August he had draped himself in a thick brown army blanket, folded double, with
a hole cut in the center, through which his bald and
knobby peanut-shaped head, festooned beneath with a
beard like Father Time's, poked out balefully and peri-
scopically as he watched me coming toward him, step by
step, staring down as I went at the scuffed-out graffiti

on the sidewalk (ZOOS φυκς AFFERDITE), then over my shoulder (not out of fear, but hoping that someone might come by and pass ahead of me), then off into an inner distance, anything to break the social contract we had sealed with that first exchange of looks, but every time I risked a glance in his direction I felt the needles of his eyes fixed and flashing in mine, it was too late, he knew I knew he knew he had me, glommed, so that I found myself unconsciously slanting toward the edge of the curb, half teetering there, in a hurry now to get past and go free, and almost had it made, I thought, when he abruptly raised and jabbed his stick like a long extended middle finger straight at me, at the same time thrusting out his neck and his jaw as far as the sinews could stretch, and barked: παρακαραττειν το νομισμα—or something like that— but with such rabid and convulsive fury that I jumped, astonished, back off the sidewalk, as if I had just heard a talking dog.

His cachinnations woke up the whole street. From a hallway nearby a junkie, nodding, roused himself from his catatonia for a moment to hold out a cupped hand and burble, "Man . . ." as I went past, shaking my head, but right into a midnight-blue black in a flowered dashiki, with a topiary afro to match, who spread-eagled his arms to stop me, "Brother . . ." so that to dodge him I had to cross over to the other side of the street, where a girl with that blue gaze (*which lies!*) and a privileged face, no doubt no more than sweet sixteen, but already turned rancid, brushed up to me, smiling her mouth, "Sir . . ." and as I shook her off, finished in one blurt, "Spare 'nychange?" and . . .

Where do they all come from? Suddenly one day, one month, one year—I'm not sure which—there they all were, as if spontaneously generated by the times. And that first character, the Cerberean dog who had snarled and barked at me from the alcove, he seemed almost uncanny, an apparition out of the ancient world, and yet in a way the leader of the whole pack. Of all the changes on the Village scene, their appearance nowadays is without doubt the most portentous.

YOU CAN RUN into them at any time along the curbs, an entirely new breed of local *bhikku,* more like bill collectors from society at large than mere beggars. They outnumber the winos from the Bowery and even outhustle the familiar Village clochards who once had the streets to themselves. And with few exceptions they are mainly young, making out from day to day by making do on small change and petty grift because why not. Except for a stash of pot, maybe some acid now and then, and a sufficiency of pills, their needs are minuscule. Accordingly, they travel light, without the usual baggage of the superego (having seen through the foutrescence of it all), refusing not only to provide a good or a service to the community but also to pay their dues, like decent panhandlers, by feigning gratitude or shame. Like Mao's guerrilla fish, they survive in the bottom sea of Village life by mingling with the hoi polloi of heads, dropouts, gynanders & androgynes, bike faggots, orgyasmic groupies, stargazers, shamans & warlocks, apocalyptic utopiates, dinamiteros, tricksters & ponces, radical chicsas, bleeders & draculae, and all the rest. Very few of them can get up the steep rents required to live here; yet they still consider the Village turf their own, as the rightful heirs of bohemia, and cling to it, though the grass may actually be greener and cheaper somewhere else. At the end of the long

—*Man, is this the same shit you laid on me the last time?*
—*No, this is some new shit. This is better shit.*
—*Man, this had better be better shit than the last shit.*
—*You know I wouldn't just shit you, man, this is the best shit around. This is good clean shit.*

Village night they go back (if not to their parental homes) via F train to the dense cloacal slums of Harlem or via crosstown bus to crash pads in the lower intestinal depths of the East Side, where they come from.

Yet as part of a still inchoate international and quasi-religious movement, they might just as well have come from communes on the shores of the Red Sea, by way of Katmandu or Marrakesh or Angkor Wat, after starting out,

perhaps, by smoking the eucharist among cells of true be-
lievers in Dubuque, say, or in the catacombs of Chatta-
nooga, or . . . from anywhere at all, in fact, where the
gospel of the Hip has penetrated—to rearrive by the
usual underground commodius vicus back to Washington
Square and environs, where it's still supposed to be at. *It*
being the Scene, *at* what you make of it. And to swell it,
also coming from all over, like the mendicant hippies, to
do their own numbers, the spear carriers of various Hip-
related causes have made their entrance in recent years.

At the corner of 8th and Sixth outside of Nathan's
Famous—as if the Village had become a freaked-out
Coney Island—there are sometimes a half-dozen different
factions competing for space and decibels: Black Panther
teen-age militants in tennis shoes and leather jackets selling
the party newspaper (*"Check it out, brother! Hip yourself
to the truth. Check it out!"*) mainly to honkie sympathizers;
also, "Legalize Marijuana" martyrs smoking pot in the open
and grabbing passersby off the streets to sign petitions;
also, Women's Lib and Gay Lib activists picketing the
sexists and straight-and-narrows; also, part-time student
anarchists, "Free Palestine" graffiti commandos, Maoists,
and the like, scattering leaflets and shouting their slogans
sometimes a yard apart. And once in a while, to blow
everybody's mind, there arrives a troupe of Hare Krishna
addicts in saffron robes banging cymbals and hopping
about while chanting their mantic chant, "Hare Krishna
Krishna Krishna   Hare Hare . . ." endlessly, with their
own surrealistically pink and earnest mid-American faces,
plain as pie despite the shaved heads and the Indian getup,
contrasting oddly with the crushed, harried municipal-gray
types that hurry on past.

Once again, it goes without saying, hardly any of the
aforementioned weirdos and agitators actually live here.
In fact, even homegrown Village weirdos and agitators
have gradually been forced out and compelled to move
somewhere else. Likewise very few starving artists can
afford to starve here any more.

For what with rent controls and the passage of laws
designating the Village a "national historic area," or whatever, to keep it from being bulldozed by speculators, the

Village has slowly become fossilized instead. Those decrepit old brownstones and sagging townhouses on the side streets, whole rows of them, where the young just starting out or people just making out could live, almost all have now been taken over as private residences by those who have made it or already had it made for them. And even those raunchy walk-up-six-flight tenements and loft buildings, with their communal johns in the hallways and warped and tilted Dr. Caligari walls and floors, but which provided large artists' studios and cheap apartments, have been eviscerated and the hulks chopped up into high-rent cubicles. The facades are the same, but the people behind them are different. Someone once remarked—maybe I did, but it doesn't matter—that the Village, with its unpredictably digressive streets and twisting free-associational byways, was divided from the straight and squared-away world uptown like the ego from the id; but the universal solvent of money on one side, and the adoption of a fashionable Hip style on the other, coming together, have blurred that distinction. Nevertheless, since the facades of the Village have remained the same, like a stage set, anyone who has lived here long enough to have passed through various personal metamorphoses and transfigurations can encounter on almost every street the ghosts of former selves, lost personae, forgotten identities. It is, not to be too analytical, the widespread Village affliction of anamnesis, or *déjà vu*, the feeling that one's past may be lurking about somewhere, psychologically equivalent to the head-swiveling backward-looking tic of people afraid of being mugged by someone coming up behind them. . . . But I digress.

Like the buildings themselves, all those avant-garde and bohemian causes first proclaimed in the Village have also, though keeping their facades, become somewhat fossilized. For instance, now that prudery in the U.S. has been wiped out almost as thoroughly as polio, the erstwhile "sublimation" of sex into vaporous spiritual inanities has been turned about, arsy-versy, by an eqally false "inspissation" of the spirit into mucky sexual inanities. Again, the feminist demands for equality and freedom, put into practice long ago in the Village, have now become the ideological dildoes of Women's Lib. In politics, too, the passionate yet sectarian radicalism that once inspired (and also consumed) a generation of Villagers has come to provide parlor patter for well-to-do ne'er-do-wells and, as staled in the mouths of the somewhat less than New Left, with their mindless and self-righteous sloganizing and

ceduceduceduceduceducedu
ce*duceduceducedu*cedu
ce**duce**duce**duce**duce**duce**du

Know Nothing violence, it has inadvertently pointed the way for any future American fascism. *Also sprach Zarathustra.* In sum, the nonconformist and dissenting spirit of the Village, in art, literature, manners & morals, has by its very success (Marx would have called it a "negation of the negation") resulted in the establishment of a new kind of disestablishmentarian Establishment. (Of which the *Village Voice,* with a circulation of over 150,000, may be said to be the echo.) Yet the facades, naturally, are still the same.

The life-style of the Village since World War II, the Hip, has undergone the same sort of transmogrification. *"Mais où, dîtes-moi, où . . ." sont* the snows and the tourists of yesteryear, who used to come down to the Village with their maps and guidebooks, cameras dangling from their necks, and nudge each other whenever they spotted a typical beatnik or maybe a boheme. They've all gone Hip. ("Yet utter the word Democratic, the word En-Masse.") For with the advent of the Hip as a mass evangelical movement, heralded by all the media, what has emerged is not, as sometimes claimed, a sub- or a counter-, but part of the boss, culture, right now the most booming and successful new stand on the American midway.

Having heard the call at last, thousands of weekend communicants from the square 9-to-5 world out there— people born with corners, but recently turned on and converted—take over the Village scene. They are the same so-called "middle" Americans, members of that "Lonely Crowd" described by sociologists, who, fifty years ago, might have attended church festivities. During the week they are involved in getting and spending, making it in one fashion or another, but the competitive "scrimmage of appetite" and status-seeking that was the mode of life for generations before theirs has lost meaning for them.

Comes the Sabbath, therefore, and as night begins to fall, tourists of all ages, colors, classes, and genders throng through the streets of the Village in long slow peristaltic waves, spilling over the sidewalks into the honking, even slower-moving traffic, going nowhere but anywhere in search of the Way Out, which is the Hip *tao,* the Far Out, past psychedelicatessens offering vibrators, electric dildoes, pot papers, water beds, hubblebubble pipes, Kama-Sutra Oil, black lights, Day-glo decals, phallic candles, stained-glass granny specs (*"Spare 'nychange?"*), and on past gay leather shops, mod schlock shops, rock record shops, past reeking incense carts and reekier pizza parlors, carts selling tacos, souvlaki, organic heroes, Tibetan prayer beads, ankhs, past newsstands stacked with the latest *Stud, Screw, Box, Eat, Flesh, Orgy,* with a pervasive sexual fever, as the night grows late, rising among them, the fairies cruising up and down for trade, girls of all ages alone or in pairs looking for action ("The Female equally with the Male I sing") just as aggressively as the men, pickups and putdowns, swaps and cross-connections being made and unmade all around, here and there a black-white or white-black couple, arm in arm, passing through, yet no one casting a stony glance, and with many in the crowd, obviously, spaced on acid or zomboid on junk, some even lighting up and passing joints around right

—*Man, where do you get this shit? You call this good shit?*
—*Just give the shit a chance, man, don't rush this shit.*

in the open, the smell mingling with all the other reeks and stinks so that no one, not even the cops, knew where it came from, or cared. The scene, after all, belonged to them. So Rome in its time must have been taken over by romanized Goths, Greece by hellenized Romans.

Sometimes the temptation arises to shope me in the

latest Hip shrouds, like Piers the Plowman, with a beard and a fright wig to match, and join that "faire felde ful of folke" . . . but the impulse as quickly fades. It's their scene. And should any long-time Villager—Hip, too, like, but of an older dispensation—happen to be caught abroad in that crowd, maneuvering his way through along the curb with a copy of the *Times* under his arm, he would no doubt appear to them the way tourists in the past had once seemed to him: displaced, cornered, and uptight.

History, as it turns, has a reverse left-handed and ironical spin of its own.

Which leads us back to our first question: *Where do they all come from?* And then another: *How did they all get here?* And finally: *Whence cometh the Hip?* Here follows then, with constant reference to the Village scene, a brief speculative discourse on the history, phenomenology, sociology, and soteriology of the Hip.

To START WITH, take the circle in Washington Square, that inverted mandala ◯ around which generations of Villagers have met and turned each other on. As the consecrated navel of bohemia, it was for them no less hallowed a spot than, say, the omphalos at Delphi for the Greeks or the double ring of menhirs at Stonehenge for the Druids. But this ◯ can also be interpreted as a kind of cryptogram of the Village ethos. Enclosed within its own Hip circle of values, the Village was able to keep its distance from, yet still orient itself ironically toward, the square world outside. But now that the Hip has become a life-style for millions, with an ever more expanding circumference, an almost miraculous presto-chango transvaluation of values has occurred: the Village has been squared within its own circle, or, as they say, blown its cover. . . . Never to be recovered.

The irony in this turnabout, with the Hip being out-hipped, is irony conceived out of and against itself: *for the Hip, as manifested in the Village, is merely the local habitation and the name assumed by irony in our times.*

Kierkegaard, himself an Ur-Hip prophet, saw it coming long ago: "Should a new manifestation of irony appear, it must be insofar as subjectivity asserts itself in a still higher form. It must be subjectivity raised to the second power, a subjectivity of subjectivity, corresponding to reflection on reflection."

The "I²" autistic and anarchist Dadaists around World War One would have been viewed by Kierkegaard as fulfillment of this prophecy. When the French Dadaist Marcel Duchamp, for instance, painted a moustache on the face of the Mona Lisa (who must have been smiling expectantly through the centuries waiting for him to do just that), it was graffiti applied to the face of the entire traditional, i.e. "square," esthetic and moral order she represented, to "*épater les bourgeois,*" as they used to say. Yet even—I mean especially—for the bourgeoisie themselves, that order has now disappeared. No case of a bourgeois being épatéd by art (except perhaps in the Soviet Union) has been reported in the last fifty years. What has taken the place of the established art of the past is, of course, the avant-garde, featuring Dada itself. How then can another moustache, "corresponding to reflection on reflection," be painted on that moustache? Come to think of it, the dadaization of Dada into official culture, enshrined in all the museums, may actually be that Higher Moustache—what Kierkegaard, in another context, must have meant by "the secret trap door through which one is suddenly hurled downward . . . into the infinite nothingness of irony."

Back now to the Village. Shortly after World War II, when the social conditions out of which the Hip emerged were still without form, and void, the prevailing mood was one of disenchantment with the jejune radical politics of the thirties. Of course there were still many faithful Stalinoid and Trotskyite utopiates around in those days, waiting patiently for the first Workers' State

> That enormous self-consuming rat
> That piecemeal nibbles itself fat

to wither away, but most of the Village intelligentsia had finally come to recognize that concentration camps, police terror, bureaucratic censorship, and even murder, of artists, the racial extinction and uprooting of whole peoples, etc., no matter how rationalized by ideologizers, were not what they had meant by "socialism" at all. The "party line" was seen for what it always had been, a "line." During the same period, the now venerable "modernism" that had kept American artists swaddled by Europe began to seem more and more constrictive. The unswaddling occurred with the so-called "Action" or "Abstract Expressionist" painters (centered around the old Cedar Tavern and the San Remo in the Village), through whom Kierkegaard's "subjectivity of subjectivity" was at last realized, and the act itself of painting the painting itself became its own content.

But the chief, if not "onlie," begetter of the Hip in those years, from which it derived both its name and intrinsic features, was jazz. I mean the "cool," oblique, and involuted jazz of the late forties and early fifties, as often cacophonous as lyrical, sometimes called "bop," conceived by Charlie Parker, Dizzy, Monk, Mingus, Miles, Coltrane, and many others not so well known. In the uptown as well as Village dives where they appeared, they came on more like a conspiracy of soliloquists than a band of "mere" musicians. The subtle and complex interiors and angles of refraction of this new jazz gave the emergent Hip its mirror image. And along with it, in the roles of performers, hangers-on, or dealers, there entered the Village scene a much larger and distinctive caste of uptown blacks (known as Negroes in those days or, if the personal coefficients worked out, spades), but all nephews of Uncle X, who brought with them—new at the time—heroin, as well as an easy supply of grass. Their cultivated "cool" —similar to the classic Greek *ataraxia*—was a practical virtue, enabling them to maintain grace under pressure of a hostile white society. For they had to remove, by whatever solvent, a stain on the psyche deep-dyed by generations of slavery and near-slavery: the black original sin of being black. Going for them, too, was an elaborately ritualized Aesopian jive, irony employed as a verbal screen, by which they could manage to remain within and yet apart from the ofay culture.

That jive, of course, has now become the *lingua franca* of the young, black and white, throughout the U.S., and so no longer Hip but square. But the intent of those original bop hipsters was no different from what the late Joe Gould, years ago, discerned as the real motive behind the boost in the subway fare from a nickel to a dime: "To keep out the hoi polloi"; and was certainly no worse, either, than what snobs and pedants intend when they create their own apartheid by quoting Greek and Latin tags.

So then, to condense this chronicle (brief enough to be printed small on one side of a strip of ZigZag): by the mid-fifties in the Village the Hip style had already been formed—*adoxia,* contempt for public opinion, whether in politics or art; *anaideia,* a profound "jemenfoutiste," or Fuck You, attitude in matters of sex, drugs, living habits, morality in general; and *adiaphoron,* a cultivated indifference to the social hangups of race, religion, status, money, etc. By the mid-fifties, too, the first psychedelic drugs, peyote and, somewhat later, LSD, appeared behind drawn shades; and to provide atmospheric cover for the sunbursts of illumination and/or hallucination imploded by these drugs, such native as well as Far Eastern esoterica as Zen, yoga, vedanta, tantric Buddhism, ESP, astrology, shamanism, and the like, found many converts. The Village scene, too, was transplanted onto college campuses, among faculty as well as students, with large colonies of the Hip in Chicago and San Francisco. Grass, tea, shit, boo, fu, hemp, birdseed . . . name your metonymy, was by now become the foison o' the glebe—and, incidentally, as an absurd cultural byproduct of the immigration of Puerto Ricans into New York, the tag for the stuff became affixed as "pot," after the Spanish *potiguaya,* meaning the crude, unstrained weed with its twigs and seeds. It had been Herbert Hoover, after all, who had warned as far back as 1932 that grass

—*Man, do you really get high on this shit? This shit's got no wings, man.*
—*Man, even if you can't get high on this shit, it'll at least turn you sideways. I mean, get lost.*

would grow in the city streets if Roosevelt were elected; and he was right; but he couldn't have foreseen that it would also spread to the previously lush suburbs . . . and so throughout middle America. And wherever there's grass, the Hip way of life is sure to follow.

Notwithstanding, there was a low-barometric dead calm of boredom during those late Eisenhower years of the sort that precedes social hurricanes and private hysteria.

When it hit the fan, finally, the newborn yawp of the Beat movement was heard across the land, then further amplified by a responsive bleat in all the media. Not too long after, Timothy Leary's Transcendental Medicine Show arrived on the scene, which by now was the American big-time, promoting Instant Hallelujah Cubes for the suffering masses under the slogan: "Tune in! Turn on! Drop out!" To millions of the young and not so young, yoked to treadmill jobs or stuck in the adolescent detention camps of high schools and schools of higher learning, it was a call to freedom and self-fulfillment. There followed, as we know, a mass conversion.

Since jazz had become both too far-out and too hermetic, as if grudging the intrusion of an audience, the gospel that suited these new converts best was rock, with its free-for-all revivalist enthusiasm. Much more was involved, however, than merely a generational shift in taste. The "cool" and ironic suspension of disbelief by the old Hip, tolerating your truth, his truth, my truth, everybody's true truth, was replaced by the clairvoyant certainties of acid and the instantaneous soap-bubble absolutes of pot. This also permitted the neo-Hip to take up a variety of social causes (including the cause of the Hip itself) with the fanatic self-righteousness and eagerness for martyrdom of a church militant.

The entire movement that originated in the Village has thus been split into what might be called a hinayana ◯ and a ◯ mahayana Hippism, with the Lesser Vehicle as doctrinally pure as ever because free from all doctrine, though now somewhat creaky and running down, and the Greater still gathering converts and momentum along the moebius curve of the seventies . . .

. . . WHICH IS A CURVE that twists backward on itself. For having taken Kierkegaard's concept of irony, in its latest avatar as the Hip, right up to the present, we now have to turn back, along the same curve, to the very source of irony among the Greeks of the fourth century B.C. And

when we do so, peering at them reflectively as through the
wrong end of a telescope until they dwindle in the mind,
dwindle and diminish into minikins, diminikins . . . we also
must do a double-take, for there *we* are, as large as life!

What I mean is that the ironic style had social consequences for the Greeks similar to our own, resulting in a
"proto-Hip" movement throughout the ancient world.

As the chief exemplar and master there stands the
baffling figure of Socrates. Since his very existence was
grounded in irony, he is as difficult to perceive in himself
(Kierkegaard well knew) as "to depict an elf wearing a hat
that renders him invisible." Of course this is not the
noble drag-queen Socrates ventriloquized by Plato in his
dialogues, too Good to be True (or Beautiful), but the
cranky, bibulous, henpecked and argumentative old lay-
about of Athens, the ironical Socrates, who confessed his
ignorance so as to confound the wise, and under the pretense of being taught, taught others. He deliberately went
about Athens seeking philosophical arguments with the
Sophists and other pretenders to the truth, making himself
a pain in the ass of hypocrisy and pomposity; and very
often, as one of his biographers relates, "he was treated
with great violence and beaten, and pulled about, and
laughed at and ridiculed by the multitude. But he bore all
this with great equanimity." The "dialectical method" (so
called) employed by Socrates in these street debates with
the Sophists, proceeding through paradox and antithesis
back to the *a priori* grounds of their beliefs, which then
gave way, to leave them dangling on the reversed hook
of his ¿, was meant as much to conceal as to reveal his
own thoughts. His irony was thus conceived by him as a
stratagem by which to bypass the mind's printed circuits
of rehearsed responses and acceptable ideas. It was, in the
old Hip word, "down."

Kierkegaard described it as "infinite absolute negativity,"
and explains: "It is negativity because it only negates; it
is infinite because it negates not this or that phenomenon
but the totality of the present age; and it is absolute because it negates by virtue of a higher [i.e., future] actuality
which is not." For the sake of freedom, but a negative
freedom, Kierkegaard adds, the Socratic ironist refuses to

cast himself in any other role than that of spectator, pre-
ferring even boredom—"this eternity void of content, this
bliss without enjoyment, this superficial profundity, this
hungry satiety"—to taking an active part in the world's farce.

When he was brought to trial for his life, as an enemy
of the Athenian democracy, he explained his apolitical
attitude (as set down by Plato in *The Defence*):

> I go round privately thrusting my advice on everybody
> and you may well wonder why I do not take my place
> on the speakers' platform and offer it to the *polis*. I
> have often told you why. It is due to the divine voice
> that has attended on me since I was a boy. This is a
> voice that never prompts me to do anything, but only
> forbids. It orders me not to engage in politics and I have
> nothing but gratitude for its advice. Well you know,
> Men of Athens, that if I had meddled in politics before
> now, I should have been dead and of no use to you or
> to myself.

And yet he was executed for his nonparticipation as
well as if he had engaged in plotting against the state.
When his wife said to him, "You die undeservedly," he is
supposed to have answered, "Would you then have me
deserve death?" Socrates, who was a stone-cutter by trade
(some say a slave), *prided* himself upon the simplicity of
his life, went about barefoot in a torn, ill-fitting leather
coat, and used to say that those who require the fewest
things are nearest to the gods.

UPON THE DEATH of Socrates in 399 B.C., one of his closest
disciples, an Athenian rhetorician named Antisthenes, determined to put into practice the preachments of the
master by living as a mendicant philosopher, indifferent
to external circumstances and public opinion. He used to
lecture, it is said, near a gymnasium called Cynosargus,
as a result of which his adherents became known as Cynics
(literally, "dogs" or "snarlers"), meant to be pejorative,
as "beatniks" and "hippies" in our own day. He himself
was tagged with the opprobrious nickname of Haplocyon
("downright dog"). Antisthenes chose to go about Athens
dirty and barefoot, let his hair and beard grow long, and

dressed winter and summer in a ragged double-folded cloak, under which he wore nothing at all, as if to show his contempt for appearances. (Once, while Socrates was still alive, Antisthenes turned a rent in his cloak outside, and Socrates is said to have remarked: "I see your vanity through the hole in your cloak.") With the addition of a walking staff and a sack to contain food and other necessities, Antisthenes' costume became the standard garb for all the Cynics. Again following the lead of their master, they went out of their way to offend and outrage convention by the use of scatological language and by defecating, masturbating, and copulating in public.

The immediate predecessors of the Cynics were itinerant and mendicant Orphic preachers, who taught that there was a blessed life after death in which all the world's wrongs would be righted; but Antisthenes inverted their doctrine, claiming that only in this world, because it was the only world, were justice and happiness possible. He advocated a return to a state of nature, without shams and hypocrisies, and the reduction of desire, ambition, pleasure, love of others as well as of possessions to a point of extinction. Antisthenes also taught the inherent equality of men and women—as, for that matter, of all classes and races of human beings—and called for the creation of a world state, or rather, non-state (coining the word *Kosmopolis*), where there would be neither ruler nor ruled. As the greatest of all blessings, he named freedom; for which reason he also chose Hercules as patron saint of the Cynics, for Hercules was a mortal who had lived without constraints and had risen to be a god by his own efforts.

It was not the founder, however, but a later disciple, the celebrated Diogenes, who became in the world's eyes the cynosure (there it is) of the Cynic movement.

Diogenes was whelped in the Milesian colony of Sinope on the Euxine Sea, an important trading center at the time between Greece and the Near and Far East. He must therefore have early become acquainted by means of travelers passing through Sinope with the religious teachings of the Magi of Babylonia and the Hindu gymnosophists of India. His father was a money-changer; and there is a disputed story that Diogenes during his youth became involved in a conspiracy to adulterate the currency of Greece. After consulting the Delphic oracle for advice on whether to continue in this fraud, he was seemingly encouraged to do so; but Diogenes did not comprehend that the oracle was really advising him to alter the *customs* of Greece, since the word νομισμα is ambiguous, meaning both "coinage" and "customs." This Delphic utterance was later adopted as the slogan of the Cynics: παραχαραττειν το νομισμα ("Change the Currency," or, "Revaluate Values").

For his crime as a forger, Diogenes was banished and sold into slavery, becoming the property of an Athenian named Xeniades. His pride was such that when he was put on the block, and the auctioneer asked him what he could do, Diogenes answered, "Govern men—give notice that if anyone wants to purchase a master, there is a master here for him." Transported to Athens, he served as a tutor in Xeniades' household for a number of years, after which he was given his freedom. He soon attached himself to the Cynics surrounding Antisthenes, becoming the most noted of all upon the death of the leader in 371 B.C.

Two tales concerning Diogenes have become legendary: first, that he made his home in a barrel (like John Q. Taxpayer in American cartoons) and took it with him wherever he went; and second, that he walked through the streets of Athens in broad daylight with a lit candle looking for an honest man. But it doesn't seem likely that the Cynic who tried to reduce his needs to nullity would have wasted a candle on such a (to him) hopeless quest; and as for the barrel, it was really a large wine jar, an idea that came to him, so he said, when he observed a snail carrying its shell around. Diogenes even gave up eating off a plate in favor of a hollowed-out loaf of bread, also threw away his bowl when he realized he could drink water out of his cupped hands. In order to inure himself against hardship, during the summer he would roll naked in the hot sands, during the winter embrace marble pillars covered with ice and snow. Once he was seen begging alms from a statue, and when asked why, replied, "To get into practice in being refused." He visited whorehouses to wrangle with the whores, hoping in this way both to sharpen his tongue and learn how to bear insults without

losing his *ataraxia*. Once when he was mocked by the people for having been sold into slavery as a forger by his
native city, he said, "The people of Sinope condemned
me to banishment, but I condemned them to be themselves
and to remain where they were." Another time, when he
was seen going into a theater while everyone was coming
out, and was asked why, replied, "It is what I have been
doing all my life." One day as he was squatting down in
the marketplace to eat his mess of leftovers, and several
bystanders reviled him by calling out "Dog!" he retorted,
"It is you who are the dogs for standing around and
drooling while I am at dinner."

Diogenes felt no shame or impropriety in stealing from
temples dedicated to the gods (just as hippies nowadays
rip off department stores and credit card agencies), arguing
as follows: "Everything belongs to the gods; wise men
are the friends of the gods; and all things are shared
among friends. Therefore, everything belongs to wise men."
He repeatedly declared that an easy life had been given
to men by the gods, but that they had spoiled it by seeking for luxuries and pleasures. By indolence and apathy
the Cynic could display his indifference toward society,
for he felt that to engage in trade or manual labor would
be to lose caste; on the contrary, as a philosopher he considered himself at least the equal of emperors and kings.
When in need of money for food, so that he had to go out
and panhandle along the curbs of Athens, he said that he
was merely reclaiming what belonged to him, not begging.
He took immediate advantage of whatever place was convenient, whether public gardens or the porticoes of temples
or the colonnades of state buildings, to sleep in or to
answer a call of nature, asserting that "the Athenians had
built him a place in which to live."

Diogenes apparently had no sexual needs, and would
lecture anyone who cared to listen that copulation was the
business of those who had nothing better to do, citing
with approval the opinion of the philosopher Democritus
that "Orgasm is merely a slight attack of apoplexy." Yet
he also held that marriage as an institution should be
nullified and all women be possessed in common, with the
children of such unions becoming the responsibility of so-

ciety at large. And . . . so forth.

Finally, Diogenes made this boast: "I have vanquished poverty, exile, disrepute; yea, and anger, pain, desire, fear and the most redoubtable beast of all, treacherous and cowardly, I mean pleasure. All alike have succumbed to her . . . all, that is, save myself."

Most of the Cynics, however, were not opposed to pleasure, sexual or otherwise, merely the excessive pursuit of it; and no doubt would have approved of the present drug culture for the immediacy of the satisfactions it offers. Diogenes' bone-dry asceticism was a function of his own personality.

When Plato, who lived in Athens at the same time, was asked to characterize Diogenes, he replied, "That man is Socrates—gone mad." A statement of which Kierkegaard (though for some reason, the Great Dane never gave the Cynics their due as the heirs of Socrates) would have approved, for he perceived that the ultimate effect of the Socratic irony would be to "reinforce vanity in its vanity and render madness more mad." Diogenes himself used to say that most men were within a finger's breadth of being mad; for, he argued, if anyone were to walk through the streets of Athens while stretching out his middle finger he would be considered mad, yet if it were his forefinger, no one would pay any mind. On one occasion, when he was asked, "What sort of man, O Diogenes, do you think Socrates?" he replied, "A madman," thereby turning the tables on Plato through his own master. What he meant was a higher madness, a condign madness, so to speak, suited to a mad world. All metaphysical speculation on the ultimate nature of reality he ridiculed as a symptom of this madness, akin to the endless cupidity of misers and the insatiable ambition of kings. Once, while Plato was discoursing at a banquet on his Ideas, and using the terms "tableness" and "cupness," Diogenes interrupted, "I, O Plato, see a table and a cup, but I see no 'tableness' or 'cupness'"; and another time, to refute Plato's definition, "Man is a featherless biped," he plucked a chicken and brought it into the Academy, saying, "This is Plato's man," then added to the definition, ". . . with broad flat nails." He loved to play the yippie clown.

The life of Diogenes (412–323) and that of Alexander the Great (356–323) were regarded by their contemporaries as mirror opposites: the anti-hero and the hero, slave and emperor, the old man who had reduced desires to nothingness and the youthful conqueror of the world who wept that there were no new worlds to conquer. It was Diogenes' claim that he enjoyed life in his wine jar as much as any king in his palace. And Alexander seemed to agree, for when asked at one time who he would rather be, other than himself, he answered, "Diogenes." According to tradition (or to the myth engendered by their contrast), Diogenes and Alexander died on the same day of the same year.

A meeting between them actually took place in Corinth, in 336 B.C., when Diogenes lay sprawled out in the market-place, basking in the sun. Alexander, who had just taken the city, saw him there and left his entourage to stand beside him, saying:

"I am Alexander, the great king."

"And I am Diogenes the dog."

"Why are you called a dog?"

"Because I fawn upon those who give me anything, bark at those who give me nothing, bite those who annoy me."

"Then ask any favor you wish."

"Cease to shade me from the sun."

This incident occurred during the first year of Alexander's reign, when he was only 22 years old; but ten years later, after the battle of the Hydaspes had opened up the whole of northern India and the Punjab to his armies, the astonished emperor encountered what must have seemed like hundreds of carbon-copy Diogeneses baked black in the sun, "a people" (Alexander wrote in a dispatch) "professing a rigid and austere philosophy, yet even more frugal than Diogenes, since they go altogether naked." These were the gymnosophists (literally, "naked philosophers") whose religious ideas Diogenes had encountered as a youth in Sinope. Quite possibly, too, Alexander and his armies might also have met with monks worshipping the Buddha, whose "Fire Sermon," preached 150 years or so earlier, was the ultimate expression of salvation through renunciation:

Everything, Bhikkus, is on fire. . . . The eye is on fire, the visible is on fire, the knowledge of the visible is on fire, the contact with the visible is on fire, the feeling which arises from the contact with the visible is on fire, be it pleasure, be it pain, be it neither pleasure nor pain. By what fire is it kindled? By the fire of lust, by the fire of hate, by the fire of delusion it is kindled, by birth age death pain lamentation sorrow grief despair it is kindled. . . .

Knowing this, Bhikkus, the wise man . . . becomes weary of the eye, he becomes weary of the visible, he becomes weary of the knowledge of the visible, he becomes weary of the contact of the visible, he becomes weary of the feeling which arises from the contact of the visible, be it pleasure, be it pain, be it neither pleasure nor pain. He becomes weary of the ear: pain. He becomes weary of the nose: pain. He becomes weary of the tongue: pain. He becomes weary of the body: pain. He becomes weary of the mind: pain.

When he is weary of these things, he becomes empty of desire. When he is empty of desire, he becomes free. When he is free he knows that he is free, that rebirth is at an end, that virtue is accomplished, that duty is done, and that there is no more returning to this world.

Upon the homecoming of Alexander's soldiers to Greece, the ascetic religious values they had absorbed and brought back gained currency—or rather, as the Cynics kept insisting, changed it—throughout the empire. The great majority of the Cynics and their supporters were drawn from the lowest classes, the slaves, outcasts, beggars, and also from among the women. From out of the same social matrix, centuries later, emerged the congregations of the primitive Christian churches. The monks and anchorites who fled from the declining Roman civilization into the wilderness were actually late heirs of the Cynics. The Cynic movement itself endured far into classical times, a familiar part of the Roman scene as it had been of the Greek . . . and is now, under another incarnation, part of our own. The Emperor Julian (the Apostate), as late—or as early—as the fourth century A.D., said of it: "Cynicism seems to be in some ways a universal philosophy, and the most natural." But it also seems to erupt most dramatically when the currency of values with which people spend their lives has been altered, and devalued, not by themselves but by historical forces beyond their control. Kierkegaard again: "For the ironic subject the given actuality has completely lost its validity; it has become for him an imperfect form which everywhere constrains. He does not possess the new, however, he only knows the present does not correspond to the idea of this future."

The death of Diogenes, when he was close to 90, befitted a man who had preached self-denial and renunciation: he simply held his breath until he was suffocated. The Corinthians are said to have erected over his grave a pillar, surmounted by a dog carved in Parian marble. Shortly before his end, he had asked to be buried on his face; and when asked why, replied, "Because in a while, everything will be turned upside down." And so it was, and many times thereafter. While he lived, however, Diogenes placed his own ! under the Socratic ?, depending his very being on it . . .

. . . WHICH IS WHERE I came in. *Where was I?* I was standing on the corner, about to step off the curb, when I suddenly remembered—*of course!*—and turned back, half running, as if late for some urgent appointment. It was one of those Village nights, after 4 A.M., when all the bars are closed, and only junkies, footpads, prowlers, muggers, and other hobgoblins seem to be abroad. Even the shadows throw their own shadowier shadows. I kept close to the curb, head down, in a hurry to get there.

At the combination Health Food & Head Shop where I had first seen him—how long ago was that?—I peered, even sniffed, around the alcove for his spoor, but he had vanished. Maybe the cops had grabbed him, I thought, maybe . . . *the park!* Where else? If he were anywhere, that's where.

Up to the corner and then down Fifth, at a lope, I passed under the Arch and then went straight to the stone circle. Except for a low moon, skulking behind clouds, there was hardly enough light to see by; but I went carefully around the rim clockwise, then counterclockwise, then clockwise again, looking into every possible nook.

Nothing. Reluctantly, still unsatisfied, I walked away, turning to glance back a couple of times.

At the base of the herm erected to Alexander P. Holley, three compacted shadows lay sprawled, an empty wine bottle poking out of a brown paper bag on the ground beside them. One of them, seeing me, roused himself and called, "Hey! Brother, c'mere . . ." and when I didn't, got up and took after me, touching my elbow. "C'mon, man, you c'n spare me some change. I'm your brother."

This time I dug into my pocket, but all I could come up with was a nickel, covered with lint, and a penny, which I then placed in his palm. Cupped there, pinched between thumb and forefinger, I could see a lit "roach" glowing like a small red third eye.

"That's it," I said. "Sorry, but all I've got else is just bills."

"Gimme a dollar, man," he told me, then pulled out a handful of coins, "and I'll change it."

Some vaguely amorphous recollection, like the contents of a bowl of oatmeal flung out and caught in midair by a circumference, momentarily passed through my mind.

"No, man," I said, dodging around him, and away.

He looked at the nickel and the penny I had given him once more, as if he couldn't believe it, then took a deep drag on his "roach," blowing out sound through the smoke, "Sh . . . sh . . . sh . . . sh . . . sh . . . sh . . . sh . . . sh . . . sh . . ." his stercoral ejaculations finally suspired in one long dieresis, "Shhhhhhhh*eeeeeeeeeeeeeeeeeee*it, man! What kinda shit is 'at?"

I heard a thunk, then a clink, as he threw the coins after me.

Down 4th St., on my way home, I went by the Maoist Peace Church—once a real honest-to-god church—in the middle of the block, then stopped, went back, and took a good look. There he was, all right, in the rear portico, laid out flat on his back in the shadows, with only his horny feet protruding into the open. The mopstick was stuck straight up into the shopping bag beside him. He seemed dead to the world . . . but was surely just asleep, like Dionysus, for the time being. Once his big left toe twitched, barely, either in blessing or derision, maybe both.

The Rabbit Fights for His Life
The Leopard Eats Lunch

C. K. Williams

for Harvey Finkle

WHAT if the revolution comes and I'm in it and my job
is to murder a child accidentally
or afterwards to get rid of the policemen?
I had a milkshake last week with a policeman
we talked about his payraise it eats shit
he told me what if I have that one? SAVAGE
the baby was easy
the baby went up in thin air
I remembered in Dostoevsky where they talked
about whether it would all be worth the death of one child
and you decided yes or no according to your character
my character
is how he got back in his car
like a tired businessman and listened to the radio
for a few minutes
and waved
is having to lug him everywhere
I go because I can't take him to his wife crying like this
the children have learned to throw their arms around you
without meaning it to kiss you without feeling it
to know there is something marvelous
and not pay attention
in order to say any of this at all to you
I have made myself up like somebody
in a novel
in order not
to go out of my mind I make it I can only do two things
hold you
bury you

Yours

I'D LIKE every girl in the world to have a poem of her own
I've written for her I don't even want to make love to them
    all anymore
just write things your body makes me delirious your face
    enchants me
you are a wonder of soul spirit intelligence one for every
    one
and then the men I don't care whether I can still beat them
    all
them too a poem for them how many?
seeing you go through woods like part of the woods seeing
    you play piano
seeing you hold your child in your tender devastating hands
and of course the children too little poems they could sing
    or dance to
this is our jumping game this our seeing game our holding
    each other
even the presidents with all their death the congressmen
    and judges
I'd give them something
they would hold awed to their chests as their proudest life
    thing
somebody walking along a road where there's no city would
    look up
and see his poem coming down like a feather out of nowhere
or on the assembly line new instructions a voice sweet as
    lunchtime
or she would turn over a stone by the fire and if she couldn't
    read
it would sing to her in her body
listen! everyone! you have your own poem now
it's yours as much as your heart as much as your own life is
you can do things to it shine it up iron it dress it in doll
    clothes

o men! o people! please stop how it's happening now please
I'm working as fast as I can I can't stop to use periods
sometimes I draw straight lines on the page because the
    words are too slow
I can only do one at a time don't die first please
don't give up and start crying or hating each other they're
    coming
I'm hurrying be patient there's still time isn't there? isn't
    there?

Stone

William Keens

> *Camille Claudel ended her liaison
> with Rodin after fifteen years, but
> was unable to forget him. She would
> come to Meudon and crouch in the
> roadside undergrowth to watch him
> pass.*

1.

WHEN I was stone my flesh again
turned in his hands.
I held my breath before his face
and it was good, his hands, that stone,
the women of me that he made.
In their faces, mine; my breasts,

my limbs, my hands,
this crease and vein.
His was a way almost witchcraft:
touch the stone, the stone breathes.
Maker! so many times of me.

2.

And if the night took hold
I dreamed of them.
Dreaming, I rose, put on my shawl;
dreaming, let my body go.
Those nights they watched me cross the garden,
open the door, stand before them.
    "This is my face." I touch the stone.
    "This is my face." The stone lips speak.
Dreaming, I stand in the dark room
that smells of their dust
and call my name.
So many voices answer: "Here! I am she."

3.

These days without end
in the tall weeds,
crouched in the grass,
surely stone.
He will not know me
from his work, if I am still.

If I am, still.

These days in the grass
of the yellow slope,
watching all day for a glimpse of my maker.
My eyes lock, my body locks:
surely I am stone.
Whatever flesh now belongs to them.

I drag my heavy body down to sleep
among the stalks and yellow wildflowers.
Sweet Maker, hear my prayer: that love was good.

Storytellers, Liars, and Bores

Leonard Michaels

I'd WORK AT a story until it was imperative to quit and go read it aloud. My friend would listen and sometimes she would say the story was good. Sometimes she would say, "I feel so embarrassed for you," and I'd go away and tear up the story and work at a new one until it was imperative to quit and read aloud. My new friend would listen and sometimes she wouldn't say good, no good, or not bad. I'd go away and tear up the story. By then I could see what should have been apparent in the beginning: there is a distinction between a story read aloud and read in silence, and the effect of a story read aloud is frequently better than the story. To me, that hadn't been apparent in the beginning. I wanted too much for the stories to succeed, and I was unable to ignore the solicitous mother in my voice which gave them encouragement and musical clarity. In silent reading a story may do nothing for itself. I came to this understanding gradually.

Meanwhile I turned to relatives and friends for things to write about and ways to make quick money. My uncle Zev told me about his years in a concentration camp. "Write it down," he said, "you'll make a million bucks. Did I tell you how they knocked out my teeth?" My friend, Tony Icona, gave me lessons in breaking and entering. What Zev told me I couldn't use, but Tony's lessons were good as gold. Criminal life was intermittent; always quick. It left me time to work at stories and learn about tearing them up.

Whenever they were disoriented by wrangles of murky feeling or feeling not intended, stories like lies, or stories which only made a shape for boredom, I tore them up. It took an unbelievable amount of time to learn to do this.

When I read stories aloud they often worked all right, but I had learned, while reading aloud, to watch for effects and yet hear the story despite any effects. I knew when my voice did work that the story didn't do well; and only saved the story from itself, not from me. Not me from myself. If I read falsetto or slurred or mumbled or fell into unnatural rhythms I'd kill the mothering voice and read gibberish. So I read in my natural voice and I watched for effects which belonged to the story, not my voice.

One evening while reading a story to my new friend she yawned. It was the fifth time I had read it to her, the hour was late, and she had to get up at down to leave for work. But I had rewritten the story and had to read it aloud from start to finish. I watched her eyes go fluid and her mouth enlarge. I saw fillings in her teeth and red ciliations in her tongue, like the bottom of a lizard's foot. By the time she completed her yawn our friendship had ended.

After I understood so much about stories and about friendship, and I had been able to consider some stories finished, and I had mastered the skill of discriminatory, diploidal hearing, it was easier to write stories and more difficult not to tear them up. There would be tension between my new friend and me when I tore up a story she liked. But I did it for her sake as well as mine. Even as she beamed and clapped with delight, I tore it up and stepped on it.

I was now better at disguising lies, and disguising the disguises, and making attractive shapes for boredom. It was urgent—to save me from myself—to tear up nearly everything, and to assimilate demons to the subject of my stories to know where the demons lurked and so escape them and repudiate myself. I needed tremendous amounts of time, and my appeals to Tony Icona for lessons in quick, remunerative work were more frequent and confessional. I told him how hard it was to write stories without being a liar or a bore, and that there was nothing, nothing, I was unwilling to do for time. He listened and picked his nose, then said if I ended up in the slam, doing time, I'd kill myself. He said one person wanted money and power; the other had ideals. Both got money and power. As for himself, he liked walking on the beach at

Coney Island, in a tight bathing suit, and lifting dumbbells in the sun. "That's purity, right?" I said, "Yeah, right."

I wondered if I could detect, in the writing of the greats, when self-hate inspired competence and, to the strains of internal dialectic, gave sweetness. I wondered about the miracles that accomplished their salvation and whether, for me, such solitude would be born at last. My wastebasket spilled into garbage pails, and trucks of the Sanitation Department hauled the contents to the steaming dump. Seagulls squealed and wheeled and feasted among rats. The dump was full of images. The more I threw out, the more my doubts remained, difficult to engage, like strange fellows beckoning to me with knives. To discover that I had written one story and read another aloud was a schizoidal shock, cleaving a distinction in my head like the path of an eighty-pound ax. My ears were tossed to either side, like kneebones in forcible rape, and they yearned to be clapped back together. A discouraging experience, made no less discouraging by repetition. But I was determined to be a writer and not an actor who needed, for the purpose of his magic, whatever fattened the moment. Protean voice, face, body, and an audience which is himself, multiplied in the gaping other. The actor's brilliance, I thought, lay in seeming to achieve the expressive intention which is the writer's achievement, preceded by nothing, concluded by no applause, audible as a big bell, swinging half a mile away, when you aren't listening.

Reading to my newest friend, the distinction was vividly in mind, like the part in the vaselined hair of Rudolph Valentino. When she said the story was good, but I knew otherwise, I'd be furious. I'd say, "Don't make me crazy." She had not heard the story right, she hadn't heard it fail. She'd let my voice tell her lies, darken her understanding, weaken her will, and give her an inclination for evil. Evil in a writer. In an actor, good, perhaps marvelous. But I wasn't an actor. To make her know it I broke her nose. In one stroke I rejected her naked pity and twisted a cage in her face. For weeks thereafter I couldn't write, because I'd left my hand inside. "Don't you want to read anything to me?" she'd ask, as if she'd swallowed the cat that swallowed the original cat.

I didn't write, but a distinction between versions of the same words obsessed me nonetheless. I'd see it in the nose I'd broken, which she made delicious in fingertips and remarks to the mirror. "It'll never be the same, you know." And I'd hear it in popular songs if I ignored the melodic adjective. "Come on, baby, light my fire," repeated again and again, sustained my desire for fire, pleased me with narcissism, allowed adumbration to pass for hard debauch. When the man associated with that song was indicted for exposing himself before his audience, I knew he'd yearned for irony and, in a gesture of extreme impatience, had seized the adjective instead of the noun. This happened in Florida where winter is summer, where the sun glorifies lust for adjectives, where surface is sensual and life is a continuous, ardent lie. Distinctions were killing me and I did not write. I was normal, I did what everyone did. I went to the movies.

As far as I was concerned they reeked of adjectives. More than life itself, they wallowed in the adjectival mood of things, the promise of immediacy which never arrives. I remember a sign outside the movie houses on Forty-second Street near Broadway—the vaults of smoky, infected air and steep balconies where armed guards trudged in the aisles and minions of normalcy came to cough and moan in the midst of gripping film, and grip your thigh. The sign read: GET MORE OUT OF LIFE. GO TO A MOVIE. For me, no movie contained a person, place, or thing that wasn't an adjective dispensable or exchangeable with another adjective. I needed them for that, for the chance to get less out of life. But isn't Fatface great in *Such and Such*? Thinface would be equally great, maybe greater. In broad daylight, I believed no movie was less an imitation of art than of life; the better the camera work and acting, the more I believed it. If I'd hated movies I'd have felt unqualified pleasure when I paid for two hours in the cave, gaping at shadows. But I didn't hate them. I went to them several times a week and when the reviews were bad I went more often. Coming home, Broken-nose listened to me explain why, despite our titillations, we hadn't had a good time. We rode the IRT and I'd have to shout. "How against such rage can beauty hold a plea?"

From Forty-second Street to Sheridan Square she agreed that we had had a rotten time and begged me not to smoke on the IRT. "You might get arrested, and it's bad for my nose which, as you see, is healing slowly."

And yet, despite grudging, ungrateful reservations, I knew Kurosawa was a genius. There were others too, directors and actors, who were geniuses. But Kurosawa, better than anyone, I thought, could make *The Magnificent Seven* over again, with a new cast of extraordinary actors and new settings, fifty times, better and better, and different each time. A story is written once.

"But don't writers compulsively repeat themselves?" she whined.

"Most of the work of most writers should have been torn up and thrown away," I answered.

Whatever such severity meant about their aesthetic condition or mine, movies struck me like stories which succeeded in loud reading and failed, in the silent word, to speak for themselves, and needed body, face, and voice, needed adjectives—camera angles, orchestras, dark vaults, bright screens, and an ocean of warm company to intensify, to justify, sensuous, sentimental experience, exceedingly like art. "So what? So what?" she said. I answered, "It is harder every day for people to read a book. To go alone and read a whole book." When I didn't go to movies, I'd read *Paradise Lost* or *Gulliver's Travels*, which are about liars. I knew a professor of English, more principled than I, who never went to any foreign movie, because, he said, he didn't go to movies to read. That seemed exactly right.

As I started again to write, and to read to my newest friend, I'd write beyond the imperative to read aloud, until the voice ran off the page amid tables and lamps to go raving out the window to the raving city. Then I'd read aloud. She'd say, "That reminds me of what happened at work. Can I tell you about it?" I'd say, "Yes, tell me."

Reading aloud was like storytelling in life, my only way of measuring my stories against a high, vital standard, which, though I couldn't point to it, hummed in my nerves like innate grammatical form. I read aloud, I listened to the words, and, even when they were exotic words which repudiated life—like "flux," "quotidian," or "suctorial proboscis"—I listened for an effect of story-telling in life. "Yes," I'd say to her, "please tell me," and I listened desperately because she so much wanted to tell me a story, and she was an astonishing bore.

Storytelling in life was the part of conversation I carried away when the rest was forgotten, sometimes when the person who told me the story was forgotten. I heard about a man in an Italian grocery on Tuesday morning, and about another man driving his 1964 Plymouth from Manhattan to Secaucus, and about an unmarried, older sister at the dentist's office, and about my uncle Zev in a concentration camp, which were stories worthy of Chekhov, or even Kafka. The people who told them never read Kafka and they didn't speak good English except in telling stories. When singing a stutterer doesn't stutter. In ordinary circumstances they engaged me with allegory, parable, and anecdote of a high order, and they were honored in their circles as storytellers who could range with daring and wit between the extremes of liar and bore. As I wrote more and threw out nearly everything, I crushed that talent in myself, lest I exhaust the urge to tell. Stories in life and in writing jumped in that urge, but, in realization, they were only brother and sister, in love, forbidden to touch. Needless to say, they wanted only to touch, to risk intimacy that led to wanting beyond all touching, to numb, then raw, sick skin. I wanted effects of storytelling in life, not life, and I tore up all my stories, finally, and never told stories, and broke into cars, climbed through windows, and poisoned dogs. I made myself ugly, lonely, and miserable, and when I explained my condition to Tony Icona, a man to whom I could speak in a theoretical way, he said, "I can't sympathize. You got one leg shorter than the other and you're walking a circle. But I'll give you a job in my delicatessen. Fifty bucks a week and you keep your tips. If the customers like you, you'll do all right. If they don't, you'll starve and be known as a dope."

The delicatessen, called "Horses," was on Broadway. A giant hall with a bar, with mirrors on the walls and ceiling, and a hundred tables. Day and night it rang plates and cutlery; it roared twenty chefs boiling at steam counters, and the floor thundered speeding waiters in black tie, jacket, and shoes. I thundered among them, a napkin slapped across my forearm. At my shoulder, a trayload of adjectives between slices of rye, with an adjectival pickle on the side. Ladies snatched my elbow. "Darling, please, please, darling. Could you be so wonderful as to bring me a lean pastrami and a piece of fresh cheesecake." They'd cling and whimper, lips white with anticipatory saliva, eyes pleading for a complicity they needed to eat. And then, if it weren't lean, they'd say, "Was it too much to ask, darling? A lean pastrami?" They made me feel guilty of revolting gristle, and the miseries which had brought them to Horses. They needed so little—a lean pastrami—so little a thing it didn't even exist. I'd swear there is no such thing as a lean pastrami, and I'd bend to them, pleading for complicity in truth. They'd look as if I'd smacked them across the chops. My tips were small. I was known as a dope. But I studied the other waiters and, gradually, I learned how to say, "Here, sweetie, just for you, a lean pastrami. Enjoy. Live." My pleasure in their pleasure was their pleasure. My tips were tremendous. When next I learned how to say, "Eat, bitch. Stop when you get to the plate," my tips were fantastic. But I wasn't writing. I was growing corns, ministering to horses for fifty bucks a week and tips. Sometimes I'd slip away into the back of the delicatessen and sit in the meat locker, smoking a cigarette in blood-rancid air, with flayed animal tonnage hooked and blazing about my head. I'd think of Gulliver among the horses he loved, how he tried to tell them about liars. But they were innocent horses. By nature they couldn't understand. They thought Gulliver meant that a liar says "the thing that is not." But that isn't a liar. That's an ironist, a storyteller, or Jonathan Swift. Or maybe that was me, among the horses of Tony Icona, saying there is no such thing as a lean pastrami when there has to be a lean pastrami. But I didn't address innocence with depravity; there was no poignant danger that the horses I fed would be made depraved. "Depraved? Sure, darling. You can bring it with the coffee."

After work I'd go to my newest friend, the one who told me what happened to her at work. Her name was Memory. She'd take off my shoes and socks, then wash my feet. A swinish indulgence, perhaps, but I had the corns of Odysseus and ancient sentiments. Besides, she had needs in her knees, and it was her way of making me uncritical when she talked. She talked incessantly, and, for my benefit, she always tried—but she could not, unnaturally could not, tell a story. Still, she was a pretty girl with generous inclinations, and also a good friend. So I listened, and it was hard not to like it, her remorseless and amazing honesty. So much like a lie. Always a bore. Once, telling me about what happened to her at work, only a few hours earlier, she began by telling me what time she got up that morning, what the weather was like, and how it differed from the weather report she'd heard the evening before. The last thing she wanted to hear, before shutting her eyes, was what tomorrow would be like. She had fears of discontinuity. The days didn't return to her bound each to each by daisies. She was a city girl, nine to five in an office. The weather report was her connection between Monday and Tuesday. "Tomorrow it will not rain." However, it rained. Gusty, slapping rain foiled her expectations, but that was all right. For her, there was as much connection in contradiction as in fulfillment. Probably more. "It rained," she said. "Isn't that strange?" She told me what bus she took, in the rain, to get the bus that took her near enough to walk, in the rain, to work. On the way, as usual, she bought a newspaper. She read it during her coffee break and at lunch to find out what movie or play she might go see, or what to watch on TV, and, generally speaking, nourish her memory.

The newspaper, the coffee break, the buses, the rain, the goodness glowing in vacant progress—all of this brought tears to my eyes. With Memory I had mortal fears. I hated her story; I wanted her to go on and on. She told me what her boss said to her before lunch, and what he said to her after lunch when they chanced to meet in the hallway outside her office as she was returning from the ladies' room. She told me that her boss—a married man with three kids—for the first time since she'd been working for him, made advances toward her. That, more or less, was the point of her story. But she didn't stop talking or lift her glance to mine. With delicate intensity she massaged my corns a bit harder, as if to impress the idea of an ending on them. But I had listened carefully and I heard not only the point but the point beside the point, flickering together, fitful as the tongue of a snake. He made his advances with suddenness and violence, not in the hallway outside her office, but in a broom closet. I don't know how they got into the broom closet. Perhaps she had been telling him a story and he nudged her and glanced significantly at the broom closet, and then, working subtly together, they sidled in among brooms and mops and the odor of detergents, and, as she persisted in her rotten story, he seized her like a dragon, with nothing in his heart but hatred for civilized intercourse, seized the very fount, and tried to express himself in it. Why she couldn't tell me this story is a problem for criticism. Not to be dismissed as a failure in mythic structure, a screwy manifestation of subterranean self, or a perversion of capitalistic imperialism. But a tough problem. I had one solution. She hated feelings, the meanings they bore, the meanings that produced them, and she didn't love form, the act in which feeling imitates itself. She couldn't tell a story. She could only fussily collect the details of her day, with no sense of which justified others, and proceed in the hope they would all justify themselves if she started at the beginning and somehow collected the end. That, she thought, made a story between her and me.

There was finally no story, only a sense that she didn't live her own life; she discovered it, from one day to the next, scattered ridiculously at her feet. She heard the weather report, got up in the morning, noticed the weather, rode a bus . . . She might as well have gotten up in the bus. Then she'd have said, "I got up this morning in the bus. It turned out to be the Fifth Avenue bus, which is not the one I take. Isn't that strange?" She lived one story and told another, the way I wrote one story and read another aloud. It wasn't strange that she woke up in the wrong bus. She was strange. She couldn't reproduce, in a story, feelings she experienced in life. That can't be done. But she also couldn't feel what represents those feelings. She had no representational feelings, the kind in which we'd have met and danced. We were often alone, and we were willing to dance, but that never happened. We lacked a drummer. She washed my feet, talked incessantly, offered hashish entrees and bennies for dessert, and, for return engagements, five, six times a night, swabbed me in anesthetics. In these rituals of boredom nothing dispelled silence. We needed a drummer, bare hands on a drumhead, smacking motion and communion out of air, with no beginning, no ending, no ideas of 1,2,3,4 and anybody's small, particular life. For us there was no drummer. I said her story was lousy and put on my shoes and socks. She said, "That's how it is with me. I thrash in a murk of days. But look. Have pity. I'm skinny and nervous and finicky. I can't tell you stories. I have problems with sublimity. I'm not Kafka."

That night, in a lucid dream, I met Kafka.

A ship had gone down. In one of its rooms, where barnacles were biting the walls, I read a story aloud. It seemed to me a perfect story, though, under water, all sound was blurry. Nevertheless, sentences issuing from my mouth took the shape of eels and went sliding away among the faces in the room, like elegant metals, slithering in subtleties, which invited and despised attention. When I finished reading, my uncle Zev rose among the faces, shoving eels aside, and he came toward me. He said nothing about my story, but only that his teeth had been knocked out. "Write it down. You can sell it to the movies. Listen to me; don't be a schmuck. They also killed my mother." Tony Icona was also there. He said, "Starting next week you'll write my menus." With his thumbs he hooked the elastic of his bathing suit and tugged up, molding the genital bulge. This room was full of light, difficult as a headache. It poured through plankton, a glaring diffusion, appropriate to the eyes of a fish. Between me and all the others, it made a translucent, palpable gap, as if we were preserved for one another, alive, in our essential habits, in formaldehyde. Broken-nose was also there, swimming in this light, her mouth like a zero. She said, "Have you met Katchka? He's here, you know. Follow me and I'll present you." I followed her to Kafka and was presented. He shook my hand with reluctance, then wiped his fingers on his tie.

Harry Truman Breakfasts at Eighty-six

Michael McMahon

1.

Wʜʏ Harry Truman still eats breakfast!

He was the tailor in my bedtime tale
Swatting three nations with one blow.
Once, I saw his daughter, Margaret,
Play piano on the Milton Berle show.

Just now his bacon's black, and fans
Want to see him more than moon rocks,
This man who sent Tom Dewey to Boot Hill,
Who shot from the hip and burst a sun.

2.

Harry Truman's coffee is too damn hot.
His face clouds.
                    He dreams beyond eggs
Of a shop where he and his cronies swap
Tall tales of the time Pecos Bill
Ran the locusts out of Missouri.

One time things got so hot Harry Truman
Fried people on the sidewalk,
Then wore the fact like a Sunday school pin
On a blue serge suit.

3.

Harry Truman, do not go out with your name.

The crowd will not suit you.

They want to see the man
History strode through like a swinging door.

So stay inside with your guns and boots on.
Give the cook till sundown to get out of town.
We will write your stories.

We can believe in you
Without seeing, Harry Truman.

Influences

Tom Wayman

I sit down at my desk
—and it turns into Pablo Neruda!
His stout face stares thoughtfully
up from between my pencils.
I say to him: *Please. I want to get on with it.*
On with being Wayman, with my own work.
Vanish. Vamos! And he goes.

But just then my chair feels uncomfortable.
I jump up and look. Neruda again.
Pablo, I tell him. *Please, I insist.*
Leave me alone. I've got to do it.
Back to your Chile. Get south.
Sud! Sud! Leave Vancouver to me.

And he goes. I draw out my papers,
my scribbles. Scratching my beard.
I pore over a fine adjustment,
searching for the perfectly appropriate sound.
Then I notice the curtain
leaning over my shoulder.
"I'd do it this way," it says, pointing.
"Change this word here."

Neruda, I say, getting real mad.
Flake off. Go bother Bly.
Teach all the poets of California.
While I'm talking to him like this
he changes from being my curtains
to a pen. And I see his eyes twinkle
as they fall on my typewriter.

Then, I get cagey.
I'll be back in a minute, I tell him
and leave, carefully shutting him
inside the room.
Out on my porch, in the cold air
I see the North Shore mountains behind the City.
I'm alone now, shivering.
There is no sound over the back yards
but traffic
and a faint Chilean chuckle.

A Very Old Man
With Enormous Wings

A TALE FOR CHILDREN

Gabriel García Márquez

On the third day of rain they had killed so many crabs inside the house that Pelayo had to cross his drenched courtyard and throw them into the sea, because the new-born child had a temperature all night and they thought it was due to the stench. The world had been sad since Tuesday. Sea and sky were a single ash-gray thing and the sands of the beach, which on March nights glimmered like powdered light, had become a stew of mud and rotten shellfish. The light was so weak at noon that when Pelayo was coming back to the house after throwing away the crabs, it was hard for him to see what it was that was moving and groaning in the rear of the courtyard. He had to go very close to see that it was an old man, a very old man, lying face down in the mud, who, in spite of his tremendous efforts, couldn't get up, impeded by his enormous wings.

Frightened by that nightmare, Pelayo ran to get Elisenda, his wife, who was putting compresses on the sick child, and he took her to the rear of the courtyard. They both looked at the fallen body with mute stupor. He was dressed like a ragpicker. There were only a few faded threads left on his bald skull and very few teeth in his mouth, and his pitiful condition of a drenched great-grandfather had taken away any sense of grandeur he might have had. His huge buzzard wings, dirty and half-plucked, were forever entangled in the mud. They looked at him so long and so closely that Pelayo and Elisenda very soon overcame their surprise and in the end found him familiar. Then they dared speak to him, and he answered in an incomprehensible dialect with a strong sailor's voice. That was how they skipped over the inconvenience of the wings and quite intelligently concluded that he was a lonely castaway from some foreign ship wrecked by the storm. And yet, they called in a neighbor woman who knew everything about life and death to see him, and all she needed was one look to show them their mistake.

"He's an angel," she told them. "He must have been coming for the child, but the poor fellow is so old that the rain knocked him down."

On the following day everyone knew that a flesh-and-blood angel was held captive in Pelayo's house. Against the judgment of the wise neighbor woman, for whom angels in those times were the fugitive survivors of a celestial conspiracy, they did not have the heart to club him to death. Pelayo watched over him all afternoon from the kitchen, armed with his bailiff's club, and before going to bed he dragged him out of the mud and locked him up with the hens in the wire chicken coop. In the middle of the night, when the rain stopped, Pelayo and Elisenda were still killing crabs. A short time afterwards the child woke up without a fever and with a desire to eat. Then they felt magnanimous and decided to put the angel on a raft with fresh water and provisions for three days and leave him to his fate on the high seas. But when they went out into the courtyard with the first light of dawn, they found the whole neighborhood in front of the chicken coop having fun with the angel, without the slightest devotion, tossing him things to eat through the openings in the wire as if he weren't a supernatural creature but a circus animal.

Father Gonzaga arrived before seven o'clock, alarmed at the strange news. By that time onlookers less frivolous than those at dawn had already arrived and they were making all kinds of conjectures concerning the captive's future. The simplest among them thought that he should be named mayor of the world. Others of sterner mind felt that he should be promoted to the rank of five-star general in order to win all wars. Some visionaries hoped that he

could be put to stud in order to implant on earth a race
of winged wise men who could take charge of the universe.
But Father Gonzaga, before becoming a priest, had been a
robust woodcutter. Standing by the wire he reviewed his
catechism in an instant and asked them to open the door so
that he could take a close look at that pitiful man who
looked more like a huge decrepit hen among the fascinated
chickens. He was lying in a corner drying his open wings
in the sunlight among the fruit peels and breakfast leftovers
that the early-risers had thrown him. Alien to the im-
pertinences of the world, he only lifted his antiquarian
eyes and murmured something in his dialect when Father
Gonzaga went into the chicken coop and said good morning to him in Latin. The parish priest had his first suspicion
of an impostor when he saw that he did not understand
the language of God or know how to greet His ministers.
Then he noticed that seen close up he was much too
human: he had an unbearable smell of the outdoors, the
back side of his wings was strewn with parasites, and his
main feathers had been mistreated by terrestrial winds,
and nothing about him measured up to the proud dignity
of angels. Then he came out of the chicken coop and in a
brief sermon warned the curious against the risks of being
ingenuous. He reminded them that the devil had the bad
habit of making use of carnival tricks in order to confuse
the unwary. He argued that if wings were not the essential
element in determining the difference between a hawk and
an airplane, they were even less so in the recognition of
angels. Nevertheless, he promised to write a letter to his
bishop so that the latter would write to his primate so that
the latter would write to the Supreme Pontiff in order to
get the final verdict from the highest courts.

His prudence fell on sterile hearts. The news of the
captive angel spread with such rapidity that after a few
hours the courtyard had the bustle of a marketplace and
they had to call in troops with fixed bayonets to disperse
the mob that was about to knock the house down. Elisenda,
her spine all twisted from sweeping up so much market-
place trash, then got the idea of fencing in the yard and
charging five cents admission to see the angel.

The curious came from far away. A traveling carnival

arrived with a flying acrobat who buzzed over the crowd several times, but no one paid any attention to him because his wings were not those of an angel but, rather, those of a sidereal bat. The most unfortunate invalids on earth came in search of health: a poor woman who since childhood had been counting her heartbeats and had run out of numbers; a Portuguese man who couldn't sleep because the noise of the stars disturbed him; a sleepwalker who got up at night to undo the things he had done while awake; and many others with less serious ailments. In the midst of that shipwreck disorder that made the earth tremble, Pelayo and Elisenda were happy with fatigue, for in less than a week they had crammed their rooms with money and the line of pilgrims waiting their turn to enter still reached beyond the horizon.

The angel was the only one who took no part in his own act. He spent his time trying to get comfortable in his borrowed nest, befuddled by the hellish heat of the oil lamps and sacramental candles that had been placed along the wire. At first they tried to make him eat some mothballs, which, according to the wisdom of the wise neighbor woman, were the food prescribed for angels. But he turned them down, just as he turned down the papal lunches that the penitents brought him, and they never found out whether it was because he was an angel or because he was an old man that in the end he ate nothing but eggplant mush. His only supernatural virtue seemed to be patience. Especially during the first days, when the hens pecked at him, searching for the stellar parasites that proliferated in his wing, and the cripples pulled out feathers to touch their defective parts with, and even the most merciful threw stones at him, trying to get him to rise so they could see him standing. The only time they succeeded in arousing him was when they burned his side with an iron for branding steers, for he had been motionless for so many hours that they thought he was dead. He awoke with a start, ranting in his hermetic language and with tears in his eyes, and he flapped his wings a couple of times, which brought on a whirlwind of chicken dung and lunar dust and a gale of panic that did not seem to be of this world. Although many thought that his reaction had not been one of rage but of pain, from then on they were careful not to annoy him, because the majority understood that his passivity was not that of a hero taking his ease but that of a cataclysm in repose.

Father Gonzaga held back the crowd's frivolity with formulas of maidservant inspiration while awaiting the arrival of a final judgment on the nature of the captive. But the mail from Rome showed no sense of urgency. They spent their time finding out if the prisoner had a navel, if his dialect had any connection with Aramaic, how many times he could fit on the head of a pin, or whether he wasn't just a Norwegian with wings. Those meager letters might have come and gone until the end of time if a providential event had not put an end to the priest's tribulations.

It so happened that during those days, among so many other carnival attractions, there arrived in town the traveling show of the woman who had been changed into a spider for having disobeyed her parents. The admission to see her was not only less than the admission to see the angel, but people were permitted to ask her all manner of questions about her absurd state and to examine her up and down so that no one would ever doubt the truth of her horror. She was a frightful tarantula the size of a ram and with the head of a sad maiden. What was most heartrending, however, was not her outlandish shape but the sincere affliction with which she recounted the details of her misfortune. While still practically a child she had sneaked out of her parents' house to go to a dance, and while she was coming back through the woods after having danced all night without permission, a fearful thunder clap rent the sky in two and through the crack came the lightning bolt of brimstone that changed her into a spider. Her only nourishment came from the meatballs that charitable souls chose to toss into her mouth. A spectacle like that, full of so much human truth and with such a fearful lesson, was bound to defeat without even trying that of a haughty angel who scarcely deigned to look at mortals. Besides, the few miracles attributed to the angel showed a certain mental disorder, like the blind man who didn't recover his sight but grew three new teeth, or the paralytic who didn't get to walk but almost won the lottery, and the leper whose sores sprouted sunflowers. Those consolation miracles, which were more like mocking fun, had already ruined the angel's reputation when the woman who had been changed into a spider finally crushed him completely. That was how Father Gonzaga was cured forever of his insomnia and Pelayo's courtyard went back to being as empty as during the time it had rained for three days and crabs walked through the bedrooms.

The owners of the house had no reason to lament. With the money they saved they built a two-story mansion with balconies and gardens and high netting so that crabs wouldn't get in during the winter, and with iron bars on the windows so that angels wouldn't get in. Pelayo also set up a rabbit warren close to town and gave up his job as bailiff for good, and Elisenda bought some satin pumps with high heels and many dresses of iridescent silk, the kind worn on Sunday by the most desirable women in those times. The chicken coop was the only thing that didn't receive any attention. If they washed it down with creoline and burned tears of myrrh inside of it every so often, it was not in homage to the angel but to drive away the dungheap stench that still hung everywhere like a ghost and was turning the new house into an old one. At first, when the child learned to walk, they were careful that he not get too close to the chicken coop. But then they began to lose their fears and got used to the smell, and before the child got his second teeth he'd gone inside the chicken coop to play, where the wires were falling apart. The angel was no less standoffish with him than with other mortals, but he tolerated the most ingenious infamies with the patience of a dog who had no illusions. They both came down with chicken pox at the same time. The doctor who took care of the child couldn't resist the temptation to listen to the angel's heart, and he found so much whistling in the heart and so many sounds in his kidneys that it seemed impossible for him to be alive. What surprised him most, however, was the logic of his wings. They seemed so natural on that completely human organism that he couldn't understand why other men didn't have them too.

When the child began school it had been some time
since the sun and rain had caused the collapse of the
chicken coop. The angel went dragging himself about
here and there like a stray dying man. They would drive
him out of the bedroom with a broom and a moment
later find him in the kitchen. He seemed to be in so many
places at the same time that they grew to think that
he'd been duplicated, that he was reproducing himself
all through the house, and the exasperated and unhinged
Elisenda shouted that it was awful living in that hell full
of angels. He could scarcely eat and his antiquarian eyes
had also become so foggy that he went about bumping
into posts. All he had left were the bare cannulas of his
last feathers. Pelayo threw a blanket over him and
extended him the charity of letting him sleep in the shed,
and only then did they notice that he had a temperature
at night, delirious with the tongue-twisters of an old
Norwegian. That was one of the few times they became
alarmed, for they thought he was going to die and not
even the wise neighbor woman had been able to tell them
what to do with dead angels.

And yet, he not only survived his worst winter, but
seemed improved with the first sunny days. He remained
motionless for several days in the farthest corner of the
courtyard, where no one would see him, and at the beginning of December some large, stiff feathers began to
grow on his wings, the feathers of a scarecrow, which
looked more like another misfortune of decrepitude. But
he must have known the reason for those changes, for he
was quite careful that no one should notice them, that
no one should hear the sea chanties that he sometimes sang
under the stars. One morning Elisenda was cutting some
bunches of onions for lunch when a wind that seemed to
come from the high seas blew into the kitchen. Then she
went to the window and caught the angel in his first
attempts at flight. They were so clumsy that his fingernails
opened a furrow in the vegetable patch and he was on the
point of knocking the shed down with the ungainly flapping
that slipped on the light and couldn't get a grip on the
air. But he did manage to gain altitude. Elisenda let out
a sigh of relief, for herself and for him, when she saw

him pass over the last houses, holding himself up in some way with the risky flapping of a senile vulture. She kept watching him even when she was through cutting the onions and she kept on watching until it was no longer possible for her to see him, because then he was no longer an annoyance in her life but an imaginary dot on the horizon of the sea.

Translated from the Spanish by Gregory Rabassa

Sum

James Nolan

MY accountant father
counts pebbles and lawn-
mowers and edges the grasses
with somber precision.
His life like machine tape
droops down in a white beard
and ends in a darkness
of double red figures
which mount like a staircase
toward some ergo sum.
With asterisk eyes braced
he dreams of a golf score
report cards and budgets

are good things to sleep on
except that they flutter
and need constant folding.
Calendrical suns stand
like forms left to fill in
as he considers the number
of hamburger patties still
stacked in the freezer.

My accountant father
made me count
one day to two
and I never made it through.

My accountant father
confides in his mother
that he really has nothing.
She calls up to ask us
about what he tells her:
we place all his things all
around where he'll be sure
to see them and count them
and sit waiting in three's.
We're all we can gather.

My accountant father
lies counting to sixty
and counting in two's
to fill up the nothing
of the second hand's shadow.

My daddy. Accounted.
A hand full of pebbles.
He never was married
divided or touched.

Seven Sketches

F. G. Tremallo

KAFKA WAS walking down the street to the grocery store, in bad clothes made for him at his parents' request by a tailor in Nusle. Very badly dressed. His pants were stiff as boards, his jacket hung in creases. But he didn't want new clothes. The old ones were comfortable, and if he got new ones they would be just as ugly as the ones he was wearing and people would notice their ugliness because they were new. He went around the corner, his back bent, his shoulders crooked, his arms and hands all over the place, and bumped into Canon Copernick who was coming back from the grocery store and was very sick, and he said to Kafka, *You look terrible, your clothes are ugly, what are your troubles?* Kafka said he found himself inescapably ugly, which was why he was afraid of mirrors, and he dressed badly because it was no use, being so ugly, to dress nicely, and coincidentally the tailor from Nusle made bad clothes, but why change tailors if you couldn't change your face and body? *I see your point,* said Copernick, *as for me, I'm about to die I'm so sick, and just today my book comes out, the one on the revolutions of the heavenly spheres, but last night I had a dream that this first edition of a thousand copies isn't ever going to sell out, whereas that ass Clavius' book is going to get nineteen reprints in fifty years.* Kafka said too bad, and they slumped away from each other. Copernick went home and died that night, and his dream was absolutely correct. Not even Galileo read his book all the way through. Kafka went on living a while and wrote a lot, but he didn't get any less ugly, and he got fed up with it all and with himself and told his friend Max to burn every one of his manuscripts after he died, which he soon did. John Tyndik, who ran the grocery store, was never read by anybody because he never wrote anything.

To get published in the *Reader's Digest*, one must be reasonable and digestible. Therefore I have prepared myself with olive oil from Lucca and holy water blessed by Saint Thomas Aquinas before launching into this anecdote about The Most Unforgettable God I Have Ever Met. He was standing fully clothed in green muslin on the corner of Spruce and Marston Streets in Epping, New Hampshire, in the midst of a hail storm. He said to me that I was the first person he'd expected to see there, and I in turn asked him forgiveness. For what? he wanted to know. For my sins, I said, and I went on to tell him all the sins I had ever committed. Those aren't sins, he said, those are good deeds. So I told him all the good things I had done. They turned out to be sins, of course, but it was a short list. *You must find it very difficult*, I said, *what with all the competition from aardvarks and theologians and English teachers*. He said it was as easy as selling canned oranges in Valencia. We went on to discuss my conversion, which is to take place on the day that war ends forever among men, perhaps Tuesday next, at which time I shall be got up in green muslin and shall stand in a hail storm on top of the Flatiron Building waving a Swahili flag that I shall buy with the money I get from the pleasant people in Niceville, New York, who are surely going to have to admit that even this that I have had to relate comes under the head of theism and as such ought to be something we can all be grateful for in these trying times of electricity and no whale oil.

This is a tough one, the funeral of Jack Kerouac. First of all his death, last announced by Ginsberg, talking at Yale, on a cardboard sign behind him IN MEMORIAM:

JACK KEROUAC, making people in the audience eight hundred miles away think Ginsberg had a grievance with Jack; but no, Jack was in fact dead and going to be buried in Lowell. Now Lowell, Massachusetts, is no place to be from unless you were brought up in Paterson, New Jersey, or were a male nurse when last the lilacs in the dooryard bloomed. Ah yes, Lowell, where there's an old, ugly church I used to drive by all the time but never saw the inside of that's where they laid him out and out of where they finally buried him, and I mean really got rid of him. Corso was there making movies of things, and they had done Jack up nicely. His second wife was harmlessly around somewhere, and his first wife took my elbow and led me off into the past for a while to talk about the second one and her father's money and the dry cleaning business. But all the while, of course, you found yourself thinking about getting back to an everlasting minute with Ginsberg, whose reputation for lack of ego was somewhat marred, you might say, by his having stolen Kerouac's funeral right out from under the corpse. Sigh. The living win, the dying lose. Has it ever been otherwise? Kaddish my foot! So let Kerouac eat that funny God's lentil soup prepared by her absent hands. Who living can grow on absent soup, lentil or otherwise? It was Ginsberg, absolutely, who came out of the tomb, not three, it is true, but maybe fourteen or fifteen days later, in Lowell.

ANOTHER anniversary. Our fourteenth, I think. The snow. Last year we celebrated in Barcelona. We had a drink on the balcony overlooking Aribau and Laforja and the kids in the vacant lot who were performing surgery on their cat. There was no snow in Barcelona for our thirteenth. The skin on the Diagonal oranges was thick as love. The juice as sweet. Diagonales are the sweetest oranges I've ever tasted. And of all our anniversaries, last year's is the one I remember best. Next year I hope I'll remember this year's best. There is snow, and the house is full of the red carnations your mother sent. The water in puddles has frozen the hair the lips the way is short but it's hard to get down deeper. There's nothing much to catch on the surface of love or memory. Break the ice, go deeper. These ruminations in the frosty meadow, overlooking the locked-in fish of love—what good are they? It is never too late to listen to a beloved voice. The wind can be such a voice, the stars have such a voice, if only you can hear it. You have to listen hard. In the anniversary of corpses there is a gnawing dissatisfaction. Life is never enough. Death is always too much. There's always either dearth or surfeit. Why is that, why is that so? Love. The years fall like cherries. Not like stars, for stars if they do fall, fall rarely and in another's direction. A cherry is a meaner thing than a star, and more like our perishable love. A worm can get to it. Its meat rots. *But it has a seed, a heartstone,* you say. *It can survive. It can regenerate. Stars have no stones, no heartseeds. A star dies. A cherry lives on,* you say. That is a good thing to say for a fourteenth anniversary in New Hampshire while the snow falls, two days before Christmas, without oranges, without sun.

WHICH COMES first, TV commercials or people? This morning I saw a TV commercial drive up in front of the house next door. It was a VW commercial with red wheelrims, a convertible with ski racks on the back (avec skis). The commercial was full of a husband, a man I know, who sat smiling in the car while his wife ran ding-a-ling up to the house next door crunch crunch in the snow with her cute little ski cap flapping behind. She's close to forty, but of course she ran like a seventeen-year-old. Merry Christmas, she ding-a-linged to the neighbors, her teeth flashing brightly, of course. And the same to you, said our neighbors, who live in the same commercial, and the same to you. They all have kids, both these cheery couples, and they all wear lots of bright sweaters and floppy ski caps, and they all drive red wheelrimmed commercials, and they drink eggnog and have ballgowns and dinner jackets, and all their teeth flash. They think they are the Kennedys, I

guess. Two guesses who they really are. You're right—
they're the Fensterstocks and the Macropoulises. What I
want to know is what they do when they're not getting
haircuts, brushing their many teeth, buying cars, knitting
ski caps, and spreading good cheer. I smell a psychiatric
rat here somewhere. Nobody can live in a TV commercial
all the time. There must be something wrong, there has to
be. The VW must be in analysis, or else they all have false
teeth, including the five-year-olds. They all have halitosis,
they're all dying of cancer. Their Christmas trees are all
flammable. Their cars will all have flat tires tomorrow
morning. Why am I such a grinch? Why can't I let people
have their pretenses? Why can't I be a TV commercial, too?
All I want for Christmas are red wheelrims and a ski rack
and a ski cap and some skis and some legs.

A PORTRAIT of the artist as a young wop at Christmas in
Little Italy of the 1940's. All the trees were festooned with
care and macaroni, only they weren't Christmas trees, they
were bent sticks from the backgarden where customarily
grew cans of tomato paste by Contadina. And not a creature
was stirring, not even Grandma Grazia who wouldn't
answer the telefono because it was an instrument of the
diavolo. Meanwhile the pipe-smoking old women, led by
Giuseppina Baldasarre and Compadre Zinna, were bedeck-
ing the Hall of the Sons of Italy with fettucine. Then jolly
Old Saint Nicolo laid his finger aside his nose and blew it
out the back window. There was a fire all this while in
Compadre Angelo Zucco's house, and we all called the
Mafia, who sent over several fire engines from Mulberry
Street in Newark. The Passaic precinct captains stopped by
to pour a little Christmas cheer. I cowered all night in the
corner of the kitchen nibbling the next morning's panettone.
A Little Irish girl wandered over from Little Ireland. A
cautious marriage was arranged between us. The marinara
snow fell, and a hush of sweet sausage was felt over all
the land as piccolo Jesu came riding by on a donkey led
by Mariuccia. The Italian cowboys stopped by, headed up

by Hopalong Casadic', on their way to shooting paisani on the Louis Prima show. The next morning there was still a star hung over in the sky above the outhouse moon, and Uncle Dominic, safely back from Saipan, Tinian, and Tarawa, was out there aiming at it with his M-1 nose.

THEY TELL ME this is the Christmas Depression. I know a nurse who works for an eighty-year-old doctor whose wife to!d her to watch out for the old man around Christmas time because of Christmas Depression. Books I have read make me believe all this has something to do with the weather and the seasons in the northern temperate zone. Not much growing, and maybe there'll never be another spring or another summer or another harvest. Maybe the food will run out, or the air. Or your wife. In any case, speaking of wives, I think I ought to start getting used to being without midnight metaphysical conversations with that good woman. Her ears can't last forever. Maybe she'll go deaf or die, and then what'll I do? And so I turn now to you to tell you how sad I am and how it feels to be thirty-five when most plants, most people, almost everything, even popsicle sticks, are younger. And then there's TV to be mentioned. What can I tell about the tube? It talks at you and looks at you, all day and all night, but it doesn't listen to a goddam word you say. Today I practiced, getting ready to talk with TV when my wife and kids are gone, but it was no good at all. So I turned the sound off. No better. It was like talking to another world on the other side of thick, peopleproof, soundproof, loveproof, meaningproof glass. This nurse I know, who is my aunt, my sister-in-law, my mother, and an old French teacher from grade school, says the same thing about TV, that it doesn't help her at all in her Christmas Depression. So she talks to me about her divorces, bereavements, and losses and debts, and deaths, operations, patients, and her eighty-year-old boss. I listen, and I talk to you, little brown notebook.

War Summer

James Applewhite

In our tin-roofed house in the big war's summer,
In a somnolent town in sunlight's dominion,
I read of the Shalott of Lord Tennyson,
Dreaming beyond guardrooms of the distant thunder
To a city in that sun's blind center.

How odd in my upstairs room, awake
In attic air, in wrath of the sun,
Except for my balsa Spitfire, alone,
Unable to descend, where my father'd mistake
My desire as he massed his jaws at steak.

Would that ardor of sunflame never relent?
My thoughts were a web as in the Lady's tower.
Tinkering tissue and sticks toward the power
Of flight, I dreamed all communion as ascent.
Our rapport in combat came only at twilight.

Through rumble of distant thunder, far
Flash of the six o'clock news. Under each
Portentous cloud, we turned from our workbench
Stunned. Radio's tone warned static; came roar
Above houses, artillery of a wide atmosphere.

Antecedentes

Edward Rivera

My PATERNAL GRANDFATHER, Xavier F. Alegría, itinerant schoolteacher, part-time painter, poetaster, guitar-picker, and Mariolater, jammed a "small gun" in his mouth and opened fire on his upper jaw. He died slowly; a lousy shot, or the hapless owner of a rusty, second-rate pistola. The hole in his palate was pretty big; the bullet lodged somewhere in his brain. He should have died right away, but the All Powerful refused to take him then and there. Instead, He let Abuelo Xavier hold on for weeks, putting him in a coma before finally cutting him loose.

Xavier F. Alegría starved himself dead when my father Geran, his third child and second son, was barely five. That was Papi's version, and my mother's. Papi said it had been a common occurrence all over Puerto Rico—all over the world, as a matter of fact. Mami, who claimed she knew little about the world, said sardonically that there had been nothing unusual in Abuelo Xavier's crash-diet death. She said that 1919, the year it happened, had been a good year for meeting the All Merciful, but not an exceptional one. "I could tell you stories, Prieto," she told me, "that would make the little hairs on your fundillo stand straight out."

In 1919, she had been a little over three years old. Poverty, she said, la pobreza, had done a lot of good people in, and some bad ones, too; and she would rattle off the names of people she'd known in Bautabarro, our home village, people whose names and lives, like the names and lives of their parents and grandparents, would disappear when Mami's generation died off. The hilly village of Bautabarro had no chroniclers; illiteracy was high in those days, headstones a luxury. Besides, who would have had time to record all the comings and goings, the births and deaths? Who would have bothered? The people of Bautabarro were peasants, not history-minded, culture-conscious scribes. You died, and a few years later people forgot where you'd been buried. Only the town church recorded the day God had cut you loose, but our town church burned down several times and its records were pretty meager.

Bautabarro was deep in the mountain range called Cordillera Central (the Rockies of Puerto Rico), an area of lush green landscape, a tangle of tropical weeds, smooth and hilly, precipitous and sloped, the monotony of greens relieved only by bald patches of soft red clay called barro, which is also the name for mud. The Bauta River, a squiggle on the map, trickles down from somewhere in the Cordillera past Bautabarro and, after coupling with the Toro Negro, flows into the Mar Caribe.

They got Xavier to a hospital somewhere, or to a village clinic, where some local G.P. probably stuffed his mouth with cotton or gauze sopping with anesthesia until a big-town surgeon arrived, took a look at his mouth, probably whispered a few prayers over him, and pronounced him technically dead. God had played a dirty joke on him: dead and alive, a breathing mummy. My grandmother's family took him home. He himself had no relatives in town; the nearest kin lived twenty-five miles away in Ponce, but they had lost track of his existence, and he of theirs. He'd been a loner, something of a snob because his parents, it was said, had been Spaniards, and because he'd received a university education. Besides, he had been too busy teaching and painting and caring for his wife and children to make close friends. They locked him up in a bedroom, though this was unnecessary, since almost no villagers came to see him. A small group of Xavier's pupils came by one day, bringing flowers and poems they had written and illustrated themselves, but his in-laws kept them out of the room. Xavier, they explained, was "muy grave," too ill to receive visitors; and the children left their gifts behind and never saw him alive again.

His in-laws waited on him day and night, kept the flies

off him, lit candles, recited rosaries and other rituals, moaned and belted their breasts, and watched him die. And God for his part let him suffer on and on with that hole in his palate. How long? Not even my aunt Celita, the family gossip, could remember for sure. "A very long time," she would say. "An eternity." He received spiritual first-aid in large doses. Padre Solivan, an Irish missionary from Nueva Jersey, was there every day, bringing prayers, blessed candles, and holy water. Xavier was his Michael-angelo, after all, and an educated man. A good father, too, and a missionary when you came down to it. For what else was a traveling schoolteacher in those days of unpaved roads, clap-trap schoolhouses, and beggar's wages? Toward the end he got Extreme Unction, that last-ditch sacrament. If you believed in that stuff, and who in those days didn't (Xavier perhaps?), then Xavier was on his way to paradise.

As a schoolteacher Xavier couldn't have earned much, a couple of dolares a day, five at most. But that was a good deal more than his neighbors, subsistence farmers, or their peones, made. Besides, he was also a painter—of canvases, not houses. But who needed art in those hills? Who could afford it? He painted portraits, tropical landscapes, birds, still-lifes, anything, everything, even church altars. The portraits and landscapes he sold to bourgeois types from Mayaguez or Ponce for next-to-nothing. He was prolific, the village Velazquez, but very formal. And self-taught. What he didn't or couldn't sell, he gave away to his pupils, neighbors, and admiring strangers. His neat wooden house was full of those portraits and landscapes. As for the religious art: Abuelo had not only designed the altar of the church he, his wife, three sons, and daughter worshiped and confessed their sins in, but decorated it as well: a large mural depicting angels in multicolored flowing gowns, puffed cheeks blowing celestial notes from golden horns and trumpets, pliant fingers plucking harps, and bow-lipped mouths choiring hallelujahs; a score of well-known saints from the comely Virgen María to Santa Barbara Bendita, patron saint of lightning; and the apostles, all twelve of them; Nuestro Señor Jesucristo, a portrait of Xavier himself, with beard and long black hair thrown in for authenticity—a handsome man; and a touch of evil, too —smirking Judas, that maricón traitor, son of the world's great whore, scowling off by himself, clutching soiled silver coins in one hand, the other propping up his pointed chin, two long-nailed, crooked fingers pointing straight down— a symbol of something or other.

The altar and the mural had been commissioned by Padre Solivan. Abuelo had been paid something, not much, but something. He wasn't starving. His children were fed, were possibly plump. They wore starched clothes; the boys got haircuts once a month in the town barbershop, next to the Sundial store, the Thom McAn of Bautabarro, where they replaced their worn-out shoes with the latest styles: patent leather, usually, with brass buckles.

Only a few months before Xavier's death, a "rare disease" (my mother's mysterious phrase) had knocked off his wife, Sara. According to Papi's cloudy recollections, she had been a perfect wife and mother, the kind Puerto Ricans, men and women, like to call "santa," meaning a docile daughter, a submissive wife, and a totally devoted mother. And a saint she died, though a little young to be leaving her husband and four children for a better life. At her funeral Solivan probably pointed out her youth. "She was only thirty-five, my children. Una muchachita. We must be ready for God's call from the day we're born. . . ." It's nine to one that he compared her to the Virgin Mary, after whose perfect life she had modeled her own.

AFTER XAVIER'S DEATH, Sara's parents adopted my father and his two brothers. Papa Santos Malanga was a poor hillbilly, a jibaro desgraciado and, said my father, who was his favorite, the kindest man he ever knew. Papa Santos was so good that whenever there wasn't enough food for everyone—and that was often—he used to steal chickens and vegetables from his neighbors. He always paid them back by doing favors, without letting them know the reason. This chicken-thief Robin Hood of Bautabarro was likely to deny himself a pair of badly needed pants or a straw hat (he worked all day in the sun) so that his three grandsons wouldn't have to walk around those hills looking like orphans. Which they did just the same; but the point was that Papa Santos would do anything for those three orphans. He'd been, in short, a saint.

His wife Josefa added much misery to Papa Santos' hard-luck life. She was a loca, and he had to look after her all the time. One time she tried to burn the house down. Another time she tried to kill Santos with his own machete. She put shit in the food, and sometimes, on a crazy whim, she would shit on the floor instead of using the chamber pot or making a trip to the outhouse. Nightmares haunted her. Seven times a week she woke up the house with her screams; she said her enemies—Papa Santos was one of them—were trying to kill her. Sometimes they tied her to a tree and tried to decapitate her with a machete, but just before the blade cut into her neck, she screamed and woke herself up. Some nights they tried to choke her by shoving human shit down her throat. To calm her down, Papa Santos would give her a concoction of boiled milk with ginger and some wild herb called "good grass," and soothe her with words while she drank it.

The worst thing about her, as far as the boys were concerned, was her violent nature. She might sneak up on one of them and clobber him on the head with the broom or the chamber pot, or empty the chamber pot on their heads. My father blamed his poor eyesight on those regular beatings she gave him. She singled him out for extra torture because he couldn't help talking back to her. One day— he was ten—when he saw a pile of her shit in a corner of the kitchen, he threw up his food and called her a disgusting old loca. She came at him with a kitchen knife. He put the table between them. When she started to climb it, determined to get him, holding the knife up for a quick stab, he upended the table and knocked her over. She cut herself with the knife, in the groin, and began screaming: "Asesino! He's killing me!" Papi was sure she'd bleed to death. He panicked, ran away, and hid in the hilly woods, living on wild fruit and coffee berries. On the second day, an attack of diarrhea almost killed him.

A posse of village men headed by Papa Santos found him at sunset of the third day. He was on his haunches, trying to move his empty bowels, when they caught up with him. He thought the men had come to hang him, but he was too proud to beg for his life. Instead, he confessed to having murdered Josefa. Accident or no accident, he had killed her, and for that he deserved to be killed in turn. At this point, Papa Santos, already weeping, knelt and pulled up Papi's pants. But what difference did it make whether his pants were up or down? They were going to hang him that very day before the sun set. But the posse, all eight of them, were laughing at him.

He broke down, sat on the ground, and wept. Papa Santos took him in his arms, and they wept together. The posse of peones stopped laughing. Papa Santos explained to him that Josefa was still very much alive. The wound had been only a scratch. Papa Santos had somehow calmed her down, and had even gotten her to forgive Papi.

Back home they had a big reunion scene. Everybody wept, especially Papi, when Josefa picked up her skirt and displayed her bandaged groin. Her hysteria, when she saw her blood flowing—her nightmares come true—had worn off. She had calmed down while sipping a cupful of Papa Santos' "good grass" potion, and even recovered some semblance of sanity. The shock of seeing her blood may have done it. And for almost a week after the incident, she behaved like the old Josefa, the sane and sound Josefa Papa Santos had eagerly married. God works in strange ways, he and his three adopted sons concluded. Instead of murdering her, as she had insisted, Papi had cured her with a knife wound. A novena was in order. They recited two of them on two successive nights; and for an entire week afterward they recited rosaries and lit votive candles in honor of Josefa's miraculous cure.

BUT HER CURE WAS MUCH TOO GOOD TO LAST. Her wound had just begun to scab when she relapsed. She got worse, in fact: screamed louder and longer at night, wet the bed and Papa Santos as well, and moved her bowels so often on the floor planks that the three brothers had to take turns cleaning it up; and once she cooked their sancocho, a vegetable and meat stew, in the chamber pot. For water she used her own piss. And as for violence, she began attacking the boys with a new passion, Papi especially, because he had tried to assassinate her. Friends of Papa Santos suggested that he have her put away; they were afraid she might attack their own children, or set fire to their fire-trap bohíos. But he refused to part with her. He was too stuck on nostalgia and pity to abandon her just like that, as if she were some kind of rabid dog. He could still remember the sweet, hefty girl who'd been as good a wife and mother as any in Bautabarro. Also, crazy or not, she was his beloved wife, she was over sixty years old, they'd been married more than forty years. The mother of his poor dead niños. True, she'd become mysteriously barren after the birth of her second child, a boy who had died of some enfermedad (smallpox probably) at the age of five; but that cut no ice: she was his mujer, a part of him, of his life. No, Papa Santos decided, if she goes, I go, and I'm not going anywhere yet.

So she stayed, for some four years, crazy and violent to the last. And when she died, suddenly, of a heart failure, he went into mourning. He mourned for the rest of his life, the old-fashioned way: extra prayers at night for the repose of her soul (he figured she must be in purgatory, possibly heaven, but for sure not hell: the insane, like infants, cannot sin); downcast gloomy looks; a self-imposed silence, broken only when speech was absolutely necessary; no more fun, no more stealing, and no music. His old guitar, which he had enjoyed plucking at night after supper, he gave to the three boys, who taught themselves quickly. But they couldn't play it in the house when he was there.

He survived Josefa by four years, and when he died of old age, the three boys and their neighbors buried him somewhere in the hills, alongside his crazy wife. No grave marker. They quickly disappeared into the wild vegetation, and even Papi, his favorite, lost sight of their graves.

THE THREE BROTHERS lived in Papa Santos' house for less than a year, planted and picked their own subsistence crops, almost starved when the land, a few acres, overworked and barren to begin with, yielded less and less. The brothers took to blaming each other for its failure. The less it yielded, the more they quarrelled, and more than once must have come close to machete blows. Elias, nineteen and the oldest, was also much taller than his brothers, and began bossing them. Papi, seventeen, and Mito, sixteen, resented Elias' arrogance. They thought of themselves as equals in their work: no boss, no peons, no unequal distribution of the labor. If anything, Papi thought *he* should be the boss, because he was smarter when it came to farming. But he kept this to himself; Elias and Mito would have laughed in his face.

The quarrels increased and finally Papi and Mito agreed they'd had enough of Elias. They told him off, called him a lazy bastard. Elias threw down his straw hat and challenged them to a fight—fists or machetes, Elias didn't give a damn. Mito backed down. Papi was mad enough to go for his machete, but chose his fists instead. He didn't want his brother's life on his hands. They would have bashed each other in if Mito hadn't stepped in and reminded them of Papa Santos: what would he think if he saw them fighting? Brothers, for God's sake. The old man would moan in his grave. The shame Mito poured on them was too much; they picked up their straw pavas and shook hands, and Mito the peacemaker had his way.

But the next day Elias quit on them. He'd had enough of that dirt-farmer's life. He said he was losing his mind in those hills, and his life was wasting away, just like Papa Santos', or worse. If he stayed, he might even take Xavier's way out. He wanted to get married and settle down somewhere to raise a family. In the big city maybe. San Juan. Papi and Mito told him the big city would kill him faster than the farm. A jibaro he was and would die one. It was in his blood. For jibaros like them the city was a cemetery. But he insisted he could cope with city life and called them timid peones. They were going to rot in that poor excuse for a farm, he warned them; their brains would rot first, then their hearts, then their balls.

He hung his pava up on a nail and left for the city. He gave them his share of the farm. Some legacy, my father said. Useless clay. Less than six months later he and Mito sold the farm for a few pesos to the family whose land adjoined theirs and hired themselves out as peones. They worked for anyone who'd hire them at something like fifty cents a day, average day's wages in those Depression years. But since they weren't always able to get work in the same finca, they gradually split up, found new friends and interests, different lodgings, and saw each other less and less.

PAPI WAS ALMOST EIGHTEEN NOW, thin, a little anemic, but not as fragile as he looked. He was quite strong. His light skin was darkened from constant exposure to the burning sun. His face was smooth and sensitive; he had thin lips, hazel eyes, curly brown hair, and a thin nose that my mother was to call Spanish because it did not round off to a pimple-pocked dome like most of the snouts in her family.

He was nineteen when he hired himself out to Gigante Hernandez as a full-time field hand. The wages were grubby even for 1933. Gigante was a thrifty patrón. He underpaid and overworked his peones, who quit on him as soon as they could find better pay. But there were always enough half-starved men looking around for work— any work—to keep Gigante's fields tilled and his strong-box full, if not overflowing. Papi was one of those hard-up jíbaros. He looked five years younger than his actual age. An undernourished niño like him couldn't compete with the mobs of full-grown men who were willing to work sixteen-hour days all week to feed their large, sickly families. So he was bound to drift toward Gigante's finca, and there he stayed for over a year, on and off. When there were no crops to plant or pick, Gigante let all his hands go, empty-handed.

Gigante Hernandez was a hard-working, puritanical dirt-farmer who found time to produce nine children. "Eight worthless daughters and one half-ass son" was how he used to put it. He could have passed for a Puerto Rican version of the hidalgo of La Mancha. At least in looks. He bore a strong resemblance to those crudely carved, imported Quixotes that pass for art in the tourist shops of Old San Juan: wooden, lanky, mournful, the face sun-burned and angular, the cheeks collapsed and the eyes dark and brooding; the bony, lantern jaw extended out of proportion. There was something Taino-Indian about his face, enough to suggest that way back somewhere in the island's hills some ancestor got down off the family tree long enough to knock up an Indian maiden. Or the reverse: that some lickerish warrior from the tribe of Chief Orocovix or Guarionex scampered up the family tree and straddled a fertile virgin of the Hernandez tribe. But if anyone had suggested this to Gigante Hernandez, he would have reached for his machete and hacked the blasphemer's balls off in a single chop. Fwop! Like sugar cane.

This *puro macho* was an old-time patriarch who took no shit from either sex, in or out of the family. He was proud, stern, and excessively strict, a boondocks tyrant who'd had the cunning to marry a submissive madonna. From his wicker rocking chair, El Sillón, he reared eight compliant daughters and one swaggering son. Hortensio more than any of his sisters, several of whom had the round pale face of their mother, was an A-1 reproduction of his old man, except that he was not quite so sullen-looking; and he took after him. Whenever padrefamilias was dropping sweat in the fields or in his querida's bed after sunset, Hortensio was in the house keeping the girls in line.

Gigante's life must have been as bitter as the cheap, home-grown tobacco he liked to chew and spit out at stinging flies and wasps. The farm he had bought as a young man—recently married and looking forward to siring five or six boys, and maybe a girl for the housework—had let him down. The land was too hilly, and too much of it was nothing but a dense mass of soft mush that sucked you in up to the ankles, and during heavy rains poured downhill in red and yellow streams. What wasn't clay or hills was maleza, a jungle of choking undergrowth that grew back as fast as he and Hortensio and his peones could clear it away with their machetes. Some sixty acres he owned, but only a fraction of that was farmable. His dreams of owning a large hacienda someday and directing the labor from his horse came to mierda. God must have had it in for him. Gigante shat on Him seven times a day.

Even his offspring came out wrong: eight girls and one, just one lousy son. "Me cago en Dios!" Eight useless daughters. No returns on that investment, just hard work to keep them fed, dressed, humble, and chaste. Hortensio was another losing proposition. He'd rather shoot craps with the village peones than squeeze the clay for whatever it still had. As for keeping an eye on his sisters, half the time the young lecher had it fixed on someone else's sisters. And, as if God hadn't rubbed Gigante's life enough in shit, Hortensio, as soon as he turned twenty-one, went and signed up for Tio Sam's army. With him gone, Gigante would have to play the master full-time once again. He cursed himself for having ever sent Hortensio and the eight girls to eight years of worthless school. He should have kept them all illiterate like himself.

Wifeless, too, he was. Abuela Socorro had died in child-birth, taking the last of her offspring, a boy, with her. Afraid he'd father still more girls, he refused to marry his querida Maritornes. What if he died first? Then she would become his legal heir and suck up a good hunk of his finca. Besides, the old Spanish customs of the countryside con-demned remarriage. Not that Gigante couldn't have re-married and gotten away with it—who of those anemic neighbors of his would dare condemn him openly? But he liked to follow the old customs, the face-saving ones espe-cially. So he stuck fast to the burdens of a viudo. Except for celibacy. That would have been too much for a puro macho.

GIGANTE'S WIFE HAD PASSED AWAY in labor pains. No photographs, no sketches of her exist. Even if Xavier had offered to paint her portrait, gratis (for Gigante would never have wasted his money on el arte), she would not have consented. She was a self-effacing woman, and to pose her face for a painter, and then to have that image of herself in the house, even stashed away under the linen —that was vanity, a pecado mayor.

My mother said that Socorro had been a saint. A foot-stool, in other words, Gigante's footstool. But according to my mother, she had been a matchless wife and mother—a kitchen martyr and a bedroom madonna. The kitchen and the bedrooms, cubicles all, were her domain, and her hus-band was her overlord. He commanded, she obeyed, eyes to the ground. No questions asked and certainly no back-talk. All day she drudged away, fixing meals for the nine and the one (plus the field hands), with help from the older girls. She always ate last, almost never with her husband, who liked to brood by himself while he chewed. She ate standing up, always on the go, piling up starchy stews, rice and beans, codfish, goat and chicken meat on wooden plates; and watchful as a finicky mother hen, double-checking to make sure they'd all had an equal share of food, urging more on them, when there was more. Several times a week, she and two or three of the girls loaded dirty laundry on their backs, or set it firmly on their heads, and dragged themselves barefoot to the nearest stream, where they squatted on a rock and scrubbed the wash clean with hard bars of Octagon soap. Socorro pounded away at her husband's soiled underwear. She insisted on doing that herself.

At night, when Gigante was home, she bestowed herself on him, put his seed in private storage, and watched her belly swell right on time year after year. She was pregnant nine months out of twelve for ten years running; and on the tenth year her overworked womb quit on her. I like to think of her dying with a scream in her gaping mouth, or even a curse on her husband and that all-fours life she'd led. But my mother said she never cursed.

Gigante's neighbors envied him his success in rearing such close-to-perfect daughters almost by himself. What hard workers they all were! What obedience and loyalty! What humility! The Hernandez girls were known as las hermanas humildes, the humble sisters. And all eight of them, or at least seven, were proud of it, to the point sometimes of committing the sin of orgullo, pride. But this the village cleric helped them overcome in the confessional. He reminded them of the Mother of God and of their own mother, a favorite of his, whose humility they could hardly hope to match. "But you can always try, Mija," he would tell each one. And they did; they bent over backwards for the Santo Espíritu, that taintless dove who had somehow made Maria Inmaculada big with child.

Las hermanas humildes: too docile for their own good, a few misguided people thought, too obedient, afraid of displeasing Papa Gigante and their brother Hortensio. They never talked back to Papa Gigante, never even asked

him for permission to smoke in his presence (he would
have made them eat the cigarettes), or to go out on dates.
Gigante regulated everything, right down to sweeping the
floor, fetching water from the stream at the bottom of a
steep hill, or feeding the pigs and chickens. Anything
that emphasized femininity—a blouse or dress that was too
colorful or fit too snugly, a new hairdo—was sure to pro-
voke Gigante's displeasure; and displeasure led to chastise-
ment; and God help the hembra who tried to defend
herself. Gigante would grab her by the hair, yank her
head down close to his chest and let her have it with the
flat of his horny right hand.

THE HEAD HE YANKED MOST was Celita's; she was the one
he couldn't break. The only one she bowed her head to,
in self-defense, not humility, was Gigante. Nobody messed
with him. But behind his back she called him an old pain
in the ass, something which the other sisters considered
blasphemous and cause for getting one's tongue cut off
with the machete.

Celita was not an attractive girl; she was short, but
rough-hewn and hard-faced like her father. Her sisters
wore their dresses above the ankle; Celita wore hers right
down to her heels; when she walked, her heavy arms
swung stiffly at her sides, as if she were clutching a pail
of water in each hand. Her thick black hair was done up
in rats. And her dark and sullen face was stippled with
tiny pits, a combination of acne and smallpox scars, which
looked like the tiny craters raindrops make on dry dust.

When Papa Gigante wasn't around, Celita liked to sit
on his old wicker rocking chair in front of the house and
keep an eye on things, the hills especially; she liked to
stare at the green, sunny mountains that surrounded the
house. Perhaps she daydreamed of hombres and of escape
from la finca; or of the lonely life she would probably have
when Gigante died and the others married and left her in
that dump with only the wild chickens and pigs, the two
horses and the half-dozen cows, and la maleza, the forest
that passed for a farm; and the bugs going at night all at
once; and especially the coquí, the little frog whose forlorn
mating call—co-quí, co-quí—could be heard all over those

hills, horny little beasts screwing away in the bushes just like some village girls she knew.

In Celita's outspoken opinion (for which her sisters avoided her as much as possible), they were "a flock of timid chickens. Papa Gallo's chickens." When Papa Rooster crowed the wrong way, displeased with his breakfast eggs or the taste of his bean sauce, his gallinitas would duck their heads and scatter off to their cubicles. Eventually Celita was bound to say something or do something that would make Papa Gallo crow the wrong way. And when that happened, there was no way she could make herself small enough and humble enough to escape the castigo of his right hand.

One of Celita's daily chores was to carry the lunch to the peones in the fields. Gigante had chosen wisely; her husky, peremptory voice was enough to scare away the most hard-up jibaro. It grated like a millstone. And like her father, she took no shit from men.

She couldn't help talking back to Gigante whenever he ordered her to do something she disliked, which was just about anything, from feeding the pigs and chickens to ironing his underwear. But of the eight sisters she was the only one he allowed to call him by his first name and to address him as tú instead of the formal, fearful usted that the others used. This indulgence of Gigante's probably came from her close resemblance to him and from her toughness that was not put-on like Hortensio's. In some subconscious way, Gigante must have seen himself as female in his third daughter. But this bond did not get Celita any special privileges. She often had to work harder than the others, almost as if Gigante were grooming her and not Hortensio to take over.

GIGANTE KEPT HIS DAUGHTERS ISOLATED. How many times had they attended a village dance? No more than five or six. And who went with them? The sons of Bautabarro? Dios help them if the sisters so much as stared sideways at those lazy chicken and plantain thieves. Brother Hortensio had gone with them every time. Hortensio was a machete wielder from the womb, just about; and it was tough tetas for any simple-minded jibaro who even looked like he was tossing florecitas at one of the sisters.

Even at dances he wore his pava, with its long fringes and pointed peak, at a sharp angle, and dusty baggy pants roped above the ankles with maguey. At his side, dangling from his maguey belt, the ends of which reached down to his cojones like a bull's pizzle, was a long, sharp, unsheathed machete. Hortensio, like his father, was all balls —in public at least, and around his eight sisters.

He'd never had to use his machete (which he took with him everywhere, as well as a small switchblade in his back pocket, just in case); every Bautabarro jibaro knew he was the son of Gigante and assumed he was a macho in his own right, and deferred to him. And stayed away from his hermanas humildes. Instead of asking one of them for a dance, a jibaro would approach Hortensio first and ask his permission. "Hortensio, may I have the privilege of dancing with Iraida?" or "Hortensio, it would be a great honor for me if you would give me permission to dance with your sister Flavia." And Hortensio, who was destined to become a police sergeant in San Juan and after that the town marshal of Bautabarro, might or might not grant them permission. Sometimes, for no clear reason, he would grant the privilege of dancing, not with the sister the jibaro had asked for, but with another one. After a while the sly jibaros learned to request the wrong sister and hope that Hortensio would give them the one they really wanted.

The only men he tolerated talking to his sisters, even on the dance floor, were married, middle-aged peones and dried-up grandfathers; but even those had to meet certain qualifications: that he know them personally inside out, that they be responsible fathers, husbands, and hard workers, and that they not hang around too long with his sisters. He was following orders from his father, but the enthusiasm he brought to his task was all his own.

This custom, and others—Catholic and Spanish, with maybe a little Indio thrown in—the seven sisters never questioned. Every now and then one of them might be tempted by el diablo and his legions to live it up, break loose from the strong grip of their father and big brother; but that was a sinful thought, and never got beyond the temptation stage. Everyone took it for granted that they were all vírgenes, and that they would remain so, until marriage sanctified the breaking of their closely guarded hymens. Dreams they couldn't help having; but even those, the sinful ones at least, they repented of and recited at Confession. (Not Celita, though. When *she* went to Confession, it was not to confess bad dreams, which she probably enjoyed too much to toss away on an old virgin priest, but to complain about her father's tyranny and her brother's meddling.) The village priest at the time, an elderly Polish one, also from the States, named Klimanskis (Solivan had died a few years before), admonished them and gave them extra prayers to say whenever one of the humilde sisters, blushing, dropping sweat in the dark confessional, confessed that last night or the one before that, she couldn't be sure, so great was her desire to perish the pecado from her mind—she had had a "bad dream."

SUCH A WAY OF LIFE Lilia had been born into and never once seriously thought to question. Even when Papa Gigante or Hortensio said or did something displeasing to her sense of right and wrong, when some diablito somewhere in the back of her head told her she'd just been insulted, or when the blackbird Celita pointed out some injustice she'd been subjected to at the hands of her papa or hermano grande, and tried to convert her to resentment, it was herself Lilia admonished, her own conscience she condemned for it: "Get behind me, Satanás." Because Mama had taught her again and again, in her saintly fashion, that our earthly life is un martirio, one trial after another, and that "it's not for us mujeres to complain, Mija, but to endure. Endure and be humble, Lilia." And endure she did, with humility to spare.

She spent her days sloshing out slops for the pigs, casting dried corn at the chickens, sweeping the dusty threshold, pulling grade-C eggs from beneath the undernourished hens, scooping out the ashes in the firewood stove, replacing the fast diminishing supply of corn husks, abrasive leaves, and brown-bag paper in the outhouse. Whenever Celita was having her period, or when she couldn't stand the sight of the peones, who taunted her for her bad looks,

Lilia exchanged tasks with her. She was happy to do it—
she looked forward to breaking her daily routine, which
was tedious and lonely, and she found the conversation of
the field hands more interesting than the grunts and clucks
of the barnyard.

Geran, the youngest peon, was her favorite. She found
him simpático, delicado though strong, serious but not lacking in humor, and sincere. Physically, they were of different
stocks. She was a shade or two darker. Her hair, thick and
long, was jet black, like a Borinquen Indian girl's; she
had high cheekbones, large limbs, and a strong constitution.
She thought nothing of standing on her wide feet all day,
from early morning to bedtime, sometimes past midnight.

He was proud-looking and uncommonly courteous. From
his weak hazel eyes with the large lids she never got the
sex-in-the-brain stares that the other men, eight or nine of
them, gave her from the time she arrived with the gunny
sack containing their lunch to the time, exactly forty-five
minutes later, that she gathered all the forks, spoons,
Thermos bottles, and leftovers and walked away with her
eyes to the ground, taking quick, barefooted strides.

There, in those steep hills dotted with cows, goats,
banana trees, and thatched huts, Lilia and Geran came to
sit together while he ate his lunch of boiled green bananas,
salty codfish, raw onion rings—the whole thing drenched
in olive oil—and fresh warm milk. He was nineteen, she
was a year younger.

He told her about his father Xavier the schoolteacher
and painter, and about Papa Santos and Josefa and his two
brothers. He told her he had no intention of staying in
Bautabarro all his life; he wanted to be more than a peon
in rags. He dreamed of having his own finca someday, a
big one, flatland, not red clay hills and jungle; but for good
land he needed a great deal of money. How could he
possibly save up when he was just barely keeping his
stomach fed on the wages Don Gigante paid him? Unless
God worked a miracle on his behalf, he would either
remain a hired slave all his life, or—something he'd been
giving serious thought to lately—move north to Los
Estados. In Nueva York, he had heard from the friends
and relatives of those who had gone there, to a place

called El Barrio, a man could get a decent job and make enough to put in the bank. Eventually, if you didn't waste your money on luxuries, you could save up enough to return to the island and buy a good finca. In Nueva York you could find work that let you live decently. Not like here, in this valle de lágrimas.

He was convinced, as she was, as most Bautabarreños were, that man is put on earth to suffer. But unlike her, he believed that man and woman are entitled to some felicidad, that life doesn't have to be totalmente un martirio. She, instinctively, knew better. In addition to that, she was too attached to those hills, to her sisters, her brother, Papa Gigante, and to the memory of her mother, to contemplate leaving it just because life there was hard.

She could see his wanting to leave the village, moving to San Juan, Santurce, Ponce, Mayaguez, or any other of the "big" cities and towns on the island where someone with ambition (and he seemed to have a good deal of that) could go into business for himself or find decent work. But Los Estados Unidos de America? No. Nunca. She knew that other villagers had done what Geran had in mind. It was nothing new. Those who could read and write sent long letters to their families telling them what a ciudad magnifica Nueva York was. They had jobs and they were making, some of them, as much as twenty dollars a week in hotels and factories. That was a lot of money, twenty dollars. Too much. She was suspicious. They were padding their paychecks with lies to impress the jibaros back home. Also, a few had come back after a year or so with different stories of Los Estados. Slums they talked about, rats and cucarachas, filth and degradation. And what had offended them most, they said, was that los americanos did not respect them, they treated nuestra gente with the kind of contempt and disgust a man feels when he sees one of his pigs wallowing in its own shit.

And even if she was willing to go with Geran to Nueva York after they got married (she assumed he wanted to marry her, otherwise why tell her all this), did he think her father was going to bestow his blessing on them and wish them a vaya con Dios? Con Satanás, if anything. Papa Gigante had nothing but odio for those who "abandoned" their families and their country and tried to make themselves into gringos. A man, he thought, a puro macho, should stick it out wherever God places him in life, not run away like a panicked sow pursued by nipping dogs. And as for las hembras, their place was with their husbands. She would never have the nerve to tell Papa Gigante she was going to Los Estados with Geran, married or—Dios mio!—not married.

WHEN WORD GOT TO GIGANTE that Lilia had been seen talking to Geran more than once, he reacted as she'd known he would. He warned her against seeing that useless orphan. But she was in love and persisted. He beat her a couple of times and forbade her to go near Geran.

The old man and his peon hadn't hit it off; necessity, cheap labor, was the only thing that kept Gigante from throwing Geran out. The patrón had a few other things against him, not the least of which was the strain of suicide and madness in his family. Since it ran in both sides of the family, the children, all three of them, had to be screwed up. Gigante didn't want any lunatic grandchildren. Bad enough that eight-ninths of his own offspring were useless females.

It wasn't Lilia's well-being that concerned him. Females, "hembras," as he called them, like jobos, a species of wild, fibrous mango that had no market value, were handicaps. Three of them at most were all he needed to keep house, feed the pigs, chickens, and cows, and help out in the fields during the busy season. The other five had been mistakes, cheap kindling, a pestilence on a man's life. Gigante would have willingly swapped them for a couple of fat pregnant sows, or a good milk cow. And now this Lilia had fallen for the first vagabundo that had sprinkled a few flowers in her path. But what rankled him most was the prospect of having grandchildren who would almost certainly carry that strain of madness in their blood. Nunca! he must have told himself during his pensive moments in the rocking chair.

Then there was the rumor among the field hands and other village men that Geran was a young stud, a skirt-lifting desgraciado. This was an unfounded rumor; in fact, it made Gigante laugh to himself that the anemic niño was capable of producing an erection, let alone laying one of those little battleaxes from Bautabarro. Even if it were true, Gigante had no objection to skirt-lifting. Hadn't he done it himself in his youth? In his childhood, for that matter. And still did when the lust came on him. That was what a real macho did. But this was his daughter, now, not Fulano so-and-so's. Let Fulano worry about his own daughters' chastity, or their loss of it, before marriage. Gigante was looking out for his own hijas.

A man with loose daughters was the victim of vicious rumors and ridicule. Gigante was sure no one in that village would have the cojones to mock him to his face, not while he still had that machete-wielding arm of his intact. But behind a man's back things were said, evil things usually, that he had no means to prevent. Some men may not be hurt by what their eyes and ears miss, but Gigante was not one of them; he heard things in his sleep— buzzing voices mocking him and his kin. On his rocking sillón, while his squinting eyes took in the sun setting, his large, leather-brown ears picked up his neighbors' gossip, the bochincherías of idle women and effeminate, henpecked men and horny young jíbaros. Already he could hear them: "Gigante's oldest daughter, Lilia, the one with the thin strong legs, is carrying on with young Geran. O sí, he's giving her las florecitas. You just wait, in no time at all he'll make her his querida." Giggle-gaggle. Querida; trapo; corteja. His oldest daughter a skinny peone's querida? If he caught her, from this day on, or even got a hint of a rumor that she was cortejando with that suicide's son—ora pro nobis, as the town priest might put it, because who was going to stay his strong right hand from violence? And who would condemn him for it? For sure not Dios. Dios the Father always took the father's side.

LILIA FOUND WAYS to steal out of the house and meet Geran. When she took the wash to the stream, he would sneak off from work and join her there. They considered themselves engaged, but who was going to break the bad news to her old man? Geran was all for it, but she wouldn't let him; she was afraid her father would hack them both to pieces. In that case, Geran told her, they should elope.

Elope? She could never do that to her father. Only loose girls eloped. Besides, didn't he know Gigante would hunt them down and kill them?

The plan was simple enough, and by no means original. Stealing a girl from her father was common in a village whose marriage customs dated back to the Spanish-Catholic conquest. It was a solemn act, matrimony; even child-bearing, another bendición, was less important than taking a young bride's "flowers." Not that Bautabarro girls were all that chaste; they were no more chaste nor yielding than other girls in other villages. But, like their counterparts all over the island, they kept up a virgin front. Had to: that was the point, a solid front, a look of vigilant virginity and cautious innocence. Even known trapos, hard-up sluts, played the chastity game in public. Both sexes played: the trapos and the men and boys who waited for them behind some stinking outhouse come blood-red sunset.

Abducting a nubile girl, then, was a common custom, an old and practical one; for it saved her menfolk's collective face, unburdened her father of an extra gut to feed and her brothers of the strain of protecting her from the local Don Juans for whom seducing unwatched girls was the first principle of machismo. Still, no honor-conscious father wanted his hijas stolen from under his snoring nose on a moonless night if he could give her hand away to any respectable, filial, up-and-coming young jibaro. But there weren't many of these young men around; they were the type who quit the village as soon as they could cut themselves off from the family. So those fathers who were tired of turning away unsuitable suitors for their virgin daughters often had to settle for a face-saving abduction.

ON A QUIET SUMMER NIGHT (no moon) in 1933, Geran met Lilia near the rock where she scrubbed her father's pee-stained underwear, and they spent the night, lying close but never touching, beneath an old, dried-up lemon tree. The next morning, while Lilia hid in his rented room, Geran smeared her underwear with chicken blood and presented Gigante with the "fact" of Lilia's womanhood.

He waited until Gigante was undressed and bathing in the stream, so that when he threw his fit and went for his machete, he would have to wade to the shore and scramble up a slope, thick with cattails and thorny weeds, to get to it. By that time, the nimble abductor would have ample time to run for his life—time, if necessary, to race for the nearest bus, with Lilia alongside him, and head for San Juan or Mayaguez.

BUT GIGANTE, without being at all conscious of it, sensed that the world was changing, knew that this was only one telltale speck in the great pile of mierda to come—women wearing pants and smoking in public, children refusing to be blessed by parents, the loss of costumbre, those venerable village customs, the end of *his* way. So he just stood there in the stream, naked, the cold morning water lapping at his brown behind, and said nothing, not even a curse for God.

For a wedding present Gigante gave them a part of his worst land, most of it hilly and overgrown with weeds and thorny bushes. The shaky shack Geran built with the help of his brother Mito and some neighbors was situated on the only level ground to be found in his two-acre wedding present, a convenient two or three up-and-down miles from Gigante's house.

Geran tried farming it, but that didn't work: somehow the clay wouldn't yield to husbanding, at least not enough to support a family's needs. Only wild things liked to grow on that finca: the prickly, starchy pear-shaped chayote; tiny, bitter oranges so inaccessible you were better off buying them six for a cent in the town market; yellow, buckshot-seeded guava; some small, sweet, slimy balls with a tough green skin and a hard white seed called quenepas; bananas, all shapes and sizes and colors; plantains; and an incredible abundance of starchy tubers whose Indian names they were never to use after they came to Nueva York, the hot dog, pizza capital of the world.

Iowa Déjà Vu

Richard Hugo

D<small>ID</small> I come from this, a hardware store
in photos long ago? No customers.
No pleasures but the forced dream pike
are cruising hungry in the lake that glows
through oaks a small walk from the farm.
The church I must attend, hard dirt and plow,
sweating horse I swear at, all the hate
that makes today tomorrow.
Next farm down the daughters married Germans.
Girls don't like me in the town.

West of here love is opportune.
I get this from the soft cry of a train,
from magazines the barber lets me take.
West, it cools at night. Stars reproduce
like insects and wild horses sing.
Here it's planting time and never harvest,
nothing but the bitterest of picnics,
the camera just invented and in first prints
women faded and the children old.

Morning again. Morning forever. The heat
all night all day. The day of sweat
and heat forever and the train gone on.
It's where I began, first choking
on a promise to be nice, first dreaming pike
were hungry in the lake I didn't try.

In Your Good Dream

Richard Hugo

From this hill they are clear, the people
in pairs emerging from churches, arm
in soft arm. And limb on green limb
the shade oaks lining the streets form
rainproof arches. All day festive tunes
explain your problems are over. You picnic
alone on clean lawn with your legend.
Girls won't make fun of you here.

Storms are spotted far off enough
to plan going home and home has fire.

It's been here forever. Two leisurely grocers
who never compete. At least ten elms
between houses and rapid grass refilling
the wild field for horses. The same mayor
year after year—no one votes anymore—
stocks bass in the ponds and monster trout
in the brook. Anger is outlawed.
The unpleasant get out. Two old policemen
stop children picking too many flowers
in May and give strangers directions.

You know they are happy. Best to stay
on the hill, drowsy witness, hearing
the music, seeing their faces beam
and knowing they marry forever, die late
and are honored in death. A local process,
no patent applied for, cuts name, born date
and died too deep in the headstone to blur.

A View

Mona Van Duyn

You DRIVE, the road aims for a mountain.
Down paving, toward the low basket of the sun,

a jackrabbit is dribbled by slaps of hot wind.
Hummocky, glazed, superficial, tanned

the landspread. I ride beside you, in the time
of life to note character, waiting for the sublime.

Enhancement of hills. Foisted up by their trite
avowals, we grow more close and hot.

Far ahead, something definite is about to occur.
The way goes flat, dusky. There they are,

the god, looming, and with him—but she is terrible!—
lying at his feet, his own foothill,

wrinkled, blue, balding, risen-above,
her back all sore from trails, child-ridden, shoved

to the ground in a dumpy heap, mined-out,
learned-on by the high one until that

moment he knew his own destiny, donned
a green-black cloak, rose up around

mid-life to stay with the stars, his face flint,
his eyes slatey and bland, and she went

into her change. Oh she was fanciful once,
garbed in dapples of yarrow, lupine and gentians,

silvery inside, always a-chatter
with rockchuck and nuthatch, point-breasted, and later

glad to be taken. Opened unmercifully,
she was used all over. Then, so accessible, she

was fair game for everyone. Even her shale
surfaces have been wrung out for oil.

He stands nearby, unmoved. He knows
how not to be. Even at sundown he flourishes.

He can sway in aspen and tender seedgrass
in his low meadows, wearing the disgrace

of his early delicacy still, where blue grouse,
calliope hummingbird, rosy finch rise

and fall in paintbrush, harebell, penstemon,
beeplant, columbine. Nothing is gone.

He shows without shame these young, soft
traces, having gone on to lift

into view rock ribs and evergreen
masculinity. He transcends every mine,

they are small scars in his potency, something
unearthly shocked, shook him and kept him ascending.

He grew rough, scrabbly, wore outlaw underbrush,
gray fox, bobcat and cougar, secret fish.

Then he was stale for a while, all bare bone, then reared
a feast of self in a head uncovered,

streaked gray and white, playing cool, leaning
on no shoulder, above raining,

oblivious of his past, in pride of escape.
Never down-hearted, he is wholly grown up.

You turn and ask how I am. I say
I'm admiring the scenery, and am O.K.

On the Perimeter

Robert Chatain

ZONE

THE TATTERED JUNGLE beyond the barbed wire had been declared a free-fire zone in late June. Looking forward to spending at least five of my remaining ten weeks of war in permanent duty on the bunker line (the unofficial transfer was complete; even my "Visit Gay, Historic Vietnam" poster had been torn from the AG barracks wall and sent along with me to the ordnance company's security platoon, so determined was Colonel Hamilton to purge from his new command any taint of the pacifist subversion he had uncovered), I decided to free-fire.

I had access, over the weeks, to M-14's, M-16's, machine guns, grenade launchers, and an occasional pistol. The M-14 had been my weapon in basic training; I was a good shot. With it I could cut down plant stalks at ten meters, hit beer cans and bottles at thirty; I drew beads on man-sized stumps and bushes as far away as I could see them and was sure some of my shots found their targets. I could also kill birds.

The M-16 I found disappointing. Its horizontal drift gave me trouble. Its ugly black stock was not long enough for my reach. The pistol grip fell awkwardly into my palm. Its sight was blunt. Obviously the weapon had not been designed for target practice. Remembering an old account of Marines dead on the slopes of Hill 881 with their M-16's broken down beside them, I wondered what it had been designed for.

The M-60 machine gun was a thrill. Fire at a patch of bare earth produced satisfying explosions of dirt, leaves, garbage, and anything else lying in the radius of my bullets. With a short burst one evening I tore a metal water can to shreds. The next night I opened up on the struts and wires of the old crippled powerline support tower I had begun to think of almost as a friend. Most of the rounds went through into empty air.

The powerlines were also a good place to aim the M-79 grenade launcher. If I connected, the grenades exploded high above the ground and fragmentation pellets clattered on the worn steel.

I discovered that pistols demanded more practice than I could manage without attracting attention. Free-fire was permitted, but some discretion was expected. Exorbitant waste of ammunition was discouraged. At the infrequent moments when a pistol found itself in my hand I shot at the rats foraging openly in the barbed wire for scraps of food. I never hit them.

I did this free-firing at dusk, after the trucks had gone back across no-man's-land through the interior perimeter gate into the ammunition depot; if the sergeant on my section of the perimeter called, I could explain that I was testing my bunker's arsenal. Firing after dark always drew such panic from the neighboring bunkers that I soon gave it up. Firing at dawn—I never fired at dawn. Dawn did not seem like the right time to fire.

Once I would have been ashamed to find myself willingly associating with these weapons. But I was alone. The guns were clean, well-made, efficient, impersonal. And I suppose that the problem of my former negative feelings toward weaponry had been solved. Guns were of some use, I admitted. In the proper circumstances I think I could have shot Colonel Hamilton without batting an eye.

FORMICARY

LYING ONE MILD afternoon on a soft wool blanket spread beneath tall birch and thick cedar, my wife-to-be had outlined her ant theories. Ants, she said, are capitalists. They're disgustingly greedy. And they're middle-class. They work twenty-four hours a day hoarding food and adding superfluous tunnels to their antholes. Did I know that some ants tend gardens? That some ants herd cows? That some keep slaves? And, of course, ants make war. Armies march into each other's territories and attack instinctively. Individual battles might last for hours. (Finishing my circuit of the bunker without finding what I'd been looking for, I returned up the hill of sandbags and slid into the half-buried enclosure. It was already too dark. I would continue the search in the morning.) Are they brave? I asked. No, she said, they're not brave, an ant might think he's brave but actually he's just doing what all the other ants are doing. If an ant were really brave, he'd refuse to fight. (At dawn and again at dusk the cracks between the sandbags were alive with large black ants. I noticed no particular pattern to their movements. Each night I spent a few minutes covering the surface of the hill looking for the main entrance to their nest.) They'd throw him in jail, I argued. It doesn't matter, she said, he would know he was a moral ant. He'd be setting an example for the other ants. But, I said, suppose he doesn't care much about the other ants? He's still better off in jail, she said, he won't get killed. But if he doesn't want to get pushed around? Ants always get pushed around, she answered. Then, I said, he plays it by ear. We laughed. And ants don't hear very well, I added. (Later we made love on the floor of the forest, sunlight through the trees camouflaging our bare skin with irregular blotches of light and darkness; I stretched this recollection out to fill my mind for an entire watch, even forgetting the discomfort of sitting upon stacked ammunition crates.)

DISCOURSE

THEY LIKED TO divide the members of the security platoon evenly along the length of the perimeter, no two "veterans" in any one bunker, and fill out the remaining positions with ordinary clerks on detail from the various units of Long Binh. Occasionally the roster put me with people from my old company, but usually I spent the night with strangers. In the intimacy of the bunker they could not keep their mouths shut. I had to listen, smoldering, to hours of rumor, complaint, prejudice, and platitude. By the time dawn carried them back to their safe barracks

I would know whether they had been drafted or had volunteered for the draft or enlisted or been tricked into enlisting or railroaded by their local boards, their families, or the courts; I would have found out where they had received training, how they had come to Vietnam, what they thought they had discovered about themselves, God, and their country, and when they would get out; I would have heard some of their most interesting Army experiences; I would have been told their opinions on the manners and morals of the peoples of Europe, Asia, and the other places their uniforms had taken them, and I would have learned their attitudes toward the war, toward international communism, toward the peace movement, and finally toward the chance that they might be killed during the night, a possibility that I sometimes came to anticipate with pleasure long before they had finished talking.

MAZE

A RAT'S SLEEK HEAD caught in the red beam of the flashlight triggered somber, fretful ruminations. How deep do they burrow? How many live in this hill with me? How do they know to avoid the pale yellow sticks of rat poison scattered in the corners of the bunker and outside under the clean starlight? Intelligent rats, well-fed on candy bars and C-ration tins, uninterested in poison. Their squeaks as they prowled around the base of my high perch on the stacked ammunition boxes. Their scuttling down below my dangling feet with cockroaches and scorpions. Don't reach down there, not for ammunition, not for anything. If you drop something, leave it until morning. Thousands in this mound of earth. Holes in the floorboards, holes in the walls, holes in the heavy timbers overhead. The sandbag slope alive with rats scurrying in the moonlight. Nocturnal. Remaining in tunnels during the day. Long tunnels, winding back upon themselves, coiling for miles. VC moving south in such tunnels, some captured with stories of traveling two hundred miles underground. Black-clad VC no older than fifteen sitting with their backs to dirt tunnel walls, singing. Underground hospitals. Operations underground, emergency lights flickering. Underground at Dien Bien Phu the wounded finding their wounds infested with maggots. The maggots beneficial, eating rotten tissue, leaving healthy. Time passing slowly. The wounded lying in darkness tended by blind worms.

I shifted my position. The rat vanished into its cavity.

TEST

JUST BEFORE MIDNIGHT the sound of a jeep on the perimeter road pulled me to the back of the bunker. Without hesitation I challenged the man who emerged; I was an old hand at the game. He identified himself as a corporal on official business. I let him climb the catwalk. He dropped into the bunker next to me and told me to relax. I relaxed. The corporal struck a match and studied his watch. I loaned him my flashlight. I saw that he carried a clipboard and a folded piece of paper. At what must have been precisely midnight, he ceremoniously handed me the paper. I asked him what the hell it was. "Black handicap message," he announced.

"What the hell is that?"

He seemed surprised. "A black handicap message," he repeated.

I looked at the piece of paper, unfolding it, and read only a small group of neatly typed numbers.

"It's a test," he said. "Don't you know what to do?"

Obviously I did not know what to do.

The corporal shook his head and sighed. "You guys are all supposed to know what to do with one of these. That's the way it goes, you don't know what you're doing, they don't know what they're doing, and I sure don't know what I'm doing."

"So what's it all about?" I asked.

"All right," he said, "you call your command bunker and tell the sergeant you've got a black handicap message. You read off the numbers. The sergeant copies them down and passes them on."

"Should I do it now?"

"Yeah, you should do it now."

I cranked the field phone, reached the sergeant in

Bunker 12, gave him my information, and hung up. The corporal retrieved his piece of paper and turned to go.

"Hold it," I said. "What the hell is going on?"

He explained. A black handicap message tested the efficiency of communications along the chain of command. Originating in my humble bunker, those numbers would be passed from one headquarters to the next until they arrived at the Pentagon itself. Crucial to the test was not only correct transmission of the number series, but also the amount of time required to pass information through command channels. "Are you bullshitting me?" I asked.

"Would anyone come way out here in the middle of the night to bullshit you?" The corporal hoisted himself up out of the bunker and descended the catwalk to his jeep.

"Hey, how long does it usually take?" I asked.

"I don't know. A couple of hours. Who gives a shit?" He wheeled his jeep around on the narrow road and raced back along the perimeter into the night, anxious for the safety of the depot.

MIAMI

THE PASSING OF the broom from one bunker to the next was a time-honored ritual that had survived the earlier attacks on the ammunition depot, the physical deterioration of the bunkers during the months since their construction, even the coming of the monsoon and subsequent reduction in the amount of dust to be swept from the bunks and floorboards. No one remembered when the last inspection of the bunker line had been made, but still the broom passed every night. It was a good chance to catch up on the news.

"You hear about Fine?"

"No."

"Got orders for the Congo. Diplomatic mission. Far out."

"Hm."

"You haven't heard about the new offensive in September?"

"No."

"Supposed to be a big offensive in September, big as Tet."

"Hm."

"You hear about all the fucking money they dug up near Qui Nhon?"

"No."

"A hundred and fifty grand, all in fifty-dollar bills. The Treasury Department says there isn't supposed to be any fifty-dollar bills over here. We're paying for both fucking sides of this war."

"Hm."

"You hear about the Republicans?"

"No."

"Nominated Richard Nixon."

"Hm."

PERFUME

WE LIT UP any time after midnight. No one traveled the perimeter road after midnight.

"Ah-ha!"

Voice and boots on the catwalk startled us.

"What is that delightful odor? Could it be—? Yes, I think it is!" A stranger climbed unhindered into our bunker. I was too stunned even to try to challenge him. But there was nothing to fear. He was a PFC from that night's reaction force, out alone for a hike and a smoke.

"We've got an IG. The fools are awake cleaning the barracks. I snuck out."

We got acquainted.

"Let me lay some of this on you people."

I inhaled.

The stranger went his way.

One of the two guards spending the night with me slept; in slow motion, the other climbed onto the upper bunk. "Jesus, what a buzz I've got. Wow, I can't stand up, I've got to sit down. Wow, I think I might get sick."

I draped my arm over the machine gun and bored into the luminous jungle with my eyes.

RELEASE

ONE OF THOSE nights of brilliant stars motionless above the earth whose grinding stones you can feel move beneath your feet. Even through thick-soled military shoes. The ground turning, tumbling around an axis fixed now nearly on the horizon, but not quite right, the wrongness more apparent at this latitude than farther north where the pole star hangs high in the air and a cold wind keeps your head clear. Eyes closed, you can hear the stones wrenching themselves slowly through each new alignment. The spindle has slipped from its proper place. The gears are binding.

I spent many watches completely outside the bunker, sitting on the roof or stretched full-length on the front of the sandbag hill gazing benignly into hostile territory. Sometimes I stood on the catwalk identifying stars and counting artillery bursts in the hills to the east. When it rained I crouched under the bunker eaves and caught the smells raised by moisture in the jungle and carried by the wind across clearings and through barbed wire. I did some undisciplined and inconclusive thinking. I daydreamed.

But the nights seemed to invite some physical participation, so from time to time I unbuttoned my fatigues and masturbated, stirring great clouds of sediment in my mind. From one of them I extracted this notion that the earth's axis had slid out of alignment and was wandering through the heavens. Under such celestial circumstances there could be no idea of progress, no notion of human accountability for human actions. Only the apocalypse could restore order. On subsequent nights I entertained further revelations of cosmic significance, all of which were cut short by the crisp sound of my sperm landing on the weathered canvas of the sandbags.

DUTY

"HELLO?"
  "Hello?"
  "Hello?"
  "Who called?"

"Bunker 18?"

"Right here."

"This is Bunker 15."

"Who called?"

"Ah, men, this is Bunker 17, ah, we've been notified of suspected movement to our immediate front, ah, I'm instructed to announce that, ah, we're going on seventy-five percent alert, ah, this means two men will be awake at all times."

"This is Bunker 17, ah, everyone on the line acknowledge please."

"Bunker 15, roger."

"Bunker 16, we read you lima charlie."

"Bunker 20, roger."

"Bunker 18?"

"Bunker 18, right, seventy-five percent alert."

"Bunker 19?"

"Bunker 19? Bunker 17 calling Bunker 19, acknowledge please."

"All right, Bunker 19, answer your fucking phone."

"Bunker 18, will you shout over to Bunker 19 and wake those people up?"

"This is Bunker 18, sarge, 19 says they're on the line and can hear you okay, but you can't hear them."

"All right, 19, sorry. Stay on the line."

"Bunker 17?"

"This is Bunker 17."

"Bunker 17, this is Bunker 15, about this seventy-five percent alert: two men awake, one asleep only makes sixty-six and two-thirds percent alert. To bring it up to a full seventy-five percent I'm going to have to wake up eight and a third percent of the last guy."

"Just do the best you can, Bunker 15."

"Hello?"

"Hello?"

"Who called?"

"Is this Bunker 17?"

"This is 17."

"Bunker 17? Come in, Bunker 17."

"This is Bunker 17, I read you lima charlie."

"Bunker 17?"

"What, for Christ's sake?"

"Hey, Bunker 17, this is Bunker 20, there's something in our wire."

"What is it?"

"Too dark to tell."

" 'Too dark to tell.' Shit, man."

"Who is that?"

"All right, 20, pop one, let's see what it is."

"Bunker 19, did you shoot off that second flare?"

"Keep observing, Bunker 18, I think it was a wild pig."

"You're a wild pig."

"Who is that? Let's keep this line clear, men!"

"Bunker 16?"

"Shut up. Go to hell."

"Bunker 17?"

"This is 17."

"Hey, Bunker 17, this is Bunker 20. All the crickets and frogs and shit have stopped making noise out in front of us. Bunker 17? Hey, Bunker 17? Bunker 17? What do we do? Come on, Bunker 17!"

AUBADE

YOU NOTICE FIRST the stilling of the night breeze. It happens abruptly; one minute your skin is cooled by the vague slow movement of air which began at dusk, the next it is not. From the jungle come tiny sounds previously masked by the whisper of leaves and branches. Then they, too, vanish. Nothing moves. Nothing. You look to the east, where you know the hills lie unevenly on the horizon you cannot see. You try to pick them out, straining to catch the first instant that they appear, staring where you think they will be; suddenly they are there, higher or lower than you had expected, the world has solidified and divided into two shades of black. Dawn is a livid, slowly spreading bruise on the face of the darkness. Birds rustle and murmur. The horizon fans to the north and south. In back of you is a strange murk, confused by several indefinable colors. Clouds form, hard shapes near the hilltops, soft shadows overhead. The sky turns blue, pink, light orange, yellow, pale gold. The buzz of a locust is followed by the flap of large wings. Details emerge in the land below the crests of the hills, some trees show their skeletons, brown and green are added to the spectrum of the visible. To the left and right other bunkers are gloomy neolithic mounds topped by thick slab roofs the color of very old rust. Flying insects rise in swarms to begin work. Grass and bushes sigh. The sky is light now, lightest just over the hump of the hill slightly to the north of east. Blue becomes white; white flashes incandescent as the tip of the sun blinds you. You turn your head away. The air is not clear; columns of smoke line the sky. Haze and fog lie in the low places. The river to the southeast is buried in white floss. Black dots of helicopters float in single file through the air above the hills, bringing night patrols home to their bases. A slight wind brings an oily smell to your nose. You itch. From somewhere comes the sound of an engine. The sun climbs. You face a day glistening, reptilian, fresh from its shell.

LOBSTER

"IMAGINE MY SURPRISE (the medic narrated loudly as four of us sprawled in a deuce-and-a-half tearing at top speed through the depot to breakfast), man, six months in this sewer of an outfit, you can't get a transfer out of here, you can't get TDY, you can't even get your ass attached to the fucking dispensary, so the complaints start up, I write some, everybody writes some, we get those Congressmen on the horn and we expect things to happen, you know? We got a union. I'm not shittin' you guys, a union. We make demands. We go up through channels like it says, you know, but we make demands. So one of our demands is about the crap we eat. That's our demand, right? Better food? Right. So last night, we head over to the mess hall, it's a Saturday and we expect hamburgers, figuring no C-ration hamburgers this time because the roads have been clear for three fucking weeks and it's about time the old ground beef turns up again. So we head over, and you know what they're serving? Lobster tails! Lobster tails? What are they doing serving lobster tails? What's going on? Drawn butter, the whole works. Lobster tails! Far fucking out. I figured that right after dinner they were going to tell us to line up for the ground assault on Hanoi, but I eat anyway. Figured they were going to make us paint the mess hall. Something like that. But I eat, and it's good, you know?"

ARMAGEDDON

LONG, VERY HOT morning, bird cries at regular intervals from the trees. Nodding over my book. When it comes, the attack rolls through the bunker line effortlessly. Some of us escape by hiding in the foliage on the other side of the road. The depot is destroyed. Long Binh's thousands of clerks are mobilized and fight holding actions for their positions. A general offensive throughout Vietnam threatens to bring down the Saigon government. Fresh U. S. combat troops are airlifted in. Unrestricted bombing of the North is resumed. South Vietnamese units sweep into the Delta and encounter fierce resistance. North Vietnamese troops emerge from Cambodian sanctuaries and strike Saigon in force. U. S. ships blockade Haiphong harbor. Communist divisions operating in the Central Highlands lay siege to isolated U. S. fire bases. A joint force of American, South Vietnamese, Korean, and Australian units engage main-strength Communist elements at the DMZ. Chinese troops join in the defense of North Vietnam. Laos is invaded simultaneously by American and Chinese armored columns attempting end-runs of the battle line. Russia calls an emergency session of the United Nations Security Council. In major clashes on both sides of the DMZ neither army gains clear advantage. Protracted artillery duels begin. Mass uprisings throw Saigon into chaos and South Vietnamese government leaders are evacuated to ships of the Sixth Fleet. A provisional government is established by neutralist and pro-Communist political leaders. High-level private negotiations begin at Geneva. Chinese and American troops withdraw from their entrenched positions along the DMZ. Formal peace talks are convened. Cease-fire is declared.

CZECHOSLOVAKIA

THE WELL-INFORMED were discussing current events over the field phone. I listened, but stayed out of it.

"If they've taken Dubček to Moscow he's probably dead by now."

"I just didn't believe they'd actually go through with it."

"The radio stations knew about it in advance and set up secret spots to broadcast from. They kept everybody cool."

"You've got to hand it to kids who throw stones at tanks."

"Well, there are good guys and bad guys in the Kremlin just as there are good guys and bad guys in Washington. The bad guys won."

A new voice cut in. "We should bomb the shit out of them."

"One war at a time, huh?"

PRODUCT

THE C-RATIONS had been packed a long time ago, everybody knew, but nobody knew just when, perhaps as far back as World War II. Most of the food tasted pretty good, considering. Inside the unmarked gray cardboard cartons there were tins of "main dish," various small tins (cheese and crackers in one, fruit dessert in another, etc.), and cellophane bags containing fork, napkin, salt, pepper, sugar, dehydrated cream, and ten cigarettes. Of the main dish selections, some were choice (tuna, ham), some not so choice (veal, hamburgers), some inedible (bacon and eggs). All of the tins were olive green; contents were printed in black according to a standard form, noun first, adjectives trailing with their commas. Brand name appeared only as a means of identifying the packer. I visualized dozens of cartoon factories turning out these uniform dark green tins and gray cardboard boxes, selfless owners and managers eschewing profitable competition to serve their country, patriotic stockholders approving, grim-faced workers unaware of any change.

In the bunkers we encountered one major problem with C-rations: the familiar ingenious government-issue P-38 can opener was not included in every C-ration box. In fact, finding a P-38 in your box was a little like finding a prize in a package of breakfast cereal. It was something to cherish, because those C-ration cans were *hard*. They conformed to *government specifications*. They were *tin cans,* not aluminum cans or vinyl-covered cardboard cans. With a good pair of pliers and a lot of time you could worry one open; artful wielding of a bayonet produced primitive but satisfactory results; blunt instruments cracked the cans but wasted most of their contents; shooting them, although entertaining, was not a good idea nourishment-wise; various other schemes occurred to me at various times, but a P-38 was the only guaranteed method of success. Without one, you might go hungry. I knew several men who carried them around their necks where they hung their dog-tags. One man wore a P-38 on the same chain with his crucifix.

GUIDANCE

MILLER CAME OUT on what was probably to be his last twenty-four-hour guard duty, managed to find out which bunker I was in and walked down early in the afternoon to say hello. He looked happy. "How many days?" I asked him.

"I won't tell you. You'll just get depressed."

Instead, Miller talked about the changes that had taken

place since Colonel Hamilton had assumed command of the office.

"The man's insane. First thing, he decides he's got to have his own private partitions, and we do the plywood and mahogany stain thing again. He scrounges another air conditioner. He hires a new secretary."

"Suzanne's gone?"

"Downstairs. This new one is a real pig. Hamilton says he wants someone to serve his guests coffee."

"Good grief."

"Then he sets up new, streamlined organizational machinery, and I've got to type such gems as this."

I took the disposition form he handed me and read, "SUBJECT: Requests for Command Guidance. TO: All AG Officers. 1. It may be necessary on occasion for you to request command guidance from the Adjutant General concerning various problems which occur. 2. Effective immediately, no problem will be presented to the Adjutant General without the accompaniment of a proposed solution, regardless of the manner of presentation, i. e., written or oral. R. A. Hamilton, LTC, AGC, Adjutant General."

"Classic," I said.

"I brought it out to make you feel better. We're all going crazy. There's a new lieutenant now, he's floundering trying to figure out your filing system, he can't get through to the units because he doesn't know any of the clerks, it takes him three drafts before the Chief of Staff will let his letters pass, and, on top of all that, Hamilton hits him with this."

I took another disposition form. "SUBJECT: Adjutant General Liaison to Information Office. TO: 1LT Robert D. Wexler. 1. You are hereby appointed to act as my liaison with the Information Officer for the purpose of insuring that all aspects of my section to include those elements under my operational control and under my staff supervision are properly recognized for their accomplishments through the use of hometown news releases and articles for various service papers. In this connection it is not necessary nor do I expect you to write articles, edit articles, or in any way act as an information specialist. All I expect you to do is to insure that the Information Officer is made aware of newsworthy items occurring in this section. 2. In connection with routine items such as arrivals, departures, awards, and promotions you are expected to make DA Form 1526 available to those individuals desiring such information to appear in hometown newspapers and to offer such assistance as may be requested. 3. In performing these duties you are authorized direct contact with the Information Officer, this command, any branch in this section, and the Commanders of all subordinate units or their authorized representatives. 4. You will clear any request for other than routine individual hometown news releases with me before presentation to the Information Officer. 5. This appointment is not intended to consume your entire working day, in fact it should not take more than five percent of your time. If it appears that you will become involved for a greater period of time, advise me, in writing, of the reasons therefor. R. A. Hamilton, LTC, AGC, Adjutant General."

I handed the copy back to him.

"He's got everybody pissed off. No crossword puzzles on duty, so Major McCarthy spends all day at the PX. No reading on duty, so we all sit around like bumps on a log waiting for mealtimes to roll around. And these mad DF's keep coming."

"I know McCarthy's no use, but can't Major Inhalt do anything?"

"Major Inhalt is threatening to become Lieutenant-Colonel Inhalt and be transferred to MACV at Tan Son Nhut."

"What about Sergeant Kroeber?"

"He's short."

"Short? You mean he didn't extend again?"

"No, he says the war's over now and the horseshit's getting started."

We talked for a little while longer, and then Pete climbed out of my bunker and scrambled down the hill. I watched his listless walk along the perimeter road, annoyed that I missed him.

RAGNAROK

WHEN IT COMES, the attack rolls through the bunker line effortlessly. Some of us escape by lying in our bunkers pretending to be dead. The depot is destroyed; Long Binh's thousands of clerks take to the woods. A general offensive throughout Vietnam panics the U. S. commanders and triggers full-scale bombing raids on Hanoi, Haiphong, the panhandle, and the Ho Chi Minh trail. We cross the DMZ and fight our way deep into North Vietnamese territory. Chinese troops enter the war and bring us to a standstill. Russian, Chinese, North Vietnamese, South Vietnamese, Laotian, and American aircraft battle in the skies. U. S. ships engage Russian and North Vietnamese craft at the approaches to Haiphong harbor. Our bombers strike at supply routes on both sides of the Chinese border. Fire storms destroy Saigon; the government falls. A provisional coalition government is formed. Plans are announced for the possible evacuation of all American troops from Indochina. The President of the United States is assassinated and right-wing pressure forces the new President to take strong military action in Southeast Asia. Our troops make amphibious landings along the North Vietnamese Red River Delta and strike directly for Hanoi. Chinese planes attack ships of the Sixth Fleet. Limited nuclear war begins. Land-based missiles are launched against enemy missile sites. China's government is destroyed. The United States suffers fifteen percent casualties. Russia suffers ten percent casualties. Ballistic missile submarines at sea are given orders to strike population centers. Everybody dies.

ORDNANCE

AT FOUR-FORTY-FIVE, if I was in one of the bunkers on the eastern side of the depot, I pulled out my borrowed watch and began to count the minutes until the five o'clock fireworks display. I had watched this show often but was still not tired of it. During the day, trucks carried the outdated ammunition a quarter-mile from the depot and left it in a clearing I could just barely make out if my bunker was on high ground. Before the detonation a helicopter flew over the site. Then there were long moments of waiting; I could not trust my watch and never turned my eyes away from the spot. If I was still looking when the explosion came I saw the smooth hemisphere of fire, the shock wave bubble, the flattened trees and the wall of dust in silence until huge noise slammed into the bunker. Sometimes other, smaller explosions followed, but more often everything went up in one grand blast. HA-*BLAM*! Smoke poured into the sky afterward. What a great sight. And what a great noise! KA-*BOOM*! Terrific.

CHICAGO

FIRST I HEARD that large demonstrations were planned, which was to be expected, and that the Mayor had announced he would keep order, which was also to be expected. Then I heard that twenty thousand troops would be on hand and that sixty black GI's had staged a sit-down strike at Fort Hood when ordered to go. From an amateur political analyst I understood that Gene had no chance, George had no chance, and if Hubert didn't take it on the first ballot, Teddy would get the nod. I was reminded that labor troubles in the city had affected transportation and communications. I discovered that the FBI had unearthed plans to dump LSD into the city's water supply. I read that the Unit Rule had been abolished, a "peace plank" had been proposed by a minority of the Platform Committee, and Georgia's Lester Maddox group had not been seated pending the outcome of a challenge by a rival delegation. A sergeant told me about a lot of violence in Lincoln Park. I found out that the peace plank had been respectably defeated. I was informed that city police had apparently gone crazy, injuring hundreds of people. A crowd had been pushed through the plate-glass window of the Hilton Hotel's Haymarket Lounge, someone reported. I saw a remarkable *Stars and Stripes* headline which read, "Police Storm Hotel, Beat McCarthy Aides." There was speculation that newsmen were being deliberately assaulted. I learned that Hubert Humphrey had received the Democratic nomination. I was told of a silent candlelight parade by delegates from the Amphitheater to the Loop.

RIOT

THE MP WAS unsympathetic. "We'll let them live in their own filth as long as they want."

"You mean they're still loose?"

"Loose? Hell, no. They got one part of the compound, is all. They're not going anywhere."

"Did some escape?"

He shrugged. "Hard to tell, with all the records gone. May be a couple of weeks before they get a good head count."

"I wonder if a guy named Forbes was in the stockade."

"No idea."

"Larry Forbes. He was in for pot. I understood that they were going to move all the narcotics guys to Okinawa."

"I don't know. I don't think so." He lit a cigarette and glanced at the rain heading toward us.

"Was a guy named Haines Cook still there?"

"What, do you know everybody in LBJ?"

I chuckled nervously.

"The whole deal was chicken-shit," the MP said.

"But somebody got killed, didn't he?"

"Yeah. Big deal. One out of seven hundred."

"Out of how many?"

"About seven hundred, more or less. Give or take a few."

"In that one spot? I've seen it; it's only two blocks long!"

"It's a lot smaller than that now, and most of what's left is charcoal."

A few drops of rain fell.

"I've got to take off, I'm going to get wet," the MP said.

"Did you guys use tear gas?"

"Shit yeah."

"Many people get hurt?"

"Mostly them."

"How come you went in?"

"Well, what are you going to do? Let a bunch of militants take the place over?"

Rain was falling harder. On the road the other men in the detail struggled to secure a tarpaulin over the trailer-load of old ammunition they had collected from the bunker. At my feet, my new shells gleamed in their fresh boxes.

"What's the status of things now?" I asked.

"Most everyone is sleeping outside; the fucking Afros are fenced off by themselves. When they feel like giving their right names, they can come out."

"I guess technically it was the worst stockade riot in Army history."

The MP sneered. "Technically."

GARBAGE

As I APPROACHED the magic thirty-day mark, that date when I could no longer be reassigned, transferred, lent out on temporary duty, or otherwise fucked with, the orderly room sent me an out-processing slip and told me to begin working on it. The next day an order arrived removing me from the guard roster and dumping me back into Headquarters Company as a nominal duty soldier, although I was expected to spend most of my time staying out of everybody's way. Reshevsky let me know that I was not supposed to report back to the AG Section. This was fine with me.

On the last night out I caught a ride from the bunker line directly back to the company area. Hart was driving; it seems that Colonel Hamilton had overheard one of his monologues on death and had reassigned him to the orderly room. I sat in the cab of the truck with him. His headlights didn't work and he wanted to make it back before the light failed; he asked me about a short cut along the perimeter road to the construction work at the new supply battalion warehouses. I had seen jeeps travel off in that direction, so we gave it a try. Hart must have missed the turn. We wound up in pitch darkness somewhere southeast of Long Binh looking for the 1st Aviation helipad. I spotted a glow on our left and we drove overland toward it. Hart bounced the truck through a series of shallow trenches and then we were in the midst of the Long Binh garbage dump. The stench was dizzying. Murky fires flickered and smoldered. Smoke blinded us. I climbed out on the running board and tried to tell Hart which way to turn. The engine stalled. Hart began to cry. I considered it, but collapsed instead into helpless laughter.

Three Hard Sonnets

Sandra McPherson

1

IF you can buy all those groceries
why do you wear those clothes?
the woman said.

The phone rang:
If you answer our
question you can take a trip.

What do you think of me? said
the gambler telling me
his life.

Are you lost asked the policeman.
Why don't you smile.

No.

She said, Sometime I'd love to talk with you.
He walked out the door without saying good-bye.

2

I parked in the driveway.
Getting out I glimpsed the body
of a tall Indian brave
framed on the floor of the station wagon.

Another time one of those big family dinners:
we invited Uncle George
and he hooked over the table
from his seat at its head.

She sewed me a red dress but said
finish this hem,
I'm going away.

An old corpse of myself obstructed
our stairwell. I covered its face
with papers and books.

3

Proof! proof! It sounds like something
going up in smoke, abracadabra
smoke, producing
the answer to nothing.

At ease! at ease! You must look
at ease. There are places for nervousness:
stand trembling over the wastebasket
till anxiety falls in.

Beautiful! beautiful! I have no
big toe, no knee.
Compliments buried them
as well as insult.

Action!
OK enough, enough, wrap it up.

Crimes of Passion: The Slasher

Terry Stokes

WHAT I like most is when
the hemline rises
& they place the high heel,
usually the right,
onto the first step of the bus,
then, they grasp the small
rod, & pull themselves up. The nylons
flare like hot butter, & as that
thigh bulges slightly, & then
taut, I gently nudge her,
& with the razor blade, one side
taped, as if a finger
were lovingly running from the back
of the knee toward the buttocks.
She will sometimes turn & smile,
feeling some part of herself freed,
only hours later does she learn
how deep my passion runs, the thick
blood of birth drips silently
to some cold floor,
& in that pool, my face returns
the wonderful smile, & then, I think,
she probably screams. She will dream of me,
& that is all
anyone can ever ask.

Authors and Writers

Roland Barthes

Who speaks? Who writes? We still lack a sociology of language. What we know is that language is a power, and that, from public body to social class, a group of men is sufficiently defined if it possesses, to various degrees, the national language. Now for a very long time—probably for the entire classical capitalist period—i.e., from the sixteenth to the nineteenth century, in France—the uncontested owners of the language were authors and they alone. If, with the exception of preachers and jurists (enclosed moreover in functional languages), no one else spoke, and this "monopoly" of the language produced a rigid order, an order less of producers than of production: it was not the literary *profession* which was stratified (it has developed greatly in three hundred years, from the domestic poet to the businessman-writer), but the very *substance* of this literary discourse which was subjected to rules of use, genre, and composition, more or less immutable from Marot to Verlaine, from Montaigne to Gide. Contrary to so-called primitive societies, in which there is witchcraft only through the agency of a witch-doctor, as Marcel Mauss has shown, the literary *institution* transcended the literary *functions*, and within this institution what presides is its essential substance, language. Institutionally, the literature of France is its language, a half-linguistic, half-aesthetic system which has not lacked a mythic dimension as well, that of its *clarity*.

When, in France, did the author cease being the only one to speak? Doubtless at the time of the Revolution, when there first appear men who appropriate the authors' language for political ends. The institution remains in place: it is still a matter of that great French language, whose lexicon and euphony are respectfully preserved throughout the greatest paroxysm of French history; but the functions change, the personnel is increased for the next hundred years; the authors themselves, from Chateaubriand or Maistre to Hugo or Zola, help broaden the literary function, transform this institutionalized language of which they are still the acknowledged owners into the instrument of a new action; and alongside these *authors*, in the strict sense of the word, a new group is constituted and develops, a new custodian of the public language. Intellectuals? The word has a complex resonance [1]; I prefer calling them here *writers*. And since the present may be that fragile moment in history when the two functions coexist, I should like to sketch a comparative typology of the author and the writer with reference to the substance they share: language.

The author performs a function, the writer an activity. Not that the author is a pure essence: he acts, but his action is immanent in its object, it is performed paradoxically on its own instrument: language. The author is the man who *labors*, who *works up* his utterance (even if he is inspired) and functionally absorbs himself in this labor, this work. His activity involves two kinds of norm: of technique (composition, genre, style) and of craft (patience, correctness, perfection). The paradox is that the substance becoming in a sense its own end, literature is at bottom a tautological activity, like that of those cybernetic machines constructed *for themselves* (Ashby's homeostat): the author is a man who radically absorbs the world's *why* in a *how-to-write*. And the miracle, so to speak, is that this narcissistic activity has always provoked an interrogation of the world: by enclosing himself in the *how-to-write*, the author ultimately discovers the open question par excellence: why the world? What is the meaning of things? In short, it is precisely when the author's work becomes its own end that it regains a mediating character: the author conceives of literature as an end, the world restores it to him as a means: and it is in

[1] Apparently the word *intellectual*, in the sense we give it today, was born at the time of the Dreyfus Affair, obviously applied by the anti-Dreyfusards to the Dreyfusards.

this perpetual *inconclusiveness* that the author rediscovers the world, an alien world moreover, since literature represents it as a question—never, finally, as an answer.

Language is neither an instrument nor a vehicle: it is a structure, as we increasingly suspect; but the author is the only man, by definition, to lose his own structure and that of the world in the structure of language. Yet this language is an (infinitely) labored substance; it is a little like a super-language. Reality is never anything but a pretext for it (for the author, *to write* is an intransitive verb); hence it can never explain the world, or at least, when it claims to explain the world, it does so only the better to conceal the world's ambiguity: once the explanation is fixed in a *work,* it immediately becomes an ambiguous product of the real, to which it is linked by perspective. In short, literature is always unrealistic, but its very unreality permits it to question the world—though these questions can never be direct: starting from a theocratic explanation of the world, Balzac finally does nothing but interrogate. Thus the author existentially forbids himself two kinds of language, whatever the intelligence or the sincerity of his enterprise: first, *doctrine,* since he converts despite himself, by his very project, every explanation into a spectacle: he is always an agent of ambiguity[2]; second, *evidence:* since he has consigned himself to language, the author cannot have a naïve consciousness, cannot "work up" an outcry without his message bearing finally much more on the working-up than on the outcry. By identifying himself with language, the author loses all claim to truth, for language is precisely that structure whose very goal (at least historically, since the Sophists), once it is no longer rigorously transitive, is to neutralize the true and the false.[3]

---

[2] An author can produce a system, but it will never be consumed as such.

[3] Structure of reality and structure of language: no better indication of the difficulty of a coincidence between the two than the constant failure of dialectic, once it becomes discourse; for language is not dialectic, it can only say *"we must be dialectical,"* but it cannot be so itself: language is a representation without perspective, except precisely for the author's; but the author dialecticizes himself, he does not dialecticize the world.

But what he obviously gains is the power to disturb the world, to afford it the dizzying spectacle of *praxis* without sanction. This is why it is absurd to ask an author for "commitment": a "committed" author claims simultaneous participation in two structures, inevitably a source of deception. What we can ask of an author is that he be responsible. Again, let there be no mistake: whether or not an author is responsible for his *opinions* is unimportant; whether or not an author assumes, more or less intelligently, the ideological implications of his work is also secondary; an author's true responsibility is to support literature as *a failed commitment,* as a Mosaic glance at the Promised Land of the real (this is Kafka's kind of responsibility, for example).

Naturally, literature is not a grace, it is the body of the projects and decisions which lead a man to fulfill himself (that is, in a sense, to essentialize himself) in language alone: an author is a man who wants to be an author. Naturally too, society, which consumes the author, transforms project into vocation, labor into talent, and technique into art. Thus is born the myth of *fine writing:* the author is a salaried priest, he is the half-respectable, half-ridiculous guardian of the sanctuary of the great French Language, a kind of national treasure, a sacred merchandise, produced, taught, consumed, and exported in the context of a sublime economy of values. This sacralization of the author's labor on his form has great consequences, and not merely formal ones: it permits society to distance the work's content when it risks becoming an embarrassment, to convert it into pure spectacle to which it is entitled to apply a liberal (i.e., an indifferent) judgment, to neutralize the revolt of passion, the subversion of criticism (which forces the "committed" author into an incessant and impotent provocation)—in short, to assimilate the author: every author is eventually digested by the literary institution, unless he scuttles himself, i.e., unless he ceases to identify his being with that of language. This is why so few authors renounce writing, for that is literally to kill themselves, to die to the being they have chosen; and if there are such authors, their silence echoes like an inexplicable conversion (Rimbaud).[4]

The *writer*, on the other hand, is a "transitive" man: he posits a goal (to give evidence, to explain, to instruct) of which language is merely a means; for him language supports a *praxis*, it does not constitute one. Thus language is restored to the nature of an instrument of communication, a vehicle of "thought." Even if the writer pays some attention to style, this concern is never ontological. The writer performs no essential technical action upon language; he employs an utterance common to all writers, a *koine* in which we can of course distinguish certain dialects (Marxist, for example, or Christian, or existentialist), but very rarely styles. For what defines the writer is the fact that his project of communication is *naïve:* he does not admit that his message is reflexive, that it closes over itself, and that we can read in it, diagnostically, anything else but what he means: what writer would tolerate a psychoanalysis of his language? He believes that his work resolves an ambiguity, institutes an irreversible explanation (even if he regards himself as a modest instructor); whereas for the author, as we have seen, it is just the other way around: he knows that his language, intransitive by choice and by labor, inaugurates an ambiguity, even if it appears to be peremptory, that it offers itself, paradoxically, as a monumental silence to be deciphered, that it can have no other motto but Jacques Rigaut's profound remark: *and even when I affirm, I am still questioning.*

The author participates in the priest's role, the writer in the clerk's; the author's language is an intransitive act (hence, in a sense, a gesture), the writer's an activity. The paradox is that society consumes a transitive language with many more reservations than an intransitive one: the writer's status, even today when writers abound, is much more problematic than the author's. This is primarily the consequence of a material circumstance: the author's language is a merchandise offered through traditional chan-

---

[4] These are the modern elements of the problem. We know that on the contrary Racine's contemporaries were not at all surprised when he suddenly stopped writing tragedies and became a royal functionary.

nels, it is the unique object of an institution created only
for literature; the writer's language, on the contrary, can
be produced and consumed only in the shadow of institutions which have, originally, an entirely different function
than to focus on language: the university, scientific and
scholarly research, politics, etc. Then, too, the writer's
language is dependent in another way: from the fact that it
is (or considers itself) no more than a simple vehicle, its
nature as merchandise is transferred to the project of which
it is the instrument: we are presumed to sell "thought"
exclusive of any art. Now the chief mythic attribute of
"pure" thought (it would be better to say "unapplied"
thought) is precisely that it is produced outside the channel
of money: contrary to form (which costs a lot, as Valéry
said), thought costs nothing, but it also does not sell itself,
it gives itself—generously. This points up at least two new
differences between author and writer. First, the writer's
production always has a free but also a somewhat "insistent" character: the writer offers society what society does
not always ask of him: situated on the margin of institutions
and transactions, his language appears paradoxically more
individual, at least in its motifs, than the author's language:
*the writer's function is to say at once and on every occasion
what he thinks* [5]; and this function suffices, he thinks, to
justify him; whence the critical, urgent aspect of the
writer's language: it always seems to indicate a conflict
between thought's irrepressible character and the inertia
of a society reluctant to consume a merchandise which no
specific institution normalizes. Thus we see *a contrario*—
and this is the second difference—that the social function
of literary language (that of the author) is precisely *to
transform thought* (or consciousness, or outcry) *into merchandise;* society wages a kind of vital warfare to appropriate, to acclimatize, to institutionalize the risk of
thought, and it is language, that model institution, which
affords it the means to do so. The paradox here is that

[5] This function of *immediate manifestation* is the very opposite of the author's: 1) the author hoards, he publishes at a
rhythm which is not that of his consciousness; 2) he mediatizes
what he thinks by a laborious and "regular" form; 3) he
permits a free interrogation of his work, he is anything but
dogmatic.

"provocative" *language* is readily accommodated by the literary institution: the scandals of language, from Rimbaud to Ionesco, are rapidly and perfectly integrated; whereas "provocative" *thought,* insofar as it is to be immediate (without mediation), can only exhaust itself in the no-man's-land of form: the scandal is never total.

I am describing here a contradiction which, in fact, is rarely pure: everyone today moves more or less openly between the two positions, the author's and the writer's; it is doubtless the responsibility of history which has brought us into the world too late to be complacent authors and too soon to be heeded writers. Today, each member of the intelligentsia harbors both roles in himself, one or the other of which he "retracts" more or less well: authors occasionally have the impulses, the impatiences of writers; writers sometimes gain access to the theater of language. We want *to write something,* and at the same time *we write* (intransitively). In short, our age produces a bastard type: the author-writer. His function is inevitably paradoxical: he provokes and exorcises at the same time; formally, his language is free, screened from the institution of literary language, and yet, enclosed in this very freedom, it secretes its own rules in the form of a common style; having emerged from the club of men-of-letters, the author-writer finds another club, that of the intelligentsia. On the scale of society as a whole, this new group has a *complementary* function: the intellectual's style functions as the paradoxical sign of a non-language, it permits society to experience the dream of a communication without system (without institution): to write without "style," to communicate "pure thought" without such communication developing any parasitical message—that is the model which the author-writer creates for society. It is a model at once distant and necessary, with which society plays something of a cat-and-mouse game: it acknowledges the author-writer by buying his books (however few), recognizing their public character; and at the same time it keeps him at a distance, obliging him to support himself by means of the subsidiary institutions it controls (the university, for instance), constantly accusing him of intellectualism, i.e., sterility (a reproach the author never incurs). In short, from an anthropological viewpoint, the author-writer is an excluded figure integrated by his very exclusion, a remote descendant of the Accursed: his function in society as a whole is perhaps related to the one Lévi-Strauss attributes to the witch-doctor: a function of complementarity, both witch-doctor and intellectual in a sense stabilizing a disease which is necessary to the collective economy of health. And naturally it is not surprising that such a conflict (or such a contract, if you prefer) should be joined on the level of language; for language is this paradox: the institutional-ization of subjectivity.

(Translated from the French by Richard Howard)

Sleeping on the Roof

Thomas Lux

TONIGHT I'm sleeping on the roof because
each night
when I sleep in bed,
I inevitably fall out of it.
The bed is only 2 feet
from the floor—

I'm sleeping near the edge
of the roof.
It's a test of my subconscious, that blind
swimmer with a candle
in his mouth.

If I fall off, it may be possible,
for the first time,
to measure the speed of sleep,
how fast and how deep we fall.
If I don't: this

is where I'll sleep every night.
I think I'll feel comfortable,
for who's never fallen
well over 100 feet, or more,
in his sleep?

Sisterhood

Marilyn Hacker

For Dora FitzGerald

No place for a lady, this
back-country gateway comes
up from dreams, the wounds
are an entrance, or a season ticket.
The morning freshness, the
summersend mountain calm:
distractions. "What do you
call this town?"

No man will love you, no
woman be your friend, your
face will go away, your body
betray you. We wrestled
to the floor, his fingers
blanching my elbows, cords
popping his neck. Don't look
into the sun. Don't squint.

He lay on the concrete
ramp of the bus terminal. I
massaged his back and shoulders through his clothes.
I opened his trenchcoat, peeled
its collar away from his thin
white shirt, his thin chest.
Staining the slashed white
yellowish pink, those wounds.

When you give the ghost
bread and water he asks
for, you incur prophecy.
"Why have you come here,
woman? Your city
is far away. We do not speak

your language. Your sister
is dead."

"Take off your rings
at the first gate. At the second
your crown of lapis lazuli.
You must leave your golden
breastplate at the third, and below
the gallows where he hangs
who forgot you, and will not rise,
break your mother's scepter."

They have killed him
often. He bled
on the concrete floor. My hands
were not healing. They took him
into the next room. I heard
gunshots. I woke screaming.
At the bottom of hell
he swings in the stinking wind. She watches.

We, women, never
trust his returnings. He takes
the bread and water, but
the words on the paper
are illegible. His body
lies severed on the white sand
and the pieces are not
food, they are stones.

We gather those
jewels and wear them,
lapis in the crown, amethysts
over the nipples, garnets
oozing on cool
fingers. The gateway
dreams itself up, and we eye the surly
guard, and strip, and go down.

A Conversation With My Father

Grace Paley

My father is eighty-six years old and in bed. His heart, that bloody motor, is equally old and will not do certain jobs anymore. It still floods his head with brainy light. But it won't let his legs carry the weight of his body around the house. Despite my metaphors, this muscle failure is not due to his old heart, he says, but to a potassium shortage. Sitting on one pillow, leaning on three, he offers last-minute advice and makes a request.

"I would like you to write a simple story just once more," he says, "the kind de Maupassant wrote, or Chekhov, the kind you used to write. Just recognizable people and then write down what happened to them next."

I say, "Yes, why not? That's possible." I want to please him, though I don't remember writing that way. I *would* like to try to tell such a story, if he means the kind that begins: "There was a woman . . ." followed by plot, the absolute line between two points which I've always despised. Not for literary reasons, but because it takes all hope away. Everyone, real or invented, deserves the open destiny of life.

Finally I thought of a story that had been happening for a couple of years right across the street. I wrote it down, then read it aloud. "Pa," I said, "how about this? Do you mean something like this?"

Once in my time there was a woman and she had a son. They lived nicely, in a small apartment in Manhattan. This boy at about fifteen became a junkie, which is not unusual in our neighborhood. In order to maintain her close friendship with him, she became a junkie too. She said it was part of the youth culture with which she felt very much at home. After a while, for a number of reasons, the boy gave it all up and left the city and his mother in disgust. Hopeless and alone, she grieved. We all visit her.

"O.K., Pa, that's it," I said, "an unadorned and miserable tale."

"But that's not what I mean," my father said. "You misunderstood me on purpose. You know there's a lot more to it. You know that. You left everything out. Turgenev wouldn't do that. Chekhov wouldn't do that. There are in fact Russian writers you never heard of, you don't have an inkling of, as good as anyone, who can write a plain ordinary story, who would not leave out what you have left out. I object not to facts, but to people sitting in trees talking senselessly, voices from who knows where . . ."

"Forget that one, Pa, what have I left out now? In this one?"

"Her looks, for instance."

"Oh. Quite handsome, I think. Yes."

"Her hair?"

"Dark, with heavy braids, as though she were a girl or a foreigner."

"What were her parents like, her stock? That she became such a person. It's interesting, you know."

"From out of town. Professional people. The first to be divorced in their county. How's that? Enough?" I asked.

"With you, it's all a joke," he said. "What about the boy's father? Why didn't you mention him? Who was he? Or was the boy born out of wedlock?"

"Yes," I said. "He was born out of wedlock."

"For Godsakes, doesn't anyone in your stories get married? Doesn't anyone have the time to run down to City Hall before they jump into bed?"

"No," I said. "In real life, yes. But in my stories, no."

"Why do you answer me like that?"

"Oh, Pa, this is a simple story about a smart woman who came to N.Y.C. full of interest love trust excitement very uptodate and about her son, what a hard time she had in this world. Married or not, it's of small consequence."

"It is of great consequence," he said.

"O.K.," I said.

"O.K. O.K. yourself," he said, "but listen. I believe you that she's good-looking but I don't think she was so smart."

"That's true," I said. "Actually that's the trouble with stories. People start out fantastic. You think they're extraordinary, but it turns out as the work goes along, they're just average with a good education, sometimes the other way around, the person's a kind of dumb innocent, but he outwits you and you can't even think of an ending good enough."

"What do you do then?" he asked. He had been a doctor for a couple of decades and then an artist for a couple of decades and he's still interested in details, craft, technique.

"Well, you just have to let the story lie around till some agreement can be reached between you and the stubborn hero."

"Aren't you talking silly, now?" he asked. "Start again," he said. "It so happens I'm not going out this evening. Tell the story again. See what you can do this time."

"O.K.," I said. "But it's not a five-minute job." Second attempt:

> Once across the street from us, there was a fine handsome woman, our neighbor. She had a son whom she loved because she'd known him since birth (in helpless chubby infancy, and in the wrestling, hugging ages, seven to ten, as well as earlier and later). This boy when he fell into the fist of adolescence became a junkie. He was not a hopeless one. He was in fact hopeful, an ideologue, and successful converter. With his busy brilliance, he wrote persuasive articles for his high school newspaper. Seeking a wider audience, using important connections, he drummed into Lower Manhattan newsstand distribution a periodical called *Oh! Golden Horse!*
>
> In order to keep him from feeling guilty (because guilt is the stony heart of nine-tenths of all clinically diagnosed cancers in America today, she said), and because she had always believed in giving bad habits room at home where one could keep an eye on them, she too became a junkie. Her kitchen was famous for a while—a center for intellectual addicts who knew what they were doing. A few felt artistic like Coleridge and others were scientific and revolutionary like Leary. Although she was often high herself, certain good mothering reflexes remained, and she saw to it that there was

lots of orange juice around and honey and milk and vitamin pills. However she never cooked anything but chili, and that no more than once a week. She explained, when we talked to her, seriously, with neighborly concern, that it was her part in the youth culture and she would rather be with the young, it was an honor, than with her own generation.

One week, while nodding through an Antonioni film, this boy was severely jabbed by the elbow of a stern and prose-lytizing girl, sitting beside him. She offered immediate apricots and nuts for his sugar level, spoke to him sharply, and took him home.

She had heard of him and his work and she herself published, edited, and wrote a competitive journal called *Man Does Live By Bread Alone*. In the organic heat of her continuous presence he could not help but become interested once more in his muscles, his arteries, and nerve connections. In fact he began to love them, treasure them, praise them with funny little songs in *Man Does Live* . . .

> the fingers of my flesh transcend
> my transcendental soul
> the tightness in my shoulders end
> my teeth have made me whole

To the mouth of his head (that glory of will and determination) he brought hard apples, nuts, wheat germ, and soybean oil. He said to his old friends: From now on, I guess I'll keep my wits about me. I'm going on the natch. He said he was about to begin a spiritual deep-breathing journey. How about you too, Mom? he asked kindly.

His conversion was so radiant, splendid, that neighborhood kids his age began to say that he had never been a real addict at all, only a journalist along for the smell of the story. The mother tried several times to give up what had become without her son and his friends a lonely habit. This effort only brought it to supportable levels. The boy and his girl took their electronic mimeograph and moved to the bushy edge of another borough. They were very strict. They said they would not see her again until she had been off drugs for sixty days.

At home alone in the evening, weeping, the mother read and reread the seven issues of *Oh! Golden Horse!* They seemed to her as truthful as ever. We often crossed the street to visit and console. But if we mentioned any of our children who were at college or in the hospital or dropouts at home, she would cry out, My baby! My baby! and burst into terrible, face-scarring, time-consuming tears. The End.

First my father was silent, then he said, "Number One: You have a nice sense of humor. Number Two: I see you can't tell a plain story. So don't waste time." Then he said, sadly, "Number Three: I suppose that means she was alone, she was left like that, his mother. Alone. Probably sick?"

I said, "Yes."

"Poor woman. Poor girl, to be born in a time of fools, to live among fools. The end. The end. You were right to put that down. The end."

I didn't want to argue, but I had to say, "Well, it is not necessarily the end, Pa."

"Yes," he said, "what a tragedy. The end of a person."

"No, Pa," I begged him. "It doesn't have to be. She's only about forty. She could be a hundred different things in this world as time goes on. A teacher or a social worker. An ex-junkie! Sometimes it's better than having a Master's in education."

"Jokes," he said. "As a writer that's your main trouble. You don't want to recognize it. Tragedy! Plain tragedy! Historical tragedy! No hope. The end."

"Oh, Pa," I said. "She could change."

"In your own life, too, you have to look it in the face." He took a couple of nitroglycerin. "Turn to five," he said pointing to the dial on the oxygen tank. He inserted the tubes into his nostrils and breathed deep. He closed his eyes and said, "No."

I had promised the family to always let him have the last word when arguing, but in this case I had a different responsibility. That woman lives across the street. She's my knowledge and my invention. I'm sorry for her. I'm not going to leave her there in that house crying. (Actually neither would Life, which unlike me has no pity.)

Therefore: She did change. Of course her son never came home again. But right now, she's the receptionist in a storefront community clinic in the East Village. Most of the customers are young people, some old friends. The head doctor has said to her—"if we only had three people in this clinic with your experiences . . ."

"The doctor said that?" my father took the oxygen tubes out of his nostrils and said. "Jokes. Jokes again."

"No, Pa, it could really happen that way, it's a funny world nowadays."

"No," he said. "Truth first. She will slide back. A person must have character. She does not."

"No, Pa," I said. "That's it. She's got a job. Forget it. She's in that storefront working."

"How long will it be?" he asked. "Tragedy! You too. When will you look it in the face?"

Lines for Leibniz

John Peck

THE hothouse flurry of the academy
Drove him to choose his life deliberately,

To let the carriage window's fluid landscape
Form his eye's garden, frame his singular grip

Upon the manifold—he would jot his notes
On whatever road sped the Duke's business.

Those notes lie now in Mainz, Hanover, Berlin,
Ungathered. How long, in wood walks, had he been

Fretting retrieval of Substantial Form
Only to lose it to the leaves?—though in time

They gave it all back to him, newly perfect.
How many designs he left to execute—

Wagon wheels that plowed themselves out of mud, and
Nails whose tiny spurs lodged them unrepentant

In the wood, and a museum that would house
Dutch sail-wagons and Chinese wind-carriages.

But it was this gift of tongues made into hands
That fated him to build in the Harz Mountains

For the Duke John of Hanover's silver mines
A windmill pump, to keep tunnels clear of rains;

The delegation came for its inspection,
And that day the wind died out of all heaven.

The wind died out of all Europe while he wrote
To hold its unity before the breeze, set

Full above the signature, *Pacidius,*
To yoke schismatics once more in the embrace

Of dialectic, strenuous, with small spurs.
What years dwindling to carriages, those letters—

Yet, the acacia boughs outside my window
Do not sway in fantasies of knowledge now,

This time their disarray holds their uphill slant
With an old, unforeseen advent of poignance:

The fern accuracy of each tiny fan
Hanging from the haphazard inflorescence

Finds place in some unguessed scheme of completeness,
Though still I feel little toward this locust, this

Thorny tree of Egypt.
                    Morning: he embarks
On *postes 'portefeuille* for the petty and grand dukes,

Taking with him on the quick trip by carriage
The *I-Ching.* It is still morning, the image

Fashions him kin to us, yet remote as well,
A profile accurate and sentimental

Looking up from the series of charmed guesses
At nothing in particular, beyond trees—

He forsook religion toward the end. Only
One came to his funeral, his secretary.

The Moon in Its Flight

Gilbert Sorrentino

THIS WAS IN 1948. A group of young people sitting on the darkened porch of a New Jersey summer cottage in a lake resort community. The host some Bernie wearing an Upsala College sweat shirt. The late June night so soft one can, in retrospect, forgive America for everything. There were perhaps eight or nine people there, two of them the people that this story sketches.

Bernie was talking about Sonny Stitt's alto on "That's Earl, Brother." As good as Bird, he said. Arnie said, bullshit: he was a very hip young man from Washington Heights, wore mirrored sunglasses. A bop drummer in his senior year at the High School of Performing Arts. Our young man, nineteen at this time, listened only to Rebecca, a girl of fifteen, remarkable in her New Look clothes. A long full skirt, black, snug tailored shirt of blue and white stripes with a high white collar and black velvet string tie, black kid Capezios. It is no wonder that lesbians like women.

At some point during the evening he walked Rebecca home. She lived on Lake Shore Drive, a wide road that skirted the beach and ran parallel to the small river that flowed into Lake Minnehaha. Lake Ramapo? Lake Tomahawk. Lake O-shi-wa-noh? Lake Sunburst. Leaning against her father's powder-blue Buick convertible, lost, in the indigo night, the creamy stars, sound of crickets, they kissed. They fell in love.

One of the songs that summer was "For Heaven's Sake." Another, "It's Magic." Who remembers the clarity of Claude Thornhill and Sarah Vaughan, their exquisite irrelevance? They are gone where the useless chrome doughnuts on the Buick's hood have gone. That Valhalla of Amos 'n' Andy and guinea fruit peddlers with golden earrings.

"Pleasa No Squeeza Da Banana." In 1948, the whole world seemed beautiful to young people of a certain milieu, or let me say, possible. Yes, it seemed a possible world. This idea persisted until 1950, at which time it died, along with many of the young people who had held it. In Korea, the Chinese played "Scrapple from the Apple" over loudspeakers pointed at the American lines. That savage and virile alto blue-clear on the sub-zero night. This is, of course, old news.

Rebecca was fair. She was fair. Lovely Jewish girl from the remote and exotic Bronx. To him, that vast borough seemed a Cythera—that it could house such fantastic creatures as she! He wanted to be Jewish. He was, instead, a Roman Catholic, awash in sin and redemption. What loathing he had for the Irish girls who went to eleven o'clock Mass, legions of blushing pink and lavender spring coats, flat white straw hats, the crinkly veils over their open faces. Church clothes, under which their inviolate crotches sweetly nestled in soft hair.

She had white and perfect teeth. Wide mouth. Creamy stars, pale nights. Dusty black roads out past the beach. The sunlight on the raft, moonlight on the lake. Sprinkle of freckles on her shoulders. Aromatic breeze.

OF COURSE THIS WAS a summer romance, but bear with me and see with what banal literary irony it all turns out—or does not turn out at all. The country bowled and spoke of Truman's grit and spunk. How softly we had slid off the edge of civilization.

The liquid moonlight filling the small parking area outside the gates to the beach. Bass flopping softly in dark waters. What was the scent of the perfume she wore? The sound of a car radio in the cool nights, collective American memory. Her browned body, delicate hair bleached golden on her thighs. In the beach pavilion they danced and drank Cokes. Mel Tormé and the Mell-Tones. Dizzy Gillespie. "Too Soon To Know." In the mornings, the sun so crystal and lucent it seemed the very exhalation of the sky, he would swim alone to the raft and lie there, the beach empty, music from the pavilion attendant's radio coming to him in splinters. At such times he would thrill himself by pretending that he had not yet met Rebecca and that he would see her that afternoon for the first time.

The first time he touched her breasts he cried in his shame and delight. Can all this really have taken place in America? The trees rustled for him, as the rain did rain. One day, in New York, he bought her a silver friendship ring, tiny perfect hearts in bas-relief running around it so that the point of one heart nestled in the cleft of another. Innocent symbol that tortured his blood. She stood before him in the pale light in white bra and panties, her shorts and blouse hung on the hurricane fence of the abandoned and weed-grown tennis court and he held her, stroking her flanks and buttocks and kissing her shoulders. The smell of her flesh, vague sweat and perfume. Of course he was insane. She caressed him so far as she understood how through his faded denim shorts. Thus did they flay themselves, burning. What were they to do? Where were they to go? The very thought of the condom in his pocket made his heart careen in despair. Nothing was like anything said it was after all. He adored her.

SHE WAS ENTERING her second year at Evander Childs that coming fall. He hated this school he had never seen, and hated all her fellow students. He longed to be Jewish, dark and mysterious and devoid of sin. He stroked her hair and fingered her nipples, masturbated fiercely on the dark roads after he had seen her home. Why didn't he at least *live* in the Bronx?

Any fool can see that with the slightest twist one way or another all of this is fit material for a sophisticated comic's routine. David Steinberg, say. One can hear his precise voice recording these picayune disasters as jokes. Yet all that moonlight was real. He kissed her luminous fingernails and died over and over again. The maimings of love are endlessly funny, as are the tiny figures of talking animals being blown to pieces in cartoons.

It was this same youth who, three years later, ravished the whores of Mexican border towns in a kind of drunken hilarity, falling down in the dusty streets of Nuevo Laredo, Villa Acuña, and Piedras Negras, the pungency of the overpowering perfume wedded to his rumpled khakis, his flowered shirt, his scuffed and beer-spattered low quarters scraping across the thresholds of the Blue Room, Ofelia's, The 1-2-3 Club, Felicia's, the Cadillac, Tres Hermanas. It would be a great pleasure for me to allow him to meet her there, in a yellow chiffon cocktail dress and spike heels, lost in prostitution.

One night, a huge smiling Indian whore bathed his member in gin as a testament to the strict hygiene she claimed to practice and he absurdly thought of Rebecca, that he had never seen her naked, nor she him, as he was now in the Hollywood pink light of the whore's room, Jesus hanging in his perpetual torture from the wall above the little bed. The woman was gentle, the light glinting off her gold incisor and the tiny cross at her throat. You good fuck, Jack, she smiled in her lying whore way. He felt her flesh again warm in that long-dead New Jersey sunlight. Turn that into a joke.

THEY WERE at the amusement park at Lake Hopatcong with two other couples. A hot and breathless night toward the end of August, the patriotic smell of hot dogs and french fries in the still air. Thin and cranky music from the carrousel easing through the sparsely planted trees down toward the shore. She was pale and sweating, sick, and he took her back to the car and they smoked. They walked to the edge of the black lake stretching out before them, the red and blue neon on the far shore clear in the hot dark.

He wiped her forehead and stroked her shoulders, worshiping her pain. He went to get a Coke and brought it back to her, but she only sipped at it, then said O God! and bent over to throw up. He held her waist while she vomited, loving the waste and odor of her. She lay down on the ground and he lay next to her, stroking her breasts until the nipples were erect under her cotton blouse. My period, she said. God, it just ruins me at the beginning. You bleeding, vomiting, incredible thing, he thought. You should have stayed in, he said. The moonlight of her teeth. I didn't want to miss a night with you, she said. It's August. Stars, my friend, great flashing stars fell on Alabama

THEY STOOD IN THE DARK in the driving rain underneath her umbrella. Where could it have been? Nokomis Road? Bliss Lane? Kissing with that trapped yet wholly innocent frenzy peculiar to American youth of that era. Her family was going back to the city early the next morning and his family would be leaving toward the end of the week. They kissed, they kissed. The angels sang. Where could they go, out of this driving rain?

Isn't there anyone, any magazine writer or avant-garde filmmaker, any lover of life or dedicated optimist out there who will move them toward a cottage, already closed for the season, in whose split log exterior they will find an unlocked door? Inside there will be a bed, whiskey, an electric heater. Or better, a fireplace. White lamps, soft lights. Sweet music. A radio on which they will get Cooky's Caravan or Symphony Sid. Billy Eckstine will sing "My Deep Blue Dream." Who can bring them to each other and allow him to enter her? Tears of gratitude and release, the sublime and elegantly shadowed configuration their tanned legs will make lying together. This was in America, in 1948. Not even fake art or the wearisome tricks of movies can assist them.

She tottered, holding the umbrella crookedly while he went to his knees and clasped her, the rain soaking him through, put his head under her skirt and kissed her belly, licked at her crazily through her underclothes.

All you modern lovers, freed by Mick Jagger and the orgasm, give them, for Christ's sake, for an hour, the use of your really terrific little apartment. They won't smoke your marijuana nor disturb your Indiana graphics. They won't borrow your Fanon or Cleaver or Barthelme or Vonnegut. They'll make the bed before they leave. They whisper good night and dance in the dark.

She was crying and stroking his hair. Ah God, the leaves of brown came tumbling down, remember? He watched her go into the house and saw the door close. Some of his life washed away in the rain dripping from his chin.

A GIRL NAMED SHEILA whose father owned a fleet of taxis gave a reunion party in her parents' apartment in Forest

Hills. Where else would it be? I will insist on purchased elegance or nothing. None of your warm and cluttered apartments in this story, cats on the stacks of books, and so on. It was the first time he had ever seen a sunken living room and it fixed his idea of the good life forever after. Rebecca was talking to Marv and Robin, who were to be married in a month. They were Jewish, incredibly and wondrously Jewish, their parents smiled upon them and loaned them money and cars. He skulked in his loud Brooklyn clothes.

I'll put her virgin flesh into a black linen suit, a single strand of pearls around her throat. Did I say that she had honey-colored hair? Believe me when I say he wanted to kiss her shoes.

Everybody was drinking Cutty Sark. This gives you an idea, not of who they were, but of what they thought they were. They worked desperately at it being August, but under the sharkskin and nylons those sunny limbs were hidden. Sheila put on "In the Still of the Night" and all six couples got up to dance. When he held her he thought he would weep.

He didn't want to hear about Evander Childs or Gun Hill Road or the 92nd Street Y. He didn't want to know what the pre-med student she was dating said. Whose hand had touched her secret thighs. It was almost unbearable since this phantom knew them in a specifically erotic way that he did not. He had touched them decorated with garters and stockings. Different thighs. She had been to the Copa, to the Royal Roost, to Lewisohn Stadium to hear the Gershwin concert. She talked about *The New Yorker* and *Vogue,* e.e. cummings. She flew before him, floating in her black patent I. Miller heels.

Sitting together on the bed in Sheila's parents' room, she told him that she still loved him, she would always love him, but it was so hard not to go out with a lot of other boys, she had to keep her parents happy. They were concerned about him. They didn't really know him. He wasn't Jewish. All right. All right. But did she have to let Shelley? Did she have to go to the Museum of Modern Art? The Met? Where were these places? What is the University of Miami? Who is Brooklyn Law? What sort of god borrows a Chrysler and goes to the Latin Quarter? What is a supper club? What does Benedictine cost? Her epic acts, his Flagg Brothers shoes.

There was one boy who had almost made her. She had allowed him to take off her blouse and skirt, nothing else! at a CCNY sophomore party. She was a little high and he —messed—all over her slip. It was wicked and she was ashamed. Battering his heart in her candor. Well, I almost slipped too, he lied, and was terrified that she seemed relieved. He got up and closed the door, then lay down on the bed with her and took off her jacket and brassiere. She zipped open his trousers. Long enough! Sheila said, knocking on the door, then opening it to see him with his head on her breasts. Oh, oh, she said, and closed the door. Of course, it was all ruined. We got rid of a lot of these repressed people in the next decade, and now we are all happy and free.

At three o'clock, he kissed her good night on Yellowstone Boulevard in a thin drizzle. Call me, he said, and I'll call you. I'll see you soon, she said, getting into Marv's car. I love you. She went into her glossy Jewish life, toward mambos and the Blue Angel.

Let me come and sleep with you. Let me lie in your bed and look at you in your beautiful pajamas. I'll do anything you say. I'll honor thy beautiful father and mother. I'll hide in the closet and be no trouble. I'll work as a stock boy in your father's beautiful sweater factory. It's not my fault I'm not Marvin or Shelley. I don't even know where CCNY is! Who is Conrad Aiken? What is Bronx Science? Who is Berlioz? What is a Stravinsky? How do you play Mah-Jongg? What is schmooz, schlepp, Purim, Moo Goo Gai Pan? Help me.

When he got off the train in Brooklyn an hour later, he saw his friends through the window of the all-night diner, pouring coffee into the great pit of their beer drunks. He despised them as he despised himself and the neighborhood. He fought against the thought of her so that he would not have to place her subtle finesse in these streets of vulgar hells, benedictions, and incense.

ON CHRISTMAS EVE, he left the office party at two, even

though one of the file girls, her Catholicism temporarily displaced by Four Roses and ginger, stuck her tongue into his mouth in the stock room.

Rebecca was outside, waiting on the corner of 46th and Broadway, and they clasped hands, oh briefly, briefly. They walked aimlessly around in the gray bitter cold, standing for a while at the Rockefeller Center rink, watching the people who owned Manhattan. When it got too cold, they walked some more, ending up at the Automat across the street from Bryant Park. When she slipped her coat off her breasts moved under the crocheted sweater she wore. They had coffee and doughnuts, surrounded by office party drunks sobering up for the trip home.

Then it went this way: We can go to Maryland and get married, she said. You know I was sixteen a month ago. I want to marry you, I can't stand it. He was excited and frightened, and got an erection. How could he bear this image? Her breasts, her familiar perfume, enormous figures of movie queens resplendent in silk and lace in the snug bedrooms of Vermont inns—shutters banging, the rain pouring down, all entangled, married! How do we get to *Maryland?* he said.

Against the table top her hand, its long and delicate fingers, the perfect moons, Carolina moons, of her nails. I'll give her every marvel: push gently the scent of magnolia and jasmine between her legs and permit her to piss champagne.

Against the table top her hand, glowing crescent moons over lakes of Prussian blue in evergreen twilights. Her eyes gray, flecked with bronze. In her fingers a golden chain and on the chain a car key. My father's car, she said. We can take it and be there tonight. We can be married Christmas then, he said, but you're Jewish. He saw a drunk going out onto Sixth Avenue carrying their lives along in a paper bag. I mean it, she said. I can't stand it, I love you. I love *you,* he said, but I can't drive. He smiled. I *mean* it, she said. She put the key in his hand. The car is in midtown here, over by Ninth Avenue. I really *can't* drive, he said. He could shoot pool and drink boilermakers, keep score at baseball games and handicap horses, but he couldn't drive.

The key in his hand, fascinating wrinkle of sweater at her waist. Of course, life is a conspiracy of defeat, a sophisticated joke, endless, endless. I'll get some money and we'll go the holiday week, he said, we'll take a train, O.K.? O.K., she said. She smiled and asked for another coffee, taking the key and dropping it into her bag. It was a joke after all. They walked to the subway and he said I'll give you a call right after Christmas. Gray bitter sky. What he remembered was her gray cashmere coat swirling around her calves as she turned at the foot of the stairs to smile at him, making the gesture of dialing a phone and pointing at him and then at herself.

Give these children a Silver Phantom and a chauffeur. A black chauffeur, to complete the America that owned them.

Now I COME to the literary part of this story, and the reader may prefer to let it go and watch her profile against the slick tiles of the IRT stairwell, since she has gone out of the reality of narrative, however splintered. This postscript offers something different, something finely artificial and discrete, one of the designer sweaters her father makes now, white and stylish as a sailor's summer bells. I grant you it will be unbelievable.

I put the young man into 1958. He has served in the army, and once told the Automat story to a group of friends as proof of his sexual prowess. They believed him: what else was there for them to believe? This shabby use of a fragile occurrence was occasioned by the smell of honeysuckle and magnolia in the tobacco country outside Winston-Salem. It brought her to him so that he was possessed. He felt the magic key in his hand again. To master this overpowering wave of nostalgia he cheapened it. Certainly the reader will recall such shoddy incidents in his own life.

After his discharge he married some girl and had three children by her. He allowed her her divers interests and she tolerated his few stupid infidelities. He had a good job in advertising and they lived in Kew Gardens in a brick semi-detached house. Let me give them a sunken living room to give this the appearance of realism. His mother died in 1958 and left the lake house to him. Since he had not been there for ten years he decided to sell it, against his wife's wishes. The community was growing and the property was worth twice the original price.

This is a ruse to get him up there one soft spring day in May. He drives up in a year-old Pontiac. The realtor's office, the papers, etc. Certainly, a shimmer of nostalgia about it all, although he felt a total stranger. He left the car on the main road, deciding to walk down to the lake, partly visible through the new-leaved trees. All right, now here we go. A Cadillac station wagon passed and then stopped about fifteen yards ahead of him and she got out. She was wearing white shorts and sneakers and a blue sweat shirt. Her hair was the same, shorter perhaps, tied with a ribbon of navy velour.

It's too impossible to invent conversation for them. He got in her car. Her perfume was not the same. They drove to her parents' house for a cup of coffee—for old times' sake. How else would they get themselves together and alone? She had come up to open the house for the season. Her husband was a college traveler for a publishing house and was on the road, her son and daughter were staying at their grandparents' for the day. Popular songs, the lyrics half-remembered. You will do well if you think of the ambience of the whole scene as akin to the one in detective novels where the private investigator goes to the murdered man's summer house. This is always in off-season because it is magical then, one sees oneself as a being somehow existing outside time, the year-round residents are drawings in flat space.

When they walked into the chilly house she reached past him to latch the door and he touched her hand on the lock, then her forearm, her shoulder. Take your clothes off, he said, gently. Oh gently. Please. Take your clothes off? He opened the button of her shorts. You see that they now have the retreat I begged for them a decade ago. If one has faith all things will come. Her flesh was cool.

In the bedroom, she turned down the spread and fluffed the pillows, then sat and undressed. As she unlaced her sneakers, he put the last of his clothes on a chair. She got up, her breasts quivering slightly, and he saw faint stretch marks running into the shadowy symmetry of her pubic hair. She plugged in a small electric heater, bending before him, and he put his hands under her buttocks and held her there. She sighed and trembled and straightened up, turning toward him. Let me have a mist of tears in her eyes, of acrid joy and shame, of despair. She lay on the bed and opened her thighs and they made love without elaboration.

In the evening, he followed her car back into the city. They had promised to meet again the following week. Of course it wouldn't be sordid. What, then, would it be? He had perhaps wept bitterly that afternoon as she kissed his knees. She would call him, he would call her. They could find a place to go. Was she happy? Really happy? God knows, he wasn't *happy!* In the city they stopped for a drink in a Village bar and sat facing each other in the booth, their knees touching, holding hands. They carefully avoided speaking of the past, they made no jokes. He felt his heart rattling around in his chest in large jagged pieces. It was rotten for everybody, it was rotten but they would see each other, they were somehow owed it. They would find a place with clean sheets, a radio, whiskey, they would just—continue. Why not?

These destructive and bittersweet accidents do not happen every day. He put her number in his address book, but he wouldn't call her. Perhaps she would call him, and if she did, well, they'd see, they'd see. But he would *not* call her. He wasn't that crazy. On the way out to Queens he felt himself in her again and the car swerved erratically. When he got home he was exhausted.

You are perfectly justified in scoffing at the outrageous transparency of it if I tell you that his wife said that he was so pale that he looked as if he had seen a ghost, but that is, indeed, what she said. Art cannot rescue anybody from anything.

Arrival

Dabney Stuart

WHAT do you love
A voice said
Myself

Where does that get you

These are the wrong questions

My daughter has begun
To linger with pages
To sleep under her pillow
Collect flies   She has told
Me
The snow is black under the mountains

She lives elsewhere
My son
Addresses the light as though he would dance
With it
He requests messages
His eyes
Read me in no language I understand
They are his
Partner

Often when the evening
Forgets its hour and the day turns
Into itself my wife
Remembers
The years before me
She keeps her
Distances

I would have it no other way

These are the wrong answers

They are not answers

Where does that get you

Here

On Meeting Keats and Shelley
in Rome, 1952

Alan Feldman

THE dark heart lay in a velvet box
Above the child's head, in a room off the Spanish Steps.
What went on? The pillars gaped at the heart bone,
All that the fire left to the friend's snatching. . . .
Outside, a hundred miles down the hill, the sea lay on the beach.
Shelley is down there; Keats, dying of tuberculosis in a small room.

The gravestones tilt, as if a tourist has been sitting on them—

The stones slide into the earth, like a man sliding into
the sea.
The ground is unplanted, the bombs have pulverized the
grass,
And no one puts it back. A paupers' cemetery.

Or, Atlantic Beach: mother's finger at the horizon pointing
to Europe.
The child, with an epigram in its mouth, makes the bathers
smile.
The baby poet slides into the sea.
The bathroom walls are a-light with paper stars. The
tourists laugh
At the child's interpretation of the art on the ceiling.
Talk gives the mouth pleasure.

Shelley beneath the ivy: the tomb flat, at rest,
Not stooping in the sun like Keats'. Trees,
And a brook near the poet's head. "But if he's buried
Beneath this stone," asks the child, "how can I have his
heart bone in my hand?"
"The bone," say the parents, "is nothing but a lambchop
bone."

The parents laugh at us.
The bleached bone, curved and pure
Like the skin on a young man's neck,
Is not authentic

Notes for a Dictionary
of Dramatic Terms

Donald Pearce

1. **Drama**, Gk. *drao*, "I do," "I play"; literally, *"doing by play."* The corresponding Latin term, *ludus,* not limited to theatrical performances but applied to games of all sorts—including sports events, athletic contests, arena shows, matches, festivals, etc. Uppermost in Roman usage, the sense of public entertainment, spectacle; in Greek, formal accomplishment, disciplined performance (the quality of the "doing"). Neither term as good as our term "Play"?

2. **Play**, Anglo-Saxon *plega,* with two distinct root meanings: *a.* "To have or display quick, nimble, dance-like movements," "animal movements," "the movements of frolic" (play as *festival*). *b.* "To commit oneself to something," "to plight oneself," "to risk or stake everything" as in a crucial move in a game, "to dedicate oneself" (play as *ritual*). Both these meanings operative in our use of the term in theater, where *to play a part* (to physically execute it, as in sense *a.*) means not merely to "perform a role" but equally—or perhaps especially—*to lose oneself in a role* (sense *b.*). Both the "festival" and "ritual" meanings of the term have to do with *transcendence:* in assuming a role an actor literally lays aside (*transcends*) his "daily self" (his "real identity") to take on an ideal self constructed of words, gestures, greasepaint; likewise, the plot of a play is a species of transcendence, being an idealization (a purged version) of those raw events we like to call "the world." Thus, (1.) *To play:* to engage in any activity in which human *concupiscence* ("utility") is suspended, or

reduced to a minimum (ideally to zero); ultimately, flight from the world. (2.) *Play:* any act of self-and-world transcendence; the categorical opposite of "work," or immersion in the world (i.e., "utility"). Punch does not work. Falstaff does not work. Hamlet and Lear do not work. An actor can "work at," or "work up," a role, after which he *plays* it—that is to say, enters its transcendent world where everything that occurs occurs solely for its own and the action's sake.

3. **Scene,** Lat. *scena,* lit. "an arbor, bower, or tent" (of branches and leaves) that forms the feigning area; the space within which the feigning is done. A "scene" is literally any enclosed, roofed, domed, framed, pictorial space; *any magical space,* within which, as within the bounding lines of a picture, *life-as-if* has the force of *life-as-is.*

4. **Plot,** Middle Eng. *plat,* "a piece of ground"; "the ground upon which a structure is built"; by extension, "the ground upon which an action is reared" (i.e., played). In the latter sense "ground" = "text." "Plot" also had (to some extent still preserves) the sense of "chart," "plan," "design" of such an action or structure. The orderly steps in a dance constituted its "plot." The weaving together ("complication") of the incidents of a story constituted its "plot." Dramatic "plot" draws on most of the above senses; it is the woven material form, or fabric, of the action; that which deploys the action; that which casts light and shade upon the action (reveals it); and that out of which the action is woven.

5. **Action,** Lat. *ago,* "I do," "I lead"; lit. *"set in motion by a doer";* a "moving sequence." Primarily, the root ("agon") denoted a "match," or "contest"; i.e., any "organized" struggle, carried on, within a framework of accepted rules ("accepted values"). Essentially, therefore, a play's action is, and ought to be viewed as, a species of *game*—either light ("comic") or heavy ("tragic").

6. **Character,** Gk. *charakter,* lit. an "instrument for making marks"; a stylus. At some early point in its history this

term ceased to mean the thing by which marks were made and came to denote the thing *on which* marks were made, and finally the *marks that had been made,* such as a price, a use, a name: in other words, a *fixed valuation.* "Dramatic characterization" is, indeed, the giving of a "fixed valuation" —moral, psychological—to a human life. A "character" is, quite literally, "a marked man"; a man with a price on his head; someone whose total life-complex has been made into a marketable commodity (given dramatic currency) by being simplified and focused around a key trait. (Othello's *character* essentially "esprit de coeur"? Iago's, "esprit geometrique"? Etc.) "Character" in drama, so far from being imperious or determinative, is in fact completely arbitrary, completely plastic, and wholly subject to the superior demands of plot and action (as Aristotle maintained).

7. **Persona,** Lat. *per-sonare,* lit. "to sound through" a mask or a pretend face. *Personare* also meant "to *resonate,*" "*to cry out,*" "to rinse with sound," with the emphasis here falling on *enhanced volume of sound:* hence, any stylized, "unnatural" mode of delivery. Additionally, the word meant "to sound or blow upon an instrument." In this sense, the *personae* of a play may be properly compared to orchestral instruments engaged in the performance of a musical score —the stress here falling quite as much, or even more, upon *precision* (i.e., synchronization) of performance, as upon quality of tonal production.

8. **Mask,** Ital. *mascara,* from Arabic *maskharah,* lit. "lending an idealized brightness or strangeness to the face by means of paint." From earliest times painting or masking the face has been intimately associated with magical practice and witchcraft—hence the suggestion of the supernatural (also the sinister) that still clings to makeup and greasepaint. Masks figured importantly in certain ancient religious rites and ceremonies; for example, in those of the god Dionysus (in which the cheeks of the devotees were daubed with the lees of wine and decorated with vine leaves) and in early Roman rites for the dead of noble families (in which a mask resembling the face of the deceased was

either worn by the celebrants, or fitted to the face of the corpse). The theatrical mask derives much of its great power from the fact that it combines both these traditions, being at one and the same time a satyr-face (an ideal "grotesque") and the face of a phantom (an apparition of the dead.) To put on a mask—or, what amounts to the same thing, to apply mascara and face powder—is analogous to taking vows: the wearer truly puts off his "natural" self to put on another "self" entirely, one of ideal passion. He becomes, in fact, a clairvoyant, a spirit-medium, manifesting the voice and person of some soul in another world—the "other world" of the script. The mask is the magical agent of this self-transcendence. But a mask is also "a protective covering for the face" (a visor). As such it is worn (as in fencing) not for the purpose of adorning the face of the wearer but to protect him *from something menacing in the text*, something that, were he without a mask, would certainly endanger his life, viz. the flashing thrust and counterthrust of logic, action, dialogue, in the ideal world of the play. But a mask protects the wearer from a yet more dangerous menace—that of unpurged (unrehearsed) nature ("real life") that lies in wait, grunting and sweating as always, just beyond the margins of his script. The donning of a mask, the merest painting of the features, transports the wearer immediately to an incorruptible country—of gods, ghosts, demons, heroes, all the brilliant spirits of the dead.

9. **Role,** Lat. *rota,* roll; originally "the roll of parchment, or papyrus, on which an actor's part had been written out"; a series of words (text) to be memorized, then synchronized in rehearsal with all the other roles in the play. Note: the root meaning of *rota* is "wheel." A play ("a system of roles") is therefore quite literally a "synchronization of rolling parts," of greater and lesser interlocking "wheels," no one wheel, moreover, being of any more importance for the final operation of the whole than any of the others. From the point of view of its roles (so to speak), a play is simply "a complex piece of engineering"; i.e., a machine.

10. **Stage,** Old Fr. *estage,* from Lat. *stare;* lit. "a standing

place" for the actors. Though the term came to denote the physical "standing area" occupied by the players, the original meaning was "enduring place," i.e., *"the place where a struggle is maintained";* literally, "the place where a *stand-to-the-end is made"* by the participants in a contest. In this primary sense, therefore, a stage is precisely *a gaming board.*

11. **Actor,** Lat. *agere,* "to drive." The actors in a play are "those who drive," "those who set in motion"; hence quite literally "goads," "whips," "thorns in each others' hides," stimuli to action and dialogue. (In *Endgame,* Beckett clearly reminds director and actor of this relationship by naming his dramatis personae Hamm-Clov, Nag-Nell, i.e., hammer-nail.) The word had numerous related secondary meanings. Depending upon context, an "actor" was a "slinger," an "accuser," an "advocate," a "reporter," "one who declaims a text" (or a pretext). Central to all these meanings, however, is the idea of *agility,* of *swift, forward movement,* "as of a ship under full sail," or "of a moving animal." *Quickness combined with grace* would be an accurate rendering of this term.

12. **Dialogue,** Lat. *dia* (between) + *logos* (speech); lit. "words tossed back and forth between speakers"; thus returned, or shuttled, speech. *Logos* had, of course, an extremely wide denotative range, depending on the sense of the context: "witty," "wise," "ornate," "weighty," "significant" speech: basically, *"speech raised above the commonplace."* In the form of *loquax* the word meant "murmurous," "rustling," "leafy" speech; obscure or ambiguous speech; hence sybilline, choral. In poetry, *logos* often denoted "the chirping or jargoning of birds"; and this sense, lingering on faintly in *dia-logus,* surely exactly suggests the quickness and brightness with which the dialogue of a play should be spoken—"trippingly on the tongue," as Hamlet insisted —the worst possible offense in an actor always having been to let the dialogue drag (really, "slow return of serve").

13. **Climax,** Gk. *klimax,* "staircase," or "ladder," of the plot; the ladder which the hero must climb, rung by rung,

to the top. Arrived there, a *peripetea* ("turning about of the feet") occurs; at which point, observing the depths below him (recognizing his true situation), he loses balance, and falls, executing the *catastrophe* ("down-turning movement") in the form of a perfect plunge to earth from forbidden (inordinate) heights (of pride). The "climax" is thus quite literally "the high point of the action." Structurally, it is, or should be, the play's most intricate moment, since it is both the end of the beginning (the ascent) and the beginning of the end (the fall), and holds both these movements in temporary equilibrium.

14. **Tragedy,** Gk. *tragos* ("goat") + *oide* ("song"); lit. "goat song." Exact significance of the *tragos* element in this word never yet settled by scholars; but we can try anyway. We know (1.) that the winner in a Greek Tragic Contest was traditionally awarded the prize of a goat; (2.) that the original lyric tragedies (or "dithyrambs," as they were called) consisted mainly, if not wholly, of choruses of "goat-singers" masked to resemble satyrs (*Poetics* of Aristotle). It seems very likely, therefore, that the ceremonious award of a goat in later festivals was a vestige, or conscious reminiscence, of the Dionysian origins of Greek tragedy. Whether or not this was so, the fact that it was always a dead goat that was awarded, and never a live one, is certainly an arresting fact, one perhaps worth considering; it may provide a clue as to the meaning both of the prize and of the idea (or "mystique") of Tragedy itself. For if one considers the goat—so unruly and lustful by nature, so notoriously lacking in all sense of propriety or decorum, with his raffish beard (which the devil, it is said, combs), so suggestive of human sexual affinities, this butting, lascivious animal, the very epitome of appetite, impulsiveness—it is, after all, hard not to see him as concupiscence incarnate, sexuality par excellence. Of all possible objects, what more appropriate (indeed, what more shocking) symbol of the death of the generative principle could have been selected than the body of a dead goat? What better Oscar awarded for proficiency in the art of Tragedy (which comes down to defeat of the generative principle, to defeat of the Year by Winter, to

phallic defeat) than the one that was, in fact, traditionally awarded? *Comedy,* on the other hand (*komos* + *oide,* "festive song") implies just the opposite—life's burgeoning, the springtime of the very principle which it was Tragedy's solemn business to annul—hence phallic victory. (If the *komos* [or "mirth"] element in *komoidia* is actually cognate with *komos* ["hairy"], as some scholars maintain, this would further augment the sexual connotations of the term, and support the point we are making.)

Drawing upon the above, we might arrive at a few definitions:

1. A play *is a seemed, or filtered, version of life; in the form of a contest; having prearranged episodes and crises; rising, in Tragedy, to a peak and thereafter falling away; whose outcome is a foregone conclusion.*

2. A stage, *the place where the contest is held, where the contestants win or lose, is essentially a playing-board.*

3. Characters *are marked, or "weighted," pieces* (*chessmen*), *confined to the board and bound by the rules of the game.*

But the chess figure is obviously too static. More mobility is needed. If you animate chessmen, what do you get? You get puppets, tumblers, minstrels, dancers, clowns—brilliant passionless beings. Thus, once more:

1. A *theater* is any roofed, enclosed, or framed magical space—i.e., any space where seeing literally is believing. (A circus tent.)

2. *Actors* are professional virtuosi; accomplished stunt men; in the same business exactly as tumblers, painted clowns, aerial performers, etc.

3. A *play* is what these performers actually do before an audience; *the sum of the "aerial routines" they have been given to memorize and master.*

4. A *plot* is the arrangement, or succession, of these

routines; the *sequence of the play's arrivals, departures, mountings, interchanges, reversals, returns.*

5. *Dialogue* is less *what is said,* than *something to be said,* i.e., *something to do,* or better, *to do with:* "the old questions, old answers—there's nothing like them," tossed back and forth at fresh speeds, new angles, different altitudes. To the professional actor, dialogue is strictly an apparatus of stunt bars—high wires, high bars, for tragedy (for dangerous, impressive effects), low wires, rubber bars, for comedy (for ludicrous effects). *Dialogue* is simply *that by means of which, or upon which, the characters' tumbling and balancing acts are, in fact, performed.*

6. A *role* is any unified set, or series, of movements in a complete consort of movements.

7. In a *Tragedy,* the leading character's special feat is to climb the play's "ladder" to the top, pause there, turn, secure undivided attention (*"Zeus, what is it you are going to do to me?"*), then execute a virtuoso leap to his perfect doom, amid a chorus of bravos (and sighs). In a *Comedy,* outstretched hands at the right instant, as if from nowhere, suddenly appear, and he is snatched away amid gales of laughter. All tragic heroes are proudest of their great swan dive; all comic heroes of their way with prearranged miracles.

House Burning

Robert Morgan

CAME TO see the house shine like quartz dilating
and spinning its facets in the sun,
so bright you can tell exactly where the flame
ends and the clear air begins.
The wood transfigures, a place leaving.
The fire gives X-ray vision
through the rooms where boards sweat
resin bombs
that drop flaring.
The ribs and soaring rafters are wrapped
tightly in flames.
Came to see the bird catch fire
and fall into the basement where cartridges
go off in a close private war.
Hot air rushes out a hundred yards
over the faces of onlookers
who came as to a hanging
to see the family sitting on a rescued sofa
under the apple trees
watching the fire preach its sermon
over the pyre.
Ash circles like buzzards
in the smoke rising straight up
before it's scattered,
huge pencil scrawling on the sky.

Came to see the black cage of studs and rafters falling
in, the timbers of black feathers,
black satin crumbling
in sour clay to nurse unheard
of growth of crabgrass.
The old folks living in a trailer,
the kids in ranchhouses around the hill.
Two chimneys facing above the cornfield.

Instructions

Michael Berryhill

"The problem with you, Mr. Berryhill,
You have no sense of form. Write sonnets."
I knew I'd had romance. "All right, I will."
And squeezed one out okay, and made it honest:
Moonlight and roses through a special lens.
(She's not here now; everything is missing.)
Getting hungry reading Solzhenitsyn's
Day in the Life, I who cannot give up kissing,
Want to open every can and gorge
And share it with the cat, a poor display.
No bread is in *my* mattress. I'll forage
On hope. My cat whose son I gave away
Yowled less and slept. Berryman, you the boss.
A lady said this morning: face up to loss.

Winter

Michael Berryhill

I finally met the abominable snow woman
Who keeps a basement apartment in our building.
A teen-ager, actually, with a weak smile,
Ashamed of the hair on her chest.
She took me to meet her father.
The palm of her hand was like shoe leather.
Her father was a brute.

Guayaquil

Jorge Luis Borges

Now I SHALL NOT journey to the Estado Occidental; now I shall not set eyes on snow-capped Higuerota mirrored in the waters of the Golfo Plácido; now I shall not decipher Bolívar's manuscripts in that library, which doubtless has its own shape and its own lengthening shadows but which from here in Buenos Aires I picture in so many different ways.

Rereading the above paragraph preparatory to writing the next, its at once melancholy and pompous tone troubles me. Perhaps one cannot speak of that Caribbean republic without, even from afar, echoing the monumental style of its most famous historian, Captain Joseph Korzeniowski—but in my case there is another reason. My opening paragraph, I suspect, was prompted by the unconscious need to infuse a note of pathos into a slightly painful and rather trivial episode. I shall with all probity recount what happened, and this may enable me to understand it. Furthermore, to confess to a thing is to leave off being an actor in it and to become an onlooker—to become somebody who has seen it and tells it and is no longer the doer.

The actual event took place last Friday, in this same room in which I am writing, at this same—though now slightly cooler—evening hour. Aware of our tendency to forget unpleasant things, I want to set down a written record of my conversation with Dr. Edward Zimmerman, of the University of Córdoba, before oblivion blurs the details. The memory I retain of that meeting is still quite vivid.

For the better understanding of my story, I shall have to set forth briefly the curious facts surrounding certain letters of General Bolívar's found among the papers of Dr. José Avellanos, whose *History of Fifty Years of Misrule*—thought to be lost under circumstances that are only too well known—was ultimately unearthed and published by his grandson, Dr. Ricardo Avellanos. To judge from references I have collected from various sources, these letters are of no particular interest, except for one dated from Cartagena on August 13, 1822, in which the Liberator places upon record details of his celebrated meeting with the Argentine national hero, General San Martín. It is needless to underscore the value of this document; in it Bolívar reveals—if only in part—exactly what had taken place during the two generals' interview the month before at Guayaquil. Dr. Ricardo Avellanos, embattled opponent of the government, refused to turn the correspondence over to his own country's Academy of History, and, instead, offered it for initial publication to a number of Latin-American republics. Thanks to the praiseworthy zeal of our ambassador, Dr. Melaza-Mouton, the Argentine government was the first to accept Dr. Avellanos' disinterested offer. It was agreed that a delegate should be sent to Sulaco, the capital of the Estado Occidental, to transcribe the letters so as to see them into print upon return here. The rector of our university, in which I hold the chair of Latin-American History, most generously recommended to the Minister of Education that I be appointed to carry out this mission. I also obtained the more or less unanimous vote of the National Academy of History, of which I am a member. The date of my audience with the Minister had already been fixed when it was learned that the University of Córdoba—which, I would rather suppose, knew nothing about these decisions—had proposed the name of Dr. Zimmerman.

Reference here, as the reader may be well aware, is to a foreign-born historian expelled from his country by the Third Reich and now an Argentine citizen. Of the doubtless noteworthy body of his work, I have glanced only at a vindication of the Semitic republic of Carthage—which posterity judges through the eyes of Roman historians, its enemies—and a sort of polemical essay which holds that government should be neither visible nor emotional. This proposal drew the unanswerable refutation of Martin Heidegger, who, using newspaper headlines, proved that the modern chief of state, far from being anonymous, is rather the protagonist, the choragus, the dancing David, who acts out the drama of his people with all the pomp of stagecraft, and resorts unhesitatingly to the overstatement inherent in the art of oration. He also proved that Zimmerman came of Hebrew, not to say Jewish, stock. Publication of this essay by the venerated existentialist was the immediate cause of the banishment and nomadic activities of our guest.

Needless to say, Zimmerman had come to Buenos Aires to speak to the Minister, who personally suggested to me, through one of his secretaries, that I see Zimmerman and, so as to avoid the unpleasant spectacle of two universities in disagreement, inform him of exactly how things stood. I of course agreed. Upon return home, I was told that Dr. Zimmerman had telephoned to announce his visit for six o'clock that same afternoon. I live, as everyone knows, on Chile Street. It was the dot of six when the bell rang.

With republican simplicity, I myself opened the door and led him to my private study. He paused along the way to look at the patio; the black and white tiles, the two magnolias, and the wellhead stirred him to eloquence. He was, I believe, somewhat ill-at-ease. There was nothing out of the ordinary about him. He must have been forty or so, and seemed to have a biggish head. His eyes were hidden by dark glasses, which he once or twice left on the table, then snatched up again. When we first shook hands, I remarked to myself with a certain satisfaction that I was the taller, and at once I was ashamed of myself, for this was not a matter of a physical or even a moral duel but was simply to be an explanation of where things stood. I am not very observant—if I am observant at all—but he brought to mind what a certain poet has called, with an ugliness that matches what it defines, an "immoderate sartorial inelegance." I can still see garments of electric blue, with too many buttons and pockets. Zimmerman's tie, I noticed, was one of those conjurer's knots held in place by two plastic clips. He carried a leather portfolio, which I presumed was full of documents. He wore a short military moustache, and when in the course of our talk he lit a cigar I felt that there were too many things on that face. *Trop meublé*, I said to myself.

The successiveness of language—since every word occupies a place on the page and a moment in the reader's mind—tends to exaggerate what we are saying; beyond the visual trivia that I have listed, the man gave the impression of having experienced an arduous life.

On display in my study are an oval portrait of my great-grandfather, who fought in the wars of Independence, and some cabinets containing swords, medals, and flags. I showed Zimmerman those old glorious things, explaining as I went along; his eyes passed over them quickly, like one who is carrying out a duty, and, not without a hint of impoliteness that I believe was involuntary and mechanical, he interrupted and finished my sentences for me. He said, for example:

"Correct. Battle of Junín. August sixth, eighteen twenty-four. Cavalry charge under Juárez."

"Under Suárez," I corrected.

I suspect his error was deliberate. He spread his arms in an Oriental gesture and exclaimed, "My first mistake, and certainly not my last! I feed on texts and slip up on facts —in you the interesting past lives." He pronounced his *v*'s like *f*'s.

Such flatteries displeased me. He was far more interested in my books, and let his eyes wander almost lovingly over the titles. I recall his saying, "Ah, Schopenhauer, who always disbelieved in history. This same set, edited by Grisebach, was the one I had in Prague. I thought I'd grow old in the friendship of those portable volumes, but it was history itself, in the flesh of a madman, that evicted me from that house and that city. Now here I am, with you, in South America, in this hospitable house of yours."

He spoke inelegantly but fluently, his noticeable German accent going hand-in-hand with a Spanish lisp. By then we were seated, and I seized upon what he had said in order to take up our subject. "History here in the Argentine is more merciful," I said. "I was born in this house and I expect to die here. Here my great-grandfather lay down his sword, which saw action throughout the continent.

Here I have pondered the past and have compiled my books. I can almost say I've never been outside this library, but now I shall go abroad at last and travel to lands I have only traveled in maps." I cut short with a smile my possible rhetorical excess.

"Are you referring to a certain Caribbean republic?" said Zimmerman.

"So I am," I answered. "And it's to this imminent trip that I owe the honor of your visit."

Trinidad served us coffee. I went on slowly and confidently. "You probably know by now that the Minister has entrusted me with the mission of transcribing and writing an introduction to the new Bolívar letters, which have accidentally turned up in Dr. Avellanos' files. This mission, by a happy stroke, crowns my lifework—the work that somehow runs in my blood."

It was a relief having said what I had to say. Zimmerman appeared not to have heard me; his averted eyes were fixed not on my face but on the books at my back. He vaguely assented, and then spoke out, saying, "In your blood. You are the true historian. Your people roamed the length and breadth of this continent and fought in the great battles, while in obscurity mine were barely emerging from the ghetto. You, according to your own eloquent words, carry history in your blood; you have only to listen closely to an inner voice. I, on the other hand, must go all the way to Sulaco and struggle through stacks of perhaps apocryphal papers. Believe me, sir, I envy you."

His tone was neither challenging nor mocking; his words were the expression of a will that made of the future something as irrevocable as the past. His arguments hardly mattered. The strength lay in the man himself, not in them. Zimmerman continued, with a schoolteacher's deliberation: "In this matter of Bolívar—I beg your pardon, San Martín —your stand, *cher maître,* is known to all scholars. *Votre siège est fait.* As yet, I have not examined Bolívar's pertinent letter, but it is obvious, or reasonable to guess, that it was written as a piece of self-justification. In any case, this much-touted letter will show us only Bolívar's side of the question, not San Martín's. Once made public, it should be weighed in the balance, studied, passed through the sieve of criticism, and, if need be, refuted. No one is better qualified for that final judgment than you, with your magnifying glass. The scalpel, the lancet—scientific rigor itself demands them! Allow me at the same time to point out that the name of the editor of the letter will remain linked to the letter. Such a link is hardly going to stand you in good stead. The public at large will never bother to look into these subtleties."

I realize now that what we argued after that, in the main, was useless. Maybe I felt it at the time. In order to avoid an outright confrontation I grasped at a detail, and I asked him whether he really thought the letters were fakes.

"That they are in Bolívar's own hand," he said, "does not necessarily mean that the whole truth is to be found in them. For all we know, Bolívar may have tried to deceive the recipient of the letter or, simply, may have deceived himself. You, a historian, a thinker, know far better than I that the mystery lies in ourselves, not in our words."

These pompous generalities irritated me, and I dryly remarked that within the riddle that surrounded us, the meeting at Guayaquil—in which General San Martín renounced mere ambition and left the destiny of South America in the hands of Bolívar—was also a riddle possibly not unworthy of our attention.

"The interpretations are so many," Zimmerman said. "Some historians believe San Martín fell into a trap; others, like Sarmiento, have it that he was a European soldier at loose ends on a continent he never understood; others again—for the most part Argentines—ascribe to him an act of self-denial; still others, weariness. We also hear of the secret order of who knows what Masonic lodge."

I said that, at any rate, it would be interesting to have the exact words spoken between San Martín, the Protector of Peru, and Bolívar, the Liberator. Zimmerman delivered his judgment.

"Perhaps the words they exchanged were irrelevant," he said. "Two men met face-to-face at Guayaquil; if one of them was master, it was because of his stronger will, not because of the weight of arguments. As you see, I have not forgotten my Schopenhauer." He added, with a smile, "Words, words, words. Shakespeare, insuperable master of words, held them in scorn. In Guayaquil or in Buenos Aires—in Prague, for that matter—words always count less than persons."

At that moment I felt that something was happening between us, or, rather, that something had already happened. In some uncanny way we were already two other people. The dusk entered into the room, and I had not lit the lamps. By chance, I asked, "You are from Prague, Doctor?"

"I *was* from Prague," he answered.

To skirt the real subject, I said, "It must be an unusual city. I've never been there, but the first book I ever read in German was Meyrink's novel *Der Golem*."

"It's the only book by Gustav Meyrink worth remembering," Zimmerman said. "It's wiser not to attempt the others, compounded as they are of bad writing and worse theosophy. All in all, something of the strangeness of Prague stalks the pages of that book of dreams within dreams. Everything is strange in Prague, or, if you prefer, nothing is strange. Anything may happen there. In London, on certain evenings, I have had the same feeling."

"You have spoken of the will," I said. "In the tales of the Mabinogion, two kings play chess on the summit of a hill, while below them their warriors fight. One of the kings wins the game; a rider comes to him with the news that the army of the other side has been beaten. The battle of the men was a mirror of the battle of the chessboard."

"Ah, a feat of magic," said Zimmerman.

"Or the display of a will in two different fields," I said. "Another Celtic legend tells of the duel between two famous bards. One, accompanying himself on the harp, sings from the twilight of morning to the twilight of evening. Then, under the stars or moon, he hands his harp over to his rival. The second bard lays the instrument aside and gets to his feet. The first bard acknowledges defeat."

"What erudition, what power of synthesis!" exclaimed Zimmerman. Then he added, more calmly, "I must confess my ignorance, my lamentable ignorance, of Celtic lore.

You, like the day, span East and West, while I am held to my little Carthaginian corner, complemented now with a smattering of Latin-American history. I am a mere plodder."

In his voice were both Jewish and German servility but I felt, insofar as victory was already his, that it cost him very little to flatter me or to admit I was right. He begged me not to trouble myself over the arrangements for his trip. ("Provisions" was the actual word he used.) On the spot, he drew out of his portfolio a letter addressed to the Minister. In it, I expounded the motives behind my resignation, and I acknowledged Dr. Zimmerman's indisputable merits. Zimmerman put his own fountain pen in my hand for my signature. When he put the letter away, I could not help catching a glimpse of his passage aboard the next day's Buenos Aires-Sulaco flight.

On his way out he paused again before the volumes of Schopenhauer, saying, "Our master, our common master, denied the existence of involuntary acts. If you stay behind in this house—in this spacious, patrician home—it is because down deep inside you want to remain here. I obey, and I thank you for your will."

Taking this last pittance without a word, I accompanied him to the front door. There, as we said good-bye, he remarked, "The coffee was excellent."

I go over these hasty jottings, which will soon be consigned to the flames. Our meeting had been short. I have the feeling that I shall give up any future writing. *Mon siège est fait.*

(*Translated from the Spanish by Norman Thomas di Giovanni in collaboration with the author.*)

Solo Crossings

Leonard S. Marcus

O F ALL people, you,
here, rowing the Atlantic, too.
It's a small world that brings neighbors
suddenly so close.

You offer me your hand, say
it's time we'd had a talk.
The first night out you dreamed
of pyramids dismantled

in stacks of ten.
The second night you found it hard
to sleep. You wonder what this night
will bring. The moon

already waits like the tip
of a finger entering water.
You know a little place in London
I ought to try. The waves are

changing the subject.
It's the rocking that keeps you
awake, you say. It reminds you
of when you arrived

and had to step over pigeons
gathering in the streets
to get inside your house.
Things have taken another turn.

You think you're ready to fall asleep.
You must be getting on.
Moonlight touches your face.
The waves, a hundred hurries, let go.

Report from a Pedestrian

Mark Halliday

THIS is one of those Stroll Poems in which
the speaker meets somebody a little weird
e.g. a leech-gatherer on a lonely moor
and is prompted to reconsider his own experience
in light of the eccentricity of his unexpected interlocutor.
I was twenty-two and worried about getting drafted
and worried about eating cereal with no nutritive value
and worried about my complicity in U.S. imperialism
so I had bloodshot vision and felt about eighty-two
so I staggered down the Avenue of the Americas
to pick up a Muffin Burger, the comfort of its grease,
and believe me the world bore no semblance to a village
in the Scottish countryside of the last century,
and I ran into this young hero-type with a ponytail
and a three-cornered hat and an accent, who said:

> "I was young and quick
> and my eyes were alive all day.
>
> So I went to the town
> and I walked myself around
> and I found my way.
>
> And when I came to love
> it was a good love
> and when the love was gone I did cry.
>
> I sit now and wait
> til my life is again in my eye."

That's all he had to say, that little ditty, or at least
that's all he got a chance to say, because I took off
in the other direction, having, as you can imagine,
nothing to say to this callow dip with his dippy romanti-
   cism.
But you know, as I think back on it I wonder, etc.

Fairview

Richard A. Selzer

My dearest Vera,

There is such a bustle and stir at the hotel. It is as though we will be visited today by an important personage. A queen or an archangel, or wild wild hope, by you, my darling. Nothing else would do to explain the "high" that one senses here today. A dozen times have I turned from my book (although it has spice enough to mesmerize De Sade) to peer expectantly down the road. Even the lilies at the gate are bobbing and ducking to get a better view. Perhaps we should all look up, as I should not be surprised if our guest were to arrive from on high—one of your silvery astronauts carrying a tiny planet for his son, or a rug merchant from Tabriz riding smugly on his merchandise. Won't he be put down to learn this hotel doesn't take used furnishings? The swank fairly oozes from the walls. I myself shall inform the cheeky carpet beggar that even the beds are discarded each morning. We never use anything twice! Well, we shall simply have to pocket our watches (pun) and try to keep from going mad with anticipation. Be still, my heart, and all that. Perhaps a walk will help. My neighbor here is an indefatigable walker. Not heath nor steppe, not veldt nor mesa is safe from his clodhoppers. All, all he violates with his lecherous prancing. No virgin territory here. Not on your life. Old Richardson has taken care of that with his mindless laying waste. I myself am an ambler, a meanderer. I just don't like to butt into Nature's business. She knew what she was about, arranging her grass and her sand that way. It doesn't need my boot to sock it askew. No ma'am. I'll slither through the blades like a little green snake leaving it all arranged just as she put it, or melt away a morning on a barnacle-bearded rock in the tide waiting for a mollusk to open wide and

say "aaah." But Richardson and I are good for each other.
We even look well together, I'm sure. So, of course, we
would have to wear each other like apparel for the benefit
of the lobby. He is big and red with white sideburns, and
I, well, you know what I look like.

Oh Vera, hurry back to me. Man cannot live forever by
whimsy and caprice. And I must get back to the serious
work of my life—you, my magnum opus, my unicorn. There
is so much left unfinished. The two spots I have neglected
to kiss, the one on your neck beneath your earlobe, luckily
I have forgotten which one and will have to do both for
the sake of completeness, and the other on your left instep.
I cannot have you sailing the seas uncovered by kisses lest
some beetling Beelzebub find these heels of Achilles, and
slay LOVE for me.

Your last letter should have been written in light on
hummingbirds' wings. It is love perfused with air. To be
loved by you is all in all.

DR. ALLAIN gunned his car up the winding road toward
the Fairview Convalescent Hospital. There was not a jot
of eagerness in him. He had not visited this one before but
knew well enough what to expect. They were of two types,
one, darkly old with wrinkled antimacassars limp upon
the chifforobes, and samplers on the walls. The other,
geometrically "decorated" in plastic and aluminum upon
which no self-respecting germ would light. In general he
disliked less the old converted houses with samplers that
said IN GOD WE TRUST, or JESUS LOVES, or even GOD BLESS
THIS PLACE. If he were to stitch one, it would say HELP,
HELP right out. This type of convalescent home made no
pretense. Just pack them in around the Victorian pieces
and dust it all once a week.

He steered his car up the winding steep street atop
which he would find the place. It had to be on top in order
to justify the inclusion of the word "view" in its name.
This one was "Fairview." Others were "Soundview," "Bay-
view," "Oceanview," "Mountainview," all precursors, he
mused dryly, of that ultimate convalescent home, "Sky-
view," where the insurance never runs out.

Beyond which turn in the road would it become visible?

Squat, flat-topped, with ramps like tongues sticking out of every orifice. He knew he had reached the site when he began to see them here and there on the lawn, propped into deck chairs or standing immobile over canes like withered cornstalks. They would wait there peering through their cataracts, drooped and dripping, until attendants came, white and grim, to coax them back to Fairview. He pulled into the parking lot, driving very slowly, half-expecting to find a stray strewn across the path. They seemed to have been flung about by an explosion. Getting them out of bed in the morning must be tantamount to disinterment, he thought. There it is, Fairview.

In front was a huge elm tree in the advanced stages of disease. It seemed devoid of life save for three or four courageous branches near the top, whose few leaves waggled still above the skeleton. The desiccated trunk was teeming with fungi which burst through the bark with all the glee of a horde of marauding goblins. It was in a state of virtual death, or technical life, depending on one's point of view.

He consulted the list of patients to be seen. Alvin Richardson was the first name—ulcer of foot.

"Where can I find Mr. Richardson?" he asked of the nurse at the desk.

"Room fifteen, Doctor. I'll send someone down to assist you."

"Thank you."

He passed a long table in the lobby where a clutch of crones sat weaving colored ribbons into potholders. Others painted flowers on clay vases. The grave-smell of wet clay seemed appropriate. Perhaps they were here just to get used to it, he thought. He passed open doors on either side of the corridor through which could be seen the still mounds of the bedridden. He heard stertorous breathing, noted the smell of feces and urine. There was a rich productive cough and the emphatic spit that followed like an exclamation point. He encouraged his step toward number fifteen. On the bed, all four extremities twisted and frozen into the shape of a pretzel, Alvin Richardson took no note of the doctor's arrival. He lay on his back staring at the tangle of his feet that hung suspended above his head like antlers. One was covered by a bandage moist with drainage from a concealed wound.

"Mr. Richardson?" He asked a tentative question. No response. He opened a package of instruments, the rubber gloves, and gauze squares, setting everything on the bedside table. He had developed an indecent curiosity about the contents of these night tables upon which the patients piled all of their keepsakes, mementos, get-well cards, and edibles. This one was bare save for a lonely glass of faintly turbid water, one sip of which, he was certain, would lay him mad and frothing.

A nurse arrived and, leaning over the bed, grasped the leg to steady it while he unwrapped the soggy gauze. The odor of rot was strong, and the wound undressed, he could see the reason. A serpiginous ulcer wound along the entire side of the foot and across the sole. He donned the gloves and proceeded to attack the scab with scissors and forceps, cutting and pulling away the hidelike tissue.

"How long has this been present?" he asked the nurse, trying to keep reproach out of his tone.

"It's grown very fast, Doctor. It wasn't there two weeks ago. He must have gotten himself into a bad position with his foot pressed against the railing somehow. Poor soul, but he moves now and then, you know. We find him in the weirdest tie-ups," she laughed ingratiatingly.

Bad boy, Mr. Richardson. You shouldn't move at all, he thought. You should just lie still where you're put. Now see where your rocking and wriggling have got you. A sore foot, and with bone showing at the bottom. We'll be a long time getting that in shape.

"Doctor, may I call the other girls? I want them to see this too."

"Of course."

Alone with the patient he bent over the dead foot, directly beyond which he could see the man's face. The eyes roved in their fissures, briefly reconnoitering the operation above, then, preoccupied with a fog of their own, moved on.

The first "pop" he did not hear, nor the second or third. It was only later that he realized them back from below the threshold of hearing. At the fourth or fifth "pop," he began to wonder idly what was causing it. The sounds were spaced irregularly, about two to three minutes apart, and were not all of the same intensity, some being stronger than others. At the sixth "pop" he turned and with a jolt realized that there was another person in the room, a second or third, depending on how much one emphasized Mr. Richardson.

He straightened completely, still holding the scissors and forceps in his gloved hands, and faced the intruder, or had he been there all the time?

"I beg your pardon. I didn't see you. You startled me."

The man was sitting in a low wheelchair with his back to Allain. He did not answer.

"I mean, have you been here all the time?"

In front of the wheelchair was an ancient typewriter, and as Allain watched, an arm flung itself from the man's body, bending and winding as though it had more joints than it should. Arched at the wrist, rotating, flailing, it swung behind the man's head. Then the other arm appeared, flying up to meet its fellow, steering by the same incomprehensible stars. As they struggled in the air, the huge head tipped forward on the neck, lolling between the shoulders, and turned to face the right hand, squinting to get it in sight. With a sudden violent jerk the hand was brought down on the typewriter and "pop" the index finger struck a key. The man's body slumped and the arms settled slowly, sinuously to his sides.

Allain caught his breath. The man was typing! He was short. This Allain could discern despite the man's sitting position. His feet, encased in the heaviest of black shoes which came to the ankles, hung freely. The shoes were far from new but strikingly unscuffed. Worn by no walker, they were either weights or ornaments. The voluminous trousers were black and suspended from his shoulders. He wore a gray undershirt from the orifices of which emerged two arms and a neck of whiteness so stark as to belie the presence of blood coursing beneath the surface. Allain had not yet seen the man's face. The right arm was again stirring, scurrying away from the torso, swinging up and out in a grandiose overshooting of the mark, falling in back of the bowed head. Again its fellow took sudden awkward flight and shot up to meet it. They tangled and turned in the air like birds. One, having spotted its prey, dipped, shuddered, then shot, finger extended, toward the key. "Pop" went the typewriter. The great head rose to eye the page and saw the doctor. The man's surprisingly red lips were pulled into a grimace that might have been a smile. To Doctor Allain they had the quality of bruised fruit.

"Hello." The doctor cleared his throat.

"Aow." The voice had the same lack of control as the arms. It gave the distinct impression that unless great care were taken, it would shoot off into outer reaches of sound that would terrify both listener and speaker.

"You're typing," he said blankly, aware at once of his awkwardness. Be careful, Allain, he said to himself. You started this. Now try to finish it. Anything you say will be stupid, or at least unworthy.

"I am Doctor Allain. I've come to treat your roommate's bad leg."

After a long pause during which he seemed to be gathering himself together, the man began to laugh. It took a few moments for Allain to define the unrestrained scraping in the throat and the heave of the shoulders as laughter. Why is he laughing? Allain wondered. Can it be that he sees some irony here, Richardson's foot, the nurse, my being here at all? Or is he merely embarrassed at being seen?

"What's your name?"

"A-Arold."

"Harold?"

"Ayss."

Allain wished ardently that he had not started the conversation. The man had not turned back to his typewriter, and seemed to be expecting more, or, at least, waiting to see if any more were said. So, he was without embarrassment. It was Allain who was ill at ease.

Pardon me for intruding, he wanted to begin. I could not help but be impressed by your ability to type. But something like intelligence sparkled in the man's eyes, and he could not say it.

"Have you been here long?"

"Ayss."

"Where are you from?"

Again there was a pause, followed by the same shaking of shoulders and scraping laugh.

Allain thought, that does it. I'll just turn around and go on working.

"Well, I've got to finish this job. Nice talking to you, Harold."

Harold did not shift his gaze but continued to watch him, holding him.

"What are you writing?"

"A ledder."

"How long does it take you to type a letter?"

"A mon."

"A month?"

"Ayss."

From where Allain was standing, he could see that the page in the typewriter was three-quarters covered with type. He had moved to within a few feet of the man, and darted a glance at the page.

"My dearest Vera," he read.

My dearest Vera! God in Heaven! He's writing to a woman, calling her "my" and "dearest"! Allain's hands shook with a fine tremor. He inched closer, knowing that he would read the letter, knowing, too, that he would be seen; caring, but feeling a compulsion to do it. Within reading distance now, he quickly scanned the page. It was almost illegible, surrealistic. There were many letters crossed out with X's (costly). Words ran together without spacing, and whole lines slanted wildly.

When he finished, he looked down to see Harold, half-turned, grinning up at him wetly through his purple lips. There was no accusation in that grin, no resentment. Only, again, an ambiguity. Allain stood silently, no longer embarrassed. It was as though the letter had broken down the experience into its component parts, stripped it of pretense and formality. They seemed to have discovered each other.

He looked at the night table near Harold's bed. It was a wasteland of tissues, postcards, loose crackers, and a carafe of water. In the center stood the framed photograph of a woman, glossy, dark. She was gazing coolly over the shoulder of the viewer, no trace of a smile on her perfect features. Her black-sequined gown dipped dangerously across her white bosom. In the lower right corner was written with a flourish,

"To Harold with love," and under that, "Joan Crawford."

Allain nodded slightly at the picture.

"Vera?" he asked quietly.

"Ayss," grinned Harold.

Treasure Map

James Richardson

Turn right
If you see anything
you are in the wrong place

Go to the land where the dust falls with tails of silence

When you come to the fork in the road keep going

If you reach a tree
execute a smart about-
face
and wait for blood

When it does not appear
proceed to the upside-
down waterfall which plummets up
from the underground stream

Walk around it once

When you come to the realization

you have made it

Congratulations

Now they will never
find you

Possibilities

James Richardson

THE STONES will not admit
that they are the fastest

They would rather deceive us
than win

Now you know what you will be
when you have forgotten everything you need
to

Their wings are approaching:
the speck of a tern on the horizon the wings
of an egg

But the darkness
will not support them and the light
astonishes

So the stones are waiting for another world

Mostly they let themselves be
used knowing they will inherit
what they become

Some turn inside
out

those are the flowers
dying before us

Friends

James Richardson

The air has some jokes on us

It turns like a star
It will not let us see

the past

It blows a little dust off us
and brings tomorrow

So it has been burying us
since we dried

It remembers that we made it
what it is
that we have the lungs and eyes and arms

So it follows us everywhere
to be remembered

No one who breathes
lives very long

Others' Dreams

Joyce Carol Oates

Matthew woke suddenly from a daydream that was not his.

He shook himself awake, startled. He dislodged the dream from himself, out of his head. No one had noticed: the place was gleaming and empty, only the three new automobiles out on the floor, brilliant and massive and unseeing, all curves and sleek precise lines; no one else was around. Peter, one of the younger salesmen, was just coming through the door at the far end of the showroom, looking nervous, perplexed. . . .

Matthew hoped that Peter would not stop at his cubicle to talk with him.

He had stirred himself from a dream that was not his. It could not have belonged to him. He had never had such a dream before, he would not acknowledge it. Not his. He never daydreamed, he never let his thoughts wander. The dream had been someone else's, not his own. The tag-end of a stranger's dream. . . . It was possible: you could be infected by the fears of strangers.

He looked through the calendar on his desk; he must make himself concentrate on something real. What was the date? His birthday was approaching—he would be forty-six in two weeks. He felt much younger. He looked much younger, a man of broad, vigorous shoulders, thighs thick and still muscular, like the trunks of small trees. That hard grainy muscularity. He was proud of his body and of his face—he had an intelligent, kindly face, marred only by the deep lines made by smiles. Years of smiling. His hair was brown, streaked with red; there was something exclamatory in the way he frequently raised his eyebrows.

He had been selling cars for twenty years here at Over-meyer Ford.

. . . On the gleaming fake-brick floor, a man of obvious energy. Excellent clothes, shoes, his hair kept carefully trimmed. He knew everything. He could answer any question about any car manufactured by Ford. He could answer the questions of the most methodical, suspicious customer. Everyone knew him, Matthew Brown, he had sold thousands of cars, old customers kept coming back to him, making appointments specifically with him . . . he knew everyone's name, he shook hands easily and yet without presumption; there was a sacred space around all men, a few feet of air, and he knew enough not to blunder into it. Though he was almost forty-six he could judge by the look in women's eyes his own youthful appearance, that blond, broad, generous Irish face, the good looks he had had for decades without especially prizing them. He was proud of his work, not of himself. Proud of his family. Not himself: his family. He was devoted to his wife and five children.

He did not think about the strange dream he had had, sitting here awake. He was a man who did not believe in dreams.

Yes, it said here on his calendar that someone was supposed to have come to see him at three o'clock. He would wait. No reason for uneasiness. Customers were often late. This month had been a slow month . . . interest rates had risen again . . . there were rumors of another dealer going bankrupt . . . but it did no good to think of any of these things. He would sit in his cubicle and wait quietly. He wondered if Peter had lost his customer—that woman with the bone-white hair, bleached and sullen, who had talked so loudly. It might be a good idea to stop by Peter's cubicle on the way out, say something kind to him, it was the least he could do. He felt sorry for Peter, who had not made any sales yet this month. . . . Waiting, he looked idly at the tiny crack on his desk top. It seemed that his daydream had sprung somehow out of that crack. It was an irritant, the crack. Faint and thin and curving as a hair. He often tried to brush it away while talking with customers. His voice could move on rapidly, knowing the answers to all questions, heading off questions before they were asked, gauging by the customers' faces how well he was doing. He usually did well. Very well. He could work swiftly with numbers, adding up long columns, subtracting, figuring out discounts, a routine performance of his that impressed customers. If the trade-in is twelve hundred, then. . . . Minus this. Minus. Plus.

Months in a long wavering column, adding up to decades.

Father came home early, about four-thirty, on that day. . . .

"Do you want some coffee, Matt? I'm going over now," Gardie said. She wore a navy blue dress, trim as a uniform. Gardie. Hildegarde. He must have said yes because in a few minutes she appeared again with coffee for him. He accepted the paper cup, touched. Women had always liked him, had always been concerned about him. She leaned against the partition, her dress stark and neutral against the frosted glass. Five or six years now of Gardie's cheerful, sagging face. Cheerful conversation, the words slightly sagging as the years passed. A troubled marriage—Matthew knew only a little, didn't want to know more. In spite of his tall, broad, leggy personality he didn't want to know much about people, resisted their hints of private, personal, grieved lives, didn't want to get snagged by them. He carried himself cautiously through crowds.

He had five children of his own and thought about them constantly.

One of us saw his car coming up the Boulevard, the big black Lincoln he drove in 1970. That was Ronnie, delivering papers. Then Len saw the car parked in front of the garage. Why wasn't it inside the garage the way Father always wanted it? He didn't want oil stains on the concrete . . . he had poured the concrete himself for the new driveway. But now the car was parked outside and might drip oil onto the concrete.

He drank the coffee slowly, grateful for its warmth. A bad habit, all this coffee. It was almost four o'clock. Someone named Mr. Yates had called Gardie yesterday to make this appointment with Matthew, but he had never heard of the man before: no Mr. Yates in his file of old customers. Should he have known him?

He would not think of Yates. Customers often came late, or showed up the next day. He would not think of the daydream that had disturbed him. Instead, he concentrated on the crack in his desk. The top was plastic, an unclean light yellow. Almost white. The crack was a stream, a river . . . a faint life-line he must follow . . . a stubborn little artery. The daydream had come from this line, somehow. It had not been about automobiles. The automobiles, those magnificent new models, were right out there on the floor, a few yards away from him, and he had only to glance up to see how massive and patient they were. He did not dream about them. Never about them. He did not dream about selling cars, about breaking his own record, made three years ago. Not about his wife Florence. Not about his sons, his daughters. . . . This strange dream had been about sleep. A dream about sleep. There had been a body, a kind of mummy, lying very still beneath heavy covers. Sheets pulled up to the chin. A faceless face. Formless bulges, ridges. A mystery. The figure had appeared in his mind's eye and had held itself there for some minutes, frightening him.

But it was not his dream. It must have belonged to someone else.

One of us, Vicky, heard Mother's voice upstairs. "Matt? What do you mean? Why is the door locked?" Vicky backed away from that sound in her mother's voice. She felt a sharp, terrified thrill in the pit of her stomach: why was Father home, up in the bedroom, at 4:30 on a Tuesday afternoon?

She noticed a crack on the living room ceiling. Had she ever seen that crack before?

Someone was infecting him with bad dreams, Matthew thought. He could hear Peter talking on the telephone— making a show of sounding efficient, talking too fast. Peter should know that customers did not trust salesmen who talked too fast. Peter was several years younger than Matthew, but he had stomach troubles, he probably had bad dreams. His commissions dissolved: too anxious to knock down prices. But Matthew had never talked with

Peter about these tactics. Better not to talk. In the long run. . . . In the long run, he thought vaguely, the best salesman does best.

A rattle of voices. Mother washing dishes as if nothing was wrong, Vicky drying. Tommy fooling around. "Is Daddy sick? Why is the door locked?" Mother using the pink sponge, which was worn out. It looked eroded. Tommy pulled his lips away from his gums, making a face. He was five years old. Vicky stood with her back to him, her shoulders thin and tense. She kept listening for Father's footsteps upstairs. First the creaking of the bedsprings, then the heavy footsteps. Mother set dishes in the drying rack, her fingers slippery with soap. "Why didn't Daddy have supper with us? Is he sick?" Tommy whined.

He followed the crack with his eyes, then with his forefinger. Strange. It was a small river leading him up, back . . . up into what, back into what? The dream had come out of that small river. But he did not want to remember it. He did not want to see that figure in bed, hardly a human figure, lying so stiffly in bed, aged and silent. Where the hell was this Mr. Yates?

The telephone rang.

Gardie answered it and he knew before she buzzed him that it would be for him. He picked up the receiver: "This is Matthew Brown." He began talking at once. No trouble. Quoting prices: the advertisement in the Sunday paper. Yes. Subtract two hundred dollars. Three years to pay. His words rattled on with a false, bright energy of their own, while he stared at the little crack on his desk top. He had a sensation of falling and only the telephone conversation kept him upright.

He hung up. Gardie hurried over.

"That guy who just called," she said in a whisper, "he was Peter's customer a few years ago . . . oh, when was it? . . . caused all that trouble, do you remember? Something about the turn-lights not working right. . . ."

He remembered exactly, every detail. No, he did not remember.

In the middle of their conversation—such a normal, conspiratorial conversation, of the kind they had every day!—he got to his feet. Not well. Sick. Must go home. Gardie's face immediately crinkling and maternal. "I have to go home. I'm not well," he said suddenly.

"Not well?" she said, shocked.

"Not well? You're not well?" Mother was saying outside the bedroom door. "Why can't you answer me?" Vicky next to her. Another one of us—Sally—was by the bathroom door, pretending to be swinging on it. Wanting attention. She had hold of the doorknob and stood with her knees on either side of the door, trying clumsily to swing on it. If Mother noticed she would be scolded. Why were Mother and Vicky standing there like that, so strange, by the bedroom door? Mother and Vicky: the same height. Vicky was thirteen then. Her hair was cut very short, almost as short as a boy's. A deeper brown than Father's. She had Father's nose, wide at the bridge, making her eyes look clear and wise because they were spaced far apart. Vicky's wise monkeyish look. Mother, with her hair in a tangle, rapped on the door to her own bedroom. A strange, formal gesture. "Why is the door locked? Why is the door locked?" she cried.

He left the agency and drove home. His car responded at once—the powerful motor made hardly any sound. So much strength, yet nearly silent. These machines were miraculous. No one could invent them if their secret were lost. The car leapt forward, hurtled itself forward. . . . Carrying him home. Safe. Back up that winding little river, safely back to something, into something, into darkness. His heart beat calmly in his chest. When he got home he would go upstairs at once and into the bedroom and lock the door. Better to lie down and rest. A short nap before dinner. He hoped that his wife would not be in the house.

Turning onto Claremont Boulevard he felt that he was losing strength, that it was somehow flowing out of his legs and into the engine of his car. Must get home, to bed. A sense of despair in his stomach—the very pit of his stomach —everything was settling down darkly, heavily. He must get home. Get to bed. He was dangerous, out here on the street, driving this large vehicle. Its mass hurtled itself across the pavement without much warning sound, a terrible danger to other people in spite of its beauty. What if he crashed into someone?—he did not even own this car—

his legs had grown very weak—what if he crashed this car into one driven by an old customer of his, a car he himself had sold?

Other cars on the Boulevard appeared to be winking and grimacing at him. Happy grillwork in front of the cars. The slope of the bumper: a happy look. Chrome, tinted windshield, whitewall tires that seemed to be winking, gesturing. . . .

His house was at the far end of the block. Two colonials had been built at the same time, identical except that one had dark orange brick and the other had pale buff brick. The dark orange brick home was his. His lawn had a birch clump of three trees, not doing well, and his neighbor's lawn had a single red-leafed tree, not doing well. Though he was nearly home he felt very weak. Maybe he should park in front of the house, not risk turning up the drive. His wrists and knees were especially weak. But he turned up the driveway and parked just in front of the garage, not daring to drive in because he feared brushing the side of the doorway. He turned off the ignition. Left the keys inside. Went into the house, through the back hall, upstairs, before anyone saw him. Florence called out, "Matt . . . ?"

He closed the bedroom door behind him and locked it.

"What is happening to me?" he thought.

We sat around the kitchen table while Mother and Vicky were upstairs. The air was all jumbled. What was happening? Tommy was snivelling. Ronnie sat with his elbows on the table and his hands pressed against his forehead, imitating Father: the way Father sometimes sat at the table, by himself, in the evening. "What are they talking about up there? Where is Daddy?" Sally kept saying.

His hands were shaking. He tore off his suit coat and threw it onto a chair. Must get these hot, heavy clothes off. They were suffocating him. Unbuttoned his shirt, took off his necktie. Everything was damp. Smelled. There was a sour, panicked smell about him. Must get his clothes off. Must get naked. Already Florence was hurrying up the stairs. "Matt? Is that you? Is something wrong?"

Already it was beginning.

He slid into bed, trembling. Pulled the covers up to his chin. Every part of his body trembled. Lying flat, he could feel the panic spread everywhere inside him, like a pool of mercury. That sharp, acrid taste. But he would force himself to think calmly, logically. He would relax, take a nap. A nap would restore his strength. Yes, a nap before supper, and then he would be feeling as good as ever . . . if only Florence would let him alone. . . . But she was right outside the door now, calling out in that surprised, slightly annoyed voice she used on the children: "Are you in there? Is the door locked? What on earth is wrong?"

He got a grip on his teeth, his jaws locked firmly together. Good. He would relax every part of his body and sleep. It would do no good to reply to his wife because he would only be lying down here for a few minutes. The sensation of panic would pass. It was a foreign sensation, not his own. He did not recognize it. . . . What was that noise? A telephone ringing. Someone was running—one of the children—there was always someone running in this house. The boys wrestled one another, elbowed one another on the stairs and at meals. He closed his eyes and saw his oldest son's face. He loved Len more than any of the other children because he was the first child. Never another child, another miraculous birth, like that. But Vicky: sweet and waifish, he loved Vicky very much, he must explain to her that he loved her. . . .

Florence was saying: "Matt, it's Gardie. She wants to know if you're all right. Matt? Matt? Did you get sick at work?"

He must have slept. He saw now that the room was darker. It was not a very large room, but he had always liked it. Florence complained that the walls and ceiling should be painted. Everything was very still. The curtains caught his eye, pale green fishnet curtains. Dime-store curtains. His wife had always been clever at sewing, fixing up cheap things, searching for bargains. The curtains and the bureau and the rocking chair were very familiar, in the proper scale. He thought that perhaps he himself was out of proportion. He felt smaller. His legs seemed shorter. The covers on his chest formed a shallow ridge and he could not look past it. His mouth tasted sour from the spread of panic. What was that smell in the air? He had carried it up here with him, to bed—the odor of gasoline, exhaust fumes, the close, smooth stench of oil. The rainbow stench of oil. He peered along his chest but could not see to the foot of the bed. His gaze skimmed the bottom of his eyebrows and came away tangled and befuddled. The fishnet material of the curtains was confused with the tangle of his eyebrows and the bumpy ridge of his chest.

Len with the screwdriver. Mother's angry tears. "Why doesn't he answer us?" Something harsh and soiled about her face. When we used to see her out on the street, shopping, the oldest of us would flinch a little from the sight of our mother—her breeziness, the rapid skittish walk of hers—as if she were free, a woman and not a mother, just a person out on her own—and we would call out to her, to bring her to a halt. The oldest of us—Len and Vicky and Ronnie—were embarrassed because she was so pretty. But that day she wasn't a pretty woman, not a woman at all but something frightened, smelling of fear. "He won't answer me! He must be sick!" Mother kept saying.

Len stood with his cheek pressed against the locked door. Silence inside. "Father, this is Len. Father? I'm going to take the lock off the door. . . . Father? Can you hear me?"

In bed he was thinking seriously about getting up. Like commandments, certain phrases were going through his head: *front-wheel drive, liquid suspension but no springs or shock absorbers, a fully synchronized transmission, a luxurious all-vinyl interior, nylon carpeting wall-to-wall, eight cylinders. . . .* These words were like summonses from another world. They were like shouts from a cliff down to him as he lay here so peacefully in bed, preparing his strength. . . . What was that about a lock on a door? What did that mean?

Someone was rapping on wood and he thought of Mr. Yates, the customer who had never shown up. Maybe he was knocking now on a door, trying to get to see Matthew. Well, let him knock. Matthew had survived many disappointments, and now he felt himself stronger, almost independent of his customers; he would not even glance up to see who was knocking. So many disappointments! But they belonged to the past, to another Matthew, and he felt that he had grown beyond them.

"No, don't open it! He doesn't want us to open it!"
Vicky cried suddenly. The screwdriver fell to the floor—
she knocked it out of Len's hand.

The problem: he had to think through his plans for the
evening. He had to think through all the moves he would
make. "Getting up"—a generalized expression that took in
a complex, an almost hopelessly complex, sequence of
particularized movements, some of them muscular and
some of them entirely cerebral. Just thinking about this
made him exhausted. It was nearly more than the human
brain could assimilate. And, behind all this, behind the
demand placed upon him by the command "Get up" was
the mysterious rapping, the jumble of voices, which seemed
to be shouting individual and uncoordinated commandments to him. The need for "getting up" was one he could
recognize clearly, privately, as originating inside himself,
but these other voices with their curious demands—they
were obviously the voices of other people, actual existing
human beings who could not even agree with one another.
. . . The world was busy and it wanted nothing so much
as to drag him out into it, sweep him along the river where
he would be lost, in all that shouting, that busyness. . . .
What a kindness, if someone should think of bringing him
a cup of coffee! But no one thought of it, and he was too
tired to get it himself.

Instead, the voices of arguing people.

Mother hurrying downstairs. She embraced Tommy and
Sally, who were crying. "Daddy is sick, just a bad cold.
Yes. He said so. I'm going to call the doctor." Ronnie
backed away from her, bumped into a table. His face stern,
rigid, small droplets of perspiration on his forehead. He
wore a T-shirt and soiled khaki pants and sneakers. Look-
ing down at himself he saw that he was dressed like a kid
and he was ashamed.

Mother was wearing old slacks and a white blouse we
thought was too sheer—you could see straps at her shoul-
ders—we hated that.

She called the doctor and Ronnie ran out to the back
fence, where everything was weedy. He pressed against the
fence.

In the corner of the room, his wife's sewing machine.

Photographs on the wall—the children when they were very young—Florence and himself—posed for Christmas cards a few years ago. How fast the children grew! A miracle. He loved them tenderly, fiercely . . . he could feel a warm, blinding haze of love for them in his own body, located in his chest . . . or in the base of his skull . . . ? He thought of Len. A healthy, husky boy. Vicky: that cap of dark close-cropped hair, her thin arms and legs, her thin face. Len was handsome. Golden-tanned, curly hair lighter than his father's, energetic arms and legs, a sudden smile that could break his father's heart. When he confessed to stealing a bicycle from school, years before, Matthew had been the one to break down. Unashamed to cry before his oldest son. The two of them in the basement of the house, talking quietly, a father and his son. Matthew was unashamed to cry. Unashamed.

If he cried now the tears would run down sideways, comically, on his cheeks. No need to cry. Florence did not cry. They had loved each other deeply for years, he had been bold and tender with her body, for years, a cascade of years, then it had ebbed. One day he stood in the doorway of the bedroom, watching her at the sewing machine, the rapid, tonguelike flicking of the needle, her skillful hands guiding the cloth, the rattling noise, the vibrations he could feel beneath his feet, the look of danger, of relentlessness about her bent head and narrowed, skillful eyes. . . . She had been unaware of him .

Dr. Crane was talking to him, suddenly. The door stood open. Florence in the doorway, a blur. Where were the children? Dr. Crane was talking to him, asking him something, and he felt his parched lips cracking into a smile. Must smile. Must communicate. Dr. Crane was wrapping something about his upper arm, tighter and tighter. The pressure was enormous. Matthew tried not to notice it. He must not seem too sensitive. What should he say to Dr. Crane? It was important to communicate. Communication was the first step in sales, in civilization itself. Nothing happened between people unless there was communication first. You could have a miraculous product but it would not sell itself. It would sit there, inert. The three enormous cars in the showroom—the sedan, the convertible, the station wagon—would remain there forever, unsold, unacknowledged, until they were explained to the customer. All their energy, their godliness inert for centuries! Unless they were explained, translated, sold. The product and the customer had to be brought together by a handshake and certain words, which were magical and very powerful. Each word was extremely important. . . . Last winter, when things had gone so slowly, the salesmen were advised to telephone old customers: "Hello. This is _____ _____ of Overmeyer Ford. I was wondering how you are. . . ." No: "I was wondering if you might happen to be in the market for a new car this winter." No, too direct. "Hello, this is _____ _____ of Overmeyer Ford. I hope I'm not disturbing you? I was wondering. . . ." But no, it was a poor idea to apologize and to suggest that the telephone call might be a disturbance. Poor psychology. Begin again: "Hello. This is _____ _____ of Overmeyer Ford. Maybe you remember, in 19__ you bought a car from me, and I was just wondering if. . . ."

Something was decided at the bedside, Dr. Crane and his wife conferring, and he felt suddenly very relieved. He would not have to explain himself tonight, then. Evidently they had decided to let him alone. He would rest. Sleep. In the morning everything would be back to normal and perhaps when he got to the agency he would come across Mr. Yates himself, that mischievous, mysterious Mr. Yates!

Eleven o'clock already. One of us turned on the news. We had forgotten about the whole evening; suddenly it was eleven o'clock. Mother heated up some chicken gumbo soup from cans. Tommy looked feverish but wouldn't go to bed. Mother's face pale and lined. We will all go to bed at once, we said. All fall asleep at once. Make a vow: we will all fall asleep at the same minute.

In the morning, a peculiar stillness to the house. A foreign stillness. He woke from troubled dreams, dreams that did not belong to him. They must have been someone else's dreams, infecting him. Diseases were spread by germs, and bad dreams could be spread by germs. Why did he dream about flesh that was rosy turning to lard? About handshakes falling away to nothing, a hand coming loose in his own grip? He refused to think about these dreams. Maybe they belonged to Peter. Or Gardie. Maybe they belonged to Florence herself. They lay together at night, every night, side by side in the same bed, and between them there was an enormous distance of inches. . . . They never spoke of this distance. They would have had to shout across it. He would have had to telephone her from the agency, an impersonal voice: "Hello. Mrs. Brown? This is _____ _____ of Overmeyer Ford. I came across your name in my files and I was wondering if. . . ."

Maybe he was dreaming his wife's dreams?

But they were such ugly dreams! Himself in bed, Matthew Brown himself, still and cold in bed, wrapped up in blankets like a mummy. Ugh! How could she dream such dreams about her husband? His face flabby and old, the color drained out of it, wormy, grainy, pale, aged, no longer a handsome man, his hair plastered close to his skull. . . .

Len said to Vicky and Ronnie: "One of us better stay home today, it better be me." Ronnie agreed at once. He wanted to get out of the house. All A's at school. Father was very proud of him, but we all knew that he loved Len best. Vicky said, "I feel sick but I want to go to school. . . . I'm afraid to stay home here. . . ." "You're crazy!" Len said, reddening.

. . . Or maybe the dreams were Mr. Overmeyer's? He was a plump, big-voiced man of about five feet eight, fat grown on the outside of his body from too much drinking, alcoholic flab, soft wrinkles in the face and neck that seemed to gesticulate like Mr. Overmeyer's hands. Matthew was his best salesman. Mr. Overmeyer liked him best because Matthew did not ask for any favors. And he sold the most cars: a fact. Statistical fact. But sales were down, the economy was crazily inflated, who could pay such interest rates . . . ? In the past no one noticed the interest rates, but now they did. The younger customers, college-educated, scanning the figures Matthew gave them, their young foreheads wrinkling as they saw what the car would really cost. . . . "Jesus Christ," one of them whispered the other day. . . . Mr. Overmeyer lived out in Hanley

Park, along the river. He had three daughters, all taller than himself.

Mr. Overmeyer came out on Saturday, four days after Father had gotten sick. Stood eye to eye with Len and shook hands gravely. "You've got to be the man of the house, until your father gets well."

"Exhaustion," someone was saying to him. "Sick leave." "Busy period." "Too much strain." It sounded like Mr. Overmeyer. But why would he be here, at Matthew's bedside? Was Florence pushing the two of them together, urging Mr. Overmeyer to get closer, to get in bed with Matthew? A crowded bed! Matthew had a sudden idea: he would telephone customers from this bed. Very simple. Gardie could bring his files over, he would prop himself up with pillows, and use the telephone. An excellent idea. He would suggest it to Mr. Overmeyer, as soon as Mr. Overmeyer stopped talking and stopped moving his hands. Why did that man always move his hands!—it marked him as common. Matthew's mother had always noted gestures that marked people as *common,* even if they had money. As soon as Mr. Overmeyer stopped talking Matthew would tell him about his plan: telephoning from bed. That way he would still be at work. It would be quite an experiment, to see how many cars he could sell like that, over the telephone. Maybe it would be written up in *Ford Times.*

The mess in the bed. The smell. Vicky imagining she carried it with her to school. Mother had to go to a medical supply store and buy a bedpan. The youngest of us were kept out of the sickroom. We hung around downstairs and watched cartoons on television all day long. Loud enough to hear all over the house. At school, Vicky thought of that pasty face, the strange dark sockets of his eyes, the flabby lips, the raspy breathing, the bedpan emptied in the bathroom, the whispering, Mother's vague hands and eyes, the television set and the endless cartoons, the smell that was in her own clothes and wouldn't come out . . . she had to excuse herself and run to the restroom, where she was sick to her stomach for the second time that day.

Ronnie hated collection day. By now many people knew about Father: stray, sly little questions, holding the money in their hands so that Ronnie couldn't escape, always asking if "things were any better at your house . . . ?"

    The hell with them all, Ronnie thought.

    The hell with his sister Vicky puking in the bathroom.

    The hell with the little kids, always giggling or bursting into tears.

    The hell with Len, bossing everyone around.

    The hell with Mother.

    The hell with Father: let him stink.

His mother came to see him, that noble ravaged face, that harsh gray hair. She must have had some news to tell him. But he could not make sense of her words. Why didn't Florence come closer, why didn't Florence make his mother speak up? He could not make sense of her words, no. All his life he had been hearing them: *Matthew! I own you! My son!* But now they eluded him. She was only inches away. She might have come here to remind him that he was not just a father but also a son, he had been a son for forty-six years and could not escape that fact, hiding in his smelly cocoon. No. But he could not hear her. He wanted to weep: why was she leaning so close?

    Mother, Len, and Vicky fed him. The doctor showed them how. The rest of us were kept downstairs. Bickering. Tommy throwing himself around. Ronnie yelled: "God damn you little bastards! I could kill you!" Father upstairs, drooling. The best thing to feed him, Dr. Crane said, is baby food. Why not? He did not spit the food out, but sometimes it came back out by itself.

    Ronnie said: "I'm going to set that bed on fire. Get that big worm up and moving fast!" Len punched him in the chest. They wrestled together, falling back against the wall. Ronnie giggled and sucked blood from his bleeding nose and began to choke.

Sounds of battle in the distance. Beyond the range of his bed the world was in perpetual twilight and turmoil. Struggle—arguing—vibrations from angry footsteps—weeping—the ringing of the telephone. Two figures standing at the foot of his bed, speaking gravely. Was that his wife? Was that the doctor? The world was filling up with strangers, people whose names he did not know. Hands he could not shake. His customers were being taken away from him . . . perhaps his files had already been divided up among the salesmen at the agency. . . . What were these two saying, were they talking about him? He strained to hear, he tried to lift himself up on one elbow. . . .

One of us was waiting out on the veranda. Dr. Crane said: "There's nothing else to do. You'd better take this opening while you can. Yes, he did move, he seemed about to get up, but then he fell back again. . . . But it isn't enough. He's very sick." Mother stumbled over something of Tommy's on the porch. She was crying again.

Mother, why did you cry so much!—small pale rivulets worn in your cheeks—it took months of sunlight to erase them—

The doorway had widened. The whole world was trooping through it, into his room, trying to get into bed with him. Over the years the children had run in here, jumping in bed with him and Florence, what a noisy giggling bunch!—but now there were strangers coming in. They gripped him hard, skillfully. Eased him up. His body ached, his spine flashed pain. Someone was saying, "Come on. That's it. Okay. Fine. Get his feet. Hold steady."

He wondered if they would let him drive his own car. Why was he being put in the back of someone else's car? A small truck? The car he drove was not really his own, but it was given to him for his use; he always had a new car. But now his legs were strangely shortened, very limp. What had happened? Maybe if he were placed in his car, behind the wheel, he would be able to reach the accelerator and the brake. His heartbeat quickened at the thought of driving his car, himself. Even if it was the last time he was allowed to drive. He was proud of that car. His sons had always been proud of the new cars he drove, because their friends' fathers did not have such expensive cars. Would they think of letting him drive, would they be that kind? Or would he have to request this favor himself?

We all watched. The stretcher, the blankets still wrapped around him, that face. Tommy, who hadn't seen him for a while, screamed: "That's not Daddy!" Len helped the attendants with the stretcher. Mother had to get out of the way, she looked vague and confused, as if she were having difficulty making sense of the scene before her.

The ambulance was driven away like an ordinary car. No siren, no red light. Down to the end of our street and onto Claremont Boulevard and out of sight. It did not seem right that Father should be taken away so quietly.

We kept waking up at night. Was somebody in the room? In bed with us? We kept running in to Mother, Tommy and Sally especially. Tommy screamed until his eyes filled up with blood. Wanted to kick at the rest of us. He pounded at his own face with his fists. Mother took him in with her every night, in the new bed. Everything new about it: a shiny, smooth headboard, a new mattress, new pillows, new box-springs, new sheets. Even there Tommy would wake up, frightened. "Was somebody here in bed?" Mother said, "No." "Wasn't there somebody?" Tommy cried. Mother said, "No."

Temporaries

Sara S. Mitter

SORRY, the extra bedroom's occupied
again. Peter's left home
and while he searches for a furnished room,
he's here. Last week Bill
turned up to think things out. We seem to tide
half our friends through crises and affairs.
To think that we're known as the stable pair!
Something about our fireside must appeal.

My willing ear? They come like orphans
ravelled, underfed,
but all they want is someone else's bed.
They should feel some loyalty to me!
Imagine, the first night Bill was here
a gang dropped in. Remember Lise?
Those monumental breasts. Billy's eyes
deepened in a way I'd never seen.
They drank my tea, and he took her home.
Came back two days later—not a word.
I wouldn't even tease him—I was mad.

Fred? He doesn't mind it, and besides
they're his friends, and honorably straight.
I only help them sort their troubles out.
Once, you know, I thought of Jane and Roy
They kept an open house, and they were well
respected and—so we thought—secure.
Then he left her for a younger girl.
His friends were hot as foxes at her door.

Staff of Life

Gail Arkley

Sundays, some days, we made bread. Although I knew the recipe, I fetched the cookbook, which obligingly fell open to the right page, stiff with milk and powdery with the flour of the last batch.

WHITE BREAD

1 oz. yeast	2 Tbsp. shortening
¼ c. lukewarm water	2 Tbsp. sugar
1 tsp. sugar	2 c. milk, scalded
1½ tsp. salt	6–7 c. sifted flour

Catman was cleaning the kitchen table with the interest and assiduity of a novice. I, more used to kitchen chores, and lazier, got out the tools, receptacles, and initial ingredients, spreading them with inchoate strategy around the kitchen: milk by the stove to be heated; butter, salt, and sugar huddled together in a bare space on the counter; measuring cups and spoons at random to be grabbed in transit; and the big old aluminum breadmaking bowl plopped down on the clean table with a wooden spoon rattling inside it.

"Let's go." I began to drag the big bargain bag of unbleached flour out of its corner and across the floor to the table.

"Here, I'll help you with that." He leaned over and around me, and with my strength now superfluous, we pulled the bag across the floor. Letting go of the bag, I straightened up, then bent over with my elbows on the table, intending to reread the recipe. Catman still encircled me from behind, his hands slipping round my waist, up my ribs, and over my breasts, bare beneath my sweater.

Add yeast to lukewarm water and sugar. Let stand for
5 min.

Pressing my behind backwards in acknowledgment, I
stood up, turned around, gave a quick squeeze, and darted
away to the sink to concoct the lukewarm water. I finger-
tested the temperature as the water flowed into the measuring cup: warm enough to urge the little yeast plants to
grow, but not hot enough to kill. I dumped in about a
teaspoonful of brown sugar and poured in a packet of yeast.
Catman, reading the recipe, decided to scald the milk—the
next preliminary. He filled the 2-cup cup with milk, poured
it in a pan, and set it on one of the front burners of the
stove, without forgetting to turn it on. When the element
glowered a dull red, I joined him at the stove. Side by
side we gazed into the pan, waiting for the foamy little
bubbles. Slowly they appeared around the pan's encircling
sides. We became engrossed; the fulminating boil startled
us and Catman yanked the pan from the burner in a flurry
of sparks. From the pan held aloft, he poured a steaming
smooth white stream of milk cooling and splashing into
the bowl.

Add shortening, salt, and remaining sugar to milk and
cool to lukewarm.

I lopped a lump of butter from the cube—it looked like
about two tablespoons—and launched it into the hot milk
where it floated and melted in a yellow circle; added a
flowing 1½ teaspoons of salt; and instead of sugar took
honey from the cupboard and poured a thick amber ribbon
from the jar into the mixture. I stirred and tasted, fascinated
by the intensely salt/sweet combination. Catman tried it
too, and when we kissed the taste mingled in our mouths.
Returning to the bread, we thought of more things to add.
Catman cracked a couple of eggs against the edge of the
table and released them into the bowl while I threw in a
handful of wheat germ. The concoction was becoming a
lumpy pottage. Catman beat it smooth and golden. Taking
the bowl, I felt the temperature of the mixture through
the aluminum: a vital warmth for the yeast.

Add softened yeast and 3 cups flour. Beat well.

I poured in the yeast, scraping it from the sides of the cup with my finger. Next, the flour. Handing bowl and spoon back to Catman, I took the measuring cup—though it was many breadmakings since I had either measured or sifted—and dipped into the bag of flour. One, two, three cups. Catman stirred and beat; I brushed off my floury hands. The mixture was now a grainy wallpaper paste with a strong fertile yeasty smell.

Add enough more flour to make a soft dough.

Four, five, and Catman began to use a little more force. The substance was becoming doughy, clinging to the spoon. Six; stirring, beating, scraping in cadence, the stringy dough rolling in shreds from the sides of the bowl, the shank of the spoon. Seven, shaken sparingly; powdering the bumpy glutinous surface. A white flurry, and the spoon began again, working it into the mass. The spoon moved slower and slower.

Place remaining flour on board, turn out dough onto board, and knead until smooth and elastic.

I messily covered about a quarter of the table with a thick dusting of flour. Catman tilted the bowl and I took the spoon and prodded the moist heavy spreading mass of dough out of the bowl and onto the table. It sprawled, relaxed. Catman held the bowl while I scraped shreds, rolls, lumps, and strings out onto the pile of dough. We reached for more flour, the rest of the seventh cup and a little more, and dumped it on. I plunged my hands into the open flour bag, and whitely coated, sank up to my wrists in the warm gluey living mass of dough. Catman, lounging against the wall, smiled and watched as I grabbed and pressed and pushed and rubbed the flour into it. Soft and clinging, the dough covered my hands thickly. Catman piled on more flour, and stiffening, it began to resist. Still sticky, it was impossible to knead. I pushed and pulled at it in fits and starts, becoming myself sticky and floury and warm. Catman suggested I take off my sweater, already spotted and grainy with flour. I did, and stood naked to the hips, wrestling with the dough. Catman, although rather attracted by my necessary nudity, remembered that this was an especially difficult phase. After a short time, the struggle became easier, the dough more and more malleable. My face hot and my arms aching, I went to the sink to wash my crusted hands which were stickier now than the dough. I dried them, ready to knead. Leaning into the ball of dough with both hands, I began the regular push-lift-fold, push-lift-fold. I accelerated the rhythm. Catman knew from past Sundays that this was a lighter part, so he turned on the radio to a pounding rock beat which flowed joyously through my body and into my work. Smoother and smoother became the dough, and Catman's hands were smooth over my bare body. We laughed and sweated and rocked into the rhythm of the music and the kneading. We were high with laughter, music, and our kneading dance, and the dough was smooth and elastic; as smooth and elastic as my naked belly, its surface like satin without the luster. Catman took the yielding dough and pressed the soft creamy ball against my soft creamy belly. It felt like cool, firm skin. I picked it up, and with both hands tingling with friction and activity, slapped it roughly against the tabletop. Still panting, I rested my elbows on the table, Catman leaning over my shoulder, my cheek almost touching the surface of the dough, and read from the now even further bespattered recipe.

> Place in greased bowl, turn over so that greased side is on top, cover with a clean cloth, and let rise until double in bulk, about 1¼ hrs.

It had become ritual to use the big old bowl for every phase, and during the cleaning and greasing we had a chance to catch our breath after the kneading. Catman turned off the radio, and silence exploded in a burst of peace around us. Tumult subsided and our pace slowed. Catman washed the bowl while I walked round and round the kitchen gathering the dirty dishes and tossing them into the sink, dodging Catman and the bowl. With a sponge I wiped up pools of spilled liquid and little piles of dry ingredients, picking bits of dough off the floor. Bread-making leaves a fallout which remains in cracks and corners long after the last loaf has been eaten.

Taking the bowl, shining, clean, and warm from hot water, that Catman handed me, I smeared it generously with soft butter. I then lifted the smooth heavy yielding mass of dough from the table, dropped it into the bowl, and then flipped it over so that the rounded top gleamed with butter. Now to find a clean cloth and a warm place. Turning on the oven, I considered. Clean cloths were usually a problem, especially if it had been a while since we had visited the laundromat, dragging several weeks' accumulation behind us. Without even bothering to search the drawers, I shook the flour from my sweater and laid it across the top of the bowl. The oven was nice and warm now. Turning it off, I slid the bowl into the cosy-looking compartment.

For the time being, the bread was on its own, and so were we. I rubbed my bloom of flour off against Catman's chest, relaxing my weight against him. We took each other's measure with experienced and easy eyes. Another recipe lent itself to an infinity of variation, and we wanted to make it, but not in the kitchen; we usually cooked this one up better somewhere else. In the bedroom we folded ourselves into the bed. Warming up, we mixed and mingled. I dissolved, liquefied; salty. He was sweet, and tasted. Kneading, molding, I softened as he rose and stiffened. Stirring faster now, we blended and finally came together. Done, we rested.

After a while, remembering the bread, I put on a robe went barefoot across cool floors to the kitchen, and opened the oven. I removed the protective cover. The dough had risen nearly to the top of the container in a smooth and delicate convexity. Taking it from the now cool oven, I set the bowl on the counter. The next step demanded some aggression.

Punch down, turn over, and let rise a second time.

Feeling very mild and almost regretful, I sunk my fist

without violence deep into the center of the warm mass.
With a soft resigned sigh the myriads of tiny gas bubbles
imploded and the light fragile sponge became dense and
heavy around my hand.

Back in the bedroom, I turned the electric blanket on to
medium, tucked the bread in next to the sleeping Catman,
slipped off my robe, climbed into bed, and slept.

I awoke some time later. I couldn't have been asleep
for too long because the dough had attained just about
the right volume of airy puffiness. I slid carefully out of
bed and put on my robe. Throwing back the blanket, I
lifted out the bowl with its soft shaky mound not quite
ballooning over the top. Catman watched, slightly surprised
and yawning. I carried the bowl back to the kitchen table.
Catman, loosely tying the belt of his velvety robe, slouched
sleepily after. I handed him the bowl. His strong brown
fist plunged solidly into the tremulous paleness, which
collapsed softly, snugly around it. I turned lazily to the
recipe.

Divide in half, round into two balls, cover, and allow
to rest 10 min.

Catman tilted the bowl and nudged the dough, causing
it to loll blowsily out onto the table. Gathering it about the
middle with both hands, I squeezed. It yielded and divided
like a rubbery hourglass into two parts. We each took one
and molded wonderfully compact and self-contained balls,
settling them comfortably side by side and covering them
again with the sweater. During the rest period, I moved
slowly around the kitchen, clearing the remaining mess
and clutter. I found the bread pans, too, and greased their
cool metal sides. With still buttery hands, I took a ball of
dough from under its cover.

Shape into loaves and place in greased bread pans.

Cookbook directions for loaf-shaping are always more
complex than necessary, and the serial positions and manip-
ulations of the dough are too rigid and professional. Keeping the classic breadloaf shape in mind (notwithstanding

occasional fantasy deviations into balls, French loaves, rings, crescents, braids, and so forth), and remembering to vigorously press out air bubbles in order to prevent a too holey loaf that leaks the filling from sandwiches, the butter from toast, and can't be spread without tearing, one can shape a very good loaf spontaneously.

I stretched and pulled the dough wide and thin, then rolled it up long and close like a cigar, then folded it over and over upon itself, pinching the folds together until it was a pleasant solid oblong. Catman pulled out the other ball of dough, and pressing it with his hands, flattened it, keeping the circle smaller and thicker than I had done. He folded it rather like an envelope and put it in the second pan. I took a pan in each hand, and for a change of scene, set them uncovered on the lukewarm radiator.

Let rise until doubled in bulk.

Returning to our warm place, we lay down, stretched, patted, rolled, pinched, enfolded, and rose.

The bread had risen too, and when we returned to the kitchen we saw it palely mooning up over the straight and confining pans, presaging in understatement the finished loafy contours.

Bake in a hot oven for 45 min., approx.

I turned the oven on to preheat. When the little red light went off, we opened the door and a blast of heat and light flashed into our faces. We slid the pans in gingerly, afraid of deflating the nascent loaves. Shutting the oven door with an exaggerated sense of completion, we turned to each other with comic-book conspiracy, symbolically dusted off our hands, and breathed a long hearty "ahh."

The next 45 min., approx., were spent in expectation. We became aware of time and did not succeed in blurring our awareness through the haze of the Sunday papers which we desultorily tried to read while we waited. When the rich odor of yeasty baking bread had become unbearably overwhelming, the forty-five minutes were almost over.

"I think it's time," said Catman, looking at the clock again.

Suddenly we were in the kitchen. Opening the oven door we were once more struck by a wave of heat, this time smelling thickly of hot fresh bread. It looked done.

The bread is done when the color is a deep golden brown, the loaf shrinks from the sides of the pan and sounds hollow when tapped.

I turned off the oven and groped for a potholder. Catman found one and took the first loaf out, then the second, placing them on the table. While he gathered the implements and ingredients necessary for the final phase—long serrated bread knife, bread board, blunt spreading knives, paper napkins, butter, and jam—I lifted the loaves from the pans. I placed one of them across a pan to cool, and the other on the square wooden bread board. We looked at it, feasting first with our eyes. Symmetrical golden sides rose to a high even rounded top, brown and slightly powdery: an essential loaf. It was still very hot. Catman took the bright knife and sliced decisively into the bread, sawing with light rapid strokes to prevent the moist steaming crumb from becoming too compact under the dragging pressure of the knife and the weight of his hand which, protected from the heat by a napkin, steadied the loaf. The first slice, the heel end, dropped away from the loaf, releasing visible steam. Then the next inner slice buckled limply outward, its shape defined by the dark confining rim of the surrounding crust. The knife had freed moist heat and rich fragrance, and had laid open the smooth creamy inside of the loaf. The shining yellow butter melted instantly on our slices, pooling in the little holes, intensifying the darkness of the crust with its oily gleam, causing tender, flavorful crumbs to adhere to our lips and fingers. As we ate, we laughed.

Fever

Edward Bonetti

It was mid-September and Nat Seever's luck had been good, with seven stripers taken on bait and three on plug. They were adequate fish, this late in the season, averaging ten pounds, some slightly more. He knew after he had taken his second within minutes that he had found the feeding hole of a school holding close to the warmer water near shore. He would wait then until two hours before the next tide was full. If he got any strikes, or if he caught another, he would fish for two more hours after full tide, and then go to sleep. It would be a little over four hours of fishing, but it would be easy work for he would have a full moon with plenty of light, the wind was lessening, and the water offshore to the hole would be calm. The ground swells too had decreased since the night before and they would give little surf to work against when he made his casts.

Seever stood now above the beach in the dusklight looking seaward. He smiled, stroked his stubble of beard, and felt again the need to look at his fish. When he reached his camp in a grove of scrub oak and pine some fifty yards back from shore he fed three small logs to his fire, sat down cross-legged before it, and looked at the stripers lying on a sheet of tarpaulin spread alongside of his jeep. After forty hours out of water they were still in almost perfect condition: there was no odor, no visible decomposition. They were still perfect in form as if he had just pulled them from the sea. He watched the play of the firelight on their bodies. He studied the lateral lines of dark and light scales along the sides receding and converging into a taper, and the taper fanning out acutely into the winglike shape of the tails. They lay stiffly, side by side, a row of pointed heads juxtaposed each with its one eye open to the firelight, the pupils clouded milky with fluid, but the stare insistent and frozen as if from a bead of glass. The belly of the nearest one exposed to the light of the flame was crystal white and its composite pattern of interlocking scales glistened like slivers of bone. "Bone," Seever said, and he got up, not fully standing, his knees still bent, and moved within reaching distance of his fish. He drew his finger along the head of one and traced the outline of the eye, then carefully along the head to the jaw and along the lower lip to the partly opened mouth. He pulled down on the lip and inserted his finger deep into the mouth. Further back in the throat he could feel the tightness of the gullet narrowing and the cold residue of fluids. With his free hand he rubbed his stubble, smiled, and looked into the stare of the fish below his face, his finger moving in and out of the mouth now slowly. "Still moist," he said. "Even to the gullet. And no smell yet." He withdrew his finger, heard the quick snap of suction close the gullet, stood up, and walked out of the clearing to check once more on the weather.

He could see the moon now full to its rim lifting out of the horizon like a stone disk above the water. A few stars were visible to the north, but a cloud bank had risen and swept up darkly to the clouds that still held motionless on the horizon inland. "It might be overcast," he said, "but it'll make no difference to me." Yes, they were in there, and overcast or not they were his for the taking. He would fish until he got them all, fish until he fished the ocean clean; if necessary, until he collapsed. He had been bit since his first fifty-pounder taken four months earlier from a chartered launch out of Cuttyhunk. Then a week later, when he felt the need to fish again as he had felt the same need some years before to hunt black bear in Maine —felt it like a purge in his bones when he brought a female down with one shot through the base of her neck and then watched the huge mass of fur, muscle, and head rise like a statue under the limb of an oak tree; watched the labor of its movement and the thick head rearing still upward with its mouth open in the circle of his scope; yes, watched the movement as if in a trance and felt his pleasure begin in an instant that held him full with excitement and with laughter; and the sound of his laughter severe against the sound of splitting wood when she took the limb in her teeth groaning still upward in her last movement before he shot again, then again and again until his rifle was empty and brought her down, brought her seven hundred pounds crashing down with the limb still in her teeth—then a week later after Cuttyhunk and his first striper he knew he had been bit, and he fished alone now as he had hunted alone whenever he got the chance.

Seever was no amateur then after Cuttyhunk. He took a fifty-pounder out of the Cape Cod canal on a monofilament line of forty-five-pound test. He carried a picture of the bass balanced in his right hand held above his head; and his raw muscular arms, his small waist and bulging buttocks, his long thick legs, even his hands with their thick fingers, all indicated a strength that could have pressed three hundred pounds, or could have broken a man's back with ease, or with his fist, held like the head of a mallet at his side, could have shattered a jaw.

THE STRIPERS Seever caught on the next tide in the flood of moonlight he had wished for averaged over twenty pounds. He had worked further out over the hole and had pulled in four. Later in camp before going to sleep he loaded his spool with a line of thirty-five-pound test. He resolved that he would go even lower if the fish got bigger. He would go to the lowest limit of what line he had, which was twenty-pound test, and he planned to use it on his nine-foot rod. The decision to use the lighter tackle was not impulsive. It was made after he figured his chances against the increasing easterly wind and the heavier surf that had developed on the falling tide just before he quit. It had been made for the same reason as his decision earlier in the year before Cuttyhunk: when his excitement then for hunting had ceased he knew he lacked the purpose and need for making repeated easy kills. The lighter tackle now, he reasoned, would prove his new ability against the odds of the heavier fish.

The following night before the tide was full he caught his biggest fish on the thirty-five-pound test line. It read forty pounds exactly on his scale. He fought it for near to an hour and a half, standing waist-high in the surf. At times the seas broke against his chest, and the sand beneath his feet was carried away in the backwash, leaving him balanced on the heels of his boots as if he stood on a floating rail. But Seever had worked his fish carefully, playing its weight delicately through the feel of his rod and feeling the stretch of line to its mouth and to the barb of the hook holding in the mouth. He thought too of the hook as he worked up and down the beach in the driving surf, holding deep through the upper lip and protruding hard between the openings of its nose; thought he could see the eyes of the fish move like turrets of light in the murk of the water, and stare like beads of glass on the curve of steel it had swallowed. Yes, Seever had worked his fish carefully, lost his footing once and went under. But he held on, came up and regained his balance without having let go of the rod. He felt then the initial force of the fish's mass and anger, and he felt his own anger while he reeled in, bucked the seas with his big chest and shoulders, sending just enough delicate pain to the hook when the striper had turned and feigned back toward shore and headed out again tiredly for the last time against the drag of his reel. And as the fish tired, so Seever's anger diminished and his laughter came out of his soaking frame like the roar of a fire high and severe above the roar of the surf as if he had conquered a nightmare of devils. The next night he went to his thirty-pound test.

THE FISH SEEVER had caught after five nights of fishing amounted to sixty school bass, twelve twenty- to thirty-pounders and the forty-pounder. He had caught three large skate about three feet across, which he had pulled in only to remove the hook. He considered the skates useless, and the lack of excitement he experienced when he caught them, the time wasted in removing the hook which was taken deep into the gullets, was not worth the loss of bait. Neither did he have any luck with the lighter tackle in taking a striper bigger than his forty-pounder. All of this, the skates and his increasing dissatisfaction with small fish, had triggered his anger and at times cramped his ability to make his casts accurately over the line of surf to the hole.

The fish he had caught—except for the forty-pounder, which he had carried up above the high-water mark and had covered with wet seaweed—were left on the beach. The six that he had lived with in camp were thrown out into the clearing beyond the grove. Those he had left out in the open, torn at during the day by gulls and terns, were mutilated out of shape and shredded through to their entrails.

In his activity of fishing, keeping camp, and digging for bait while he waited for the tides, Seever was unconcerned with the carcasses lying along the beach, and by the end of the week the odor of rotting fish hung palpable in the air. But he worked the hole methodically on each tide. If he landed a striper over his forty-pounder he would go to the limit of his tackle, fish until he landed a bigger one, and then leave.

So Seever fished for two nights before he landed a striper that weighed forty-eight pounds. He had little difficulty with it and took it within an hour in a low rolling surf. After this he went to his light tackle. He caught school bass and a few more skates and several large cod and flounder which he threw up with the others. While he fished the daytime tides the beach behind him was alive with yelping gulls, terns, and sheldrakes that had landed to feed on their way south. Against this background of noise, and in the stench which carried now even to his campsite, Seever fished, and he waited.

IT WAS twelve-thirty in the morning. The half moon shone through an expanse of open sky and lit up a path across the water. In front of Seever, as if powdered with a fine covering of snow, the beach was visible in the light. Inland he could see the range of dunes like mounds of chalk, and the marshes spreading black to the inlet where he had dug more bait that afternoon. He stood fixed now above the beach, with his pole at his side and his gaff-hook hanging from his waist. His rubber waders, his boots, and his parka glinted in the moonlight. The vertical mass of his frame, with its thick head and face raised above his chest, was like a silhouette of wood, immobile and singular on the lay of the sloping beach and against the shifting expanse of water in front of him. With his pole held off the sand and the stench of the rotting fish laced heavily in the force of the breeze that swept about him, Seever moved down the grade of beach across some five feet of remaining flats and entered the water smiling. It was three hours before full tide. With a minimum of ground swells the surf was irregular, running no more than a foot high over the flats and tonguing smoothly up to the edge of sand that marked the beach behind him. Once in the water he made his first cast toward the hole, and after an hour's fishing, he landed three. From their size he figured they weighed at least twenty pounds. His anger increased and he considered them as useless as skate.

There was no warning. When the fish struck it struck totally, bending the rod down to its butt end. Seever leaned forward to release the tension. "The drag must have jammed," he yelled. "If the bastard's gone, I'll . . ." The drag had jammed, but he had it working in seconds. The line drew taut down through the eyes of the rod, with four feet or more of it spinning off from the spool of the reel, and he knew he still had him. He let the line pay out over his finger, and felt the heft of the butt end in his hands. From this he calculated the fish to weigh at least sixty pounds, maybe a little more. He cranked the reel then until the line took up against the drag. When he secured his footing he began the play.

Seever gave the fish no advantage, gave it no more tension of line than enough to give himself the feel of its position in the dark somewhere out beyond him. Once he thought of moving up on shore, playing the fish from there and then gaffing it while still in the backwash; but he resolved finally to work it first over the line of the breakers some fifty yards out and then move up to the beach when it started its final run seaward from the shallow water near shore.

After two hours had passed the fish was still in the water. Seever began to feel the stiffness in his arms, the cramping muscles of his legs, and the increasing inflexibility of his wrists each time he eased back on the rod. But he continued to work carefully, rhythmically, moving with the fish down-surf when it fought for more line, his head matted with soaked hair, his shoulders and chest laboring beneath his parka slicked smooth with water, and all of him, the head rearing high above his chest, the laboring shoulders, and the arms braced out straight from the shoulders to the gripped hands around the butt end of the rod, all of him down to his waist and to his buttocks that showed hard against the strain of his waders in the back-wash—all of him contiguous with the movement of water about him. And as he reeled in on each downstroke of the rod now he cursed aloud to the increasing wind and to the spray lifting like pellets of sleet out of the driving surf. But he knew it would not be long. The fish was tiring.

When a half hour more had passed he could see the striper lying half up on its side in the crests and wallowing closer to shore on each successive wave. Seever let it come then, reeling in slack until he saw it leap out of the water, arching from the end of the leader down, a curve of muscle and scales flashing once in the moonlight, then turning sea-ward in its leap. When it fell to the water Seever was laughing, and again his laugh was severe and high above the roar of the surf. "Bastard, I've got you," he yelled, and he moved up backwards out of the surf onto the shoreline. When the striper began its last run in the shallow water he was ready. He started to give it line, all the line its run would take, no tension, no heft or pull, no weight, all slack and freedom on its run seaward before he would take it back with one final pull on the rod.

When the drag jammed again Seever had only seconds to make his choice. Within the period of those seconds, and with the anger swelling in his chest, he followed up on his first choice: he let go of the rod, and in one movement was in the water with his arm around the striper's girth and his free fist like a sledge coming down upon its head. He wrestled it—shaking under him, bounc-ing like a coil spring snapped free from its mounts, slapping the sand with its tail, flanks, belly, and head, its eyes like chips of crystal in the moonlight flashing on the angle of its stare. And as Seever fought his fish in the shallows of the surf he felt its weight of sixty-five pounds or more in the wash of sand gravel and stone when the sea pulled back to leave it higher yet than the first shock of land against its flesh.

The first blow of his gaff-hook cracked deep into the striper's head. The second blow was halfway down when the wave came up. It rose hissing, broke, and then fell with a suddenness that held Seever immobile and useless under its weight. When it receded the fish was gone. The rod too with its tangled line was gone, and he stood in the wake of the wave's backwash exhausted, looking seaward. He felt the pain now in his right arm just below the elbow. When he saw the sleeve of his parka ripped opened he knew he had been cut. He knew with anger too it had been the horny, spikelike cartilage in the striper's dorsal fin that had cut him. In the moonlight he could see the slash and his blood pulsing out of it. He stared at it absently. "I should have killed him," he said. He gripped his arm and applied pressure, and without picking up his gaff-hook, he headed back to camp.

The next morning after packing his gear into the jeep, Seever returned to the shoreline and picked up his gaff-hook. Then he walked to the ridge of the beach where it sloped upward a few feet into a mound of compass grass, holly, and tangled briar. In one movement he swung up the bank and stood in the grass, his eyes narrowing and his jaw set hard above the lapel of his open jacket. The cut in his arm throbbed under its dressing, but it was not unbearable. He looked a long time over the spread of sand below him. He could see the forty-pounder uncovered now and rotting, and the torn carcasses of the other stripers putrefying. His eyes held a while on the cartilage that had turned yellow in the open sides of their heads. Seever smiled. The odor of dead flesh hung like a shroud above the beach. Along the high-water mark he could see mounds of seaweed and the bones of the flounder and cod, the kelp and the weed mixed with sand, more mutilated fish and black casings of skate eggs. Overhead a few remaining gulls hawked intermittently, soared and dipped in the sunlight. He looked up at the gulls. After a while, as if he had forgotten something, he faced the beach once more and smiled again. "I slipped," he said. "That's all." Then he turned away and with his gaff-hook and chain swinging from his fist, he walked through the briar, through the grass, back to the grove of scrub oak and pine, to his jeep.

Atlantis on $5.00 a Day

John Haag

For Clarity

Prologue: THE MEDIUM OF EXCHANGE

Atlantis never sank. She slipped her moorings and floated off on a trip of her own. After she had been everywhere at least once or longer, she tried the Moon, and almost settled there. But the Moon sank to the bottom of the sea—a landscape draped with festivals, wearing most of its jewels and finest costumes—leaving only its indecisive ghost afloat in the night sky.

Atlantis might have stayed—did stay long enough that hearsay sunk her too—but grew tired of sea creatures nesting in her hair, and returned to teach the Egyptians how to make glass and think in pyramids.

One summer she spent a century in Greece, staying only in the best temples; then, with ten thousand amphorae in her reticule and all her old lovers folded like shadows, she began her leisurely tour of the Western capitals. But always she moved on before an atrophy of salons could carve her in ivory.

And while they changed magic into money, she moved sunward to another ocean—to a city of sugar hills and spun bridges. When it, too, hardened, she moved with the current to another, younger city of hills and water, and she lies beneath it now.

Here she lives in the mouth of the rain, like a Pacific calm of constant motion flowing for every lover in tides of color, coming like nectar in the seven senses, filling our mouths and fingers till we too flow like bells.

If you do not know her, you cannot stay for any price, but her lovers live freely in her thighs, unable to tell giving from receiving, time from motion, sound from the chromatic air. The flow opens to all who escape the vaults, who bank only in the blood and body, who know neither profit nor loss—only increase—who cannot give because they have given all, and therefore have all and can no longer tell where they leave off and their lovers begin, whose nerves extend through spaces the closed mind cannot travel.

Here they gather, the genes of genesis, while all of the places that tried to inter her among their inventories wither into the hard edges of institutions.

The $5.00 is for the needy, who build institutions instead of living them.

Chapter I: DUCK STAMPS

WHEN I LIVED HERE before, I remember, some of us knew of her, believed in her, though only a couple could truly claim to have felt her touch—those troutfeather fingers, her tongue inside their skulls. We did so many things we didn't understand then—not knowing it was preparation.

Sweeney put a tree trunk in the middle of his houseboat, then tore out all the walls but one. John Pym spent a lot of time down at the docks because he felt someone should watch the sea, and the ferryboats came and went like the days of the week, paying no attention to him. Cliff tried to learn to play the guitar, even though—or maybe because—he wasn't a very good poet, and couldn't drink. Clark took a plaster casting of some petroglyphs, and Irene spent a lot of time reading on buses, tearing the pages out of the book as she finished them so she would never lose her place. Lubin painted, but only when he couldn't help it.

Jack the Bear used to sabotage billboards, and did a lot of good until he started using dynamite and got caught and sent to a rest home even though he told them he wasn't tired and no one but the public defender thought he was more than average insane. Rusty quit paying her psychiatrist and Robin tried to make booze out of potatoes, most of which we used to clean our paintbrushes. Hannah went AWOL from the Salvation Army and began dipping candles. Walt the Fisherman painted his mailbox a different color every week, but they kept bringing him mail anyhow.

I could go on, but they were all things that seemed irrelevant, like postage stamps on a duck, until you realized they were the things people do while waiting when they're not sure what they're waiting for. But we all kept making things, and Jim had a theory about why we all used to go to the Blue Moon, and I see now that he was right.

Chapter II: GOING

JUST A LITTLE while ago someone referred to that time as the good-ol'-days. I could see that they were good, and that they were old—and they were definitely days—but I couldn't see any reason to run the words all together that way. They were more like something nice made out of pewter, or like the time a friend you thought wasn't going to make it, did.

But it was about then that some unaccountable things began to happen—things we knew weren't good, but not why. But then "why" seldom has enough color or form to be seen anyhow. We couldn't believe it when they tore down Sun Love the Two Moon Hand Laundry—as though traffic were more important than clothing scented with love of sun and moons.

I was living by the lake then, in a shack set on stilts because one corner leaned against the hill and the rest hung out over a large hole. One night Dewey King got drunk and said: Let's all get drunk an' be somebody. Then he fell off my porch into the hole. And Ed Giddings tried to tear out Sweeney's tree trunk. They fought till they knocked each other in the lake and Ed sobered up. Now this wouldn't be so strange except that both Ed and Dewey were architects who weren't building anything.

That was the winter it rained a lot and the big rock slid down the hill and into my shack.

Also about then the bills began to arrive: three thousand pounds of yams they said I shipped to Biloxi; five tons of barbwire and miles of black cotton armbands; hundreds of dollars of postage due—things I didn't remember anything about, except for Jack the Bear's dynamite, which I knew I hadn't ordered. I hadn't understood the transactions, or just how I was involved, but the obligations seemed urgent.

Besides, my woman wasn't well—she worried a lot and the rock had upset her and she was afraid of many things here for some reason she couldn't explain. Sometimes she'd stay in bed three days at a time and couldn't touch anything—but worse, she was afraid to be touched. She didn't seem to like the sea, so I thought it might be a good idea to move inland.

So I took a job in a mill back East—well, not a mill exactly, more of an enormous press where they squeeze the juice out of all sorts of buds. When I took the job I thought they made something out of the juice—they said they did—and it took me a while to understand that they really considered it a waste product. I stayed on anyway, for I thought someone should let the flattened buds know that they could still become flowers. But hardly any of them thought that that would be a good idea.

Of course nobody can flow without juice, but I hadn't realized how hard it is to get started again once you've been flattened. I used a lot of my own, trying to get some of them started again. It didn't work very well.

Chapter III: LEAVING

BY THE TIME I had begun to realize this, my woman had figured out a way not to let anyone touch her. She had been talking to a shrinker, who had taught her to seal up whatever juice she had because that was what made her hurt when touched. I guess he didn't know that when you let it flow the pain of touch turns to joy. Anyhow she shriveled up and left. (I had a letter from her not long ago, telling me how fine it was to be dry and safe and able to bump other dry ones without injury. She said I'd be better off if I'd shrivel up too.)

But I want to tell you about the flower that came back. I'm not sure what kind of a flower she is because she's the only one of her kind I've ever seen—fragile, but strong, and more beautiful than . . . well, I don't know how to explain, because you have to see inside her to appreciate her. She'd been through the bud-press where I worked, and I guess she'd been bruised badly, but she had managed to give up very little of her juices. She said I'd helped somehow, and if I did I guess the job wasn't a total waste.

But the important thing here is that she helped me to see that the yams and the postage and some of the other strange things had been bad debts and that I didn't have to pay them—at least not with juice. I had already known that working at the mill was bad for me and that I should leave, but she helped me to see how, and she helped me to learn to flow again, for I'd been getting kind of shut up because people around the mill were really afraid of juice, even though they said it was important, so I'd been getting confused. That, and other things.

Actually I didn't get the flow going very well until after she left—and that's the part that's hard to tell about. I'm not sure just how, but it has something to do with Atlantis, so I have to mention it. Anyhow it had been getting harder for her to flow when she was with me, and she had to leave me. I don't think it should have been that way, but I guess it had to be. To tell the truth, I think she's related to Atlantis—even an incarnation. Maybe. I haven't figured that out yet. I don't think she has either.

Anyhow I told them at the mill that I thought I'd better leave, and I came out here because I used to flow pretty well here. I had no idea Atlantis was living here now, but she certainly seemed to have known that I was coming again.

Chapter IV: COMING

I WASN'T GOING to use that for a chapter title, but it seems right—it's so beautiful a word because all of its meanings are good—always approaching, getting closer, arriving. I can feel a poem coming sometimes, all the ways the word means, for making a poem and making love are the same thing to me, or come from the same place when they're both coming right. When making something flows, it's like a constant coming. We were like that sometimes—like a dream I had later.

Sometimes writing in this book is like that—like the most beautiful dream I ever had. I was so deeply inside her in every way, and yet she seemed to be reaching in through me—as though our souls were coming inside each other at the same time. But I hate to say soul, because I don't know what one is—maybe it's just a way of feeling. I think it's like Blake says:

> Man has no Body distinct from his Soul; for that
> call'd Body is a portion of Soul discern'd by the
> five Senses, the chief inlets of Soul in this age.

—and right after that he says: "Energy is the only life, and is from the Body . . . Energy is Eternal Delight." He's right.

But then everything good is hard to name—like that sweet bird between her thighs. Whoever invented those names for it must have hated it, because they're all harsh and ugly. They don't make sense. We were talking about it once, trying to think of the right name for it. I even wrote a kind of poem . . .

> Name it?—of course we must—
> that velvet vault, that reliquary,
> oh that pretty pocket, furled with fur
> for welcome, full of pride well come,
> oh come, we'll call it Paradisio—
> yes, death and resurrection daily
> as the tall cock calls
> the ends of the world
> together . . .

As you can see, I couldn't find a name half as beautiful as what I wanted to name.

She's like that—very hard to name. Right now she's away trying to name herself—that may be the main reason she can't be with me now, because she thinks that if I help her find her name—even if I don't do or say anything—it won't be her true name, but partly mine, and she'll never find her true name. I think that's why she began having trouble flowing—she was afraid that if we came together too much her name would get confused with mine and she'd lose it—but I don't think that's right. I think that the way you come is who you are, and a lover you truly flow with is part of you, but there's a source where your name begins that stays constant—and that's where you come from, and the more you come the stronger it gets, and the more you flow with each other, the more your names become like each other's, but that's not because where you come from changes, but because your name grows bigger. I think that if you try to come by yourself all the time your name dries up and gets very short. Maybe that's what the sin of Onan is all about. I think people should have very long names. I think your name is how you come.

Chapter V: BACK

I wasn't going to tell you just about coming, but about coming back—what I've been doing—which can be very hard when you don't know how you went away. I was trying to come back when she came to me. Maybe she became afraid with me because she could feel that sometimes I wasn't flowing right. I wasn't.

But with the bad debts and working in the mill and watching my woman shrivel up—I don't think she realized how confusing it is when you've been gone so long and forgotten so much and don't even know which way you went. And then neither of us knew our names well enough.

When she had to leave me, I still wasn't back, but I was sure she was part of my name, and I was afraid I'd never find it at all without her. I know now that that isn't exactly true, but there is a part of it I can never find unless we're together again. But actually it takes all of your life to find your name, and you never find it all because as long as you keep looking it keeps growing longer. So sometimes I don't think it's a matter of finding an exact name, but of making your name grow as long as it can, and you have to come a lot to do that, so you have to be with someone. If she was with me now, our names would get longer every day.

After she left, I could hardly flow at all—I was clogged up till I was afraid I couldn't keep what little name I had. It seemed like all my life was going to turn out like letters to nobody—I even wrote this miserable little poem about it . . .

> Not even my name
> on the envelope
> which I opened
> to find another
> envelope, inside
> of which another and
> another inside it—
> and so for forty-two
> enigmatic envelopes
> and soon my forty-third
> birthday will arrive
> without an address.

Oh, I know why it's bad, but when you're down like that you can lose your sense of proportion—and writing it didn't feel at all like flowing. More like stopping.

Then a friend said something to me that was so right that I realized—just like that—how I'd been clogging *myself* up, and I started cleaning out the fountain and getting it to flow again. What she said was only two words, but it meant: Look, you're so busy telling people your name that it sounds like an alias. And she was right, and I could see that when the juice had begun to get low my name had begun to get shorter, and I'd started saying it over and over, as though I was afraid I might forget it. But just saying your name is no good—you have to live it and flow it and let it come or it isn't any better than one of those little boards people put on their desks like a label.

Anyhow, I began to flow pretty well again, and soon my name was as long as it had been before. And I left the mill and came back here because this seemed a good place to make it longer. And that's when I found out Atlantis was here, flowing and making it the loveliest place in the world to come.

Chapter VI: HOME

I DIDN'T MENTION the trip to anyone but Al, and I'm sure he didn't tell anyone, but Atlantis has her own ways of knowing. I'd been down in Sugartown, where she was living the last I'd heard, but I couldn't seem to find her there, so I flew up here, for I've always felt more at home here than anywhere else—which means quite a bit when you've never been any place that seemed like home.

I'd just hit the street when Randy and NM pulled up at the light, looked over at me and hollered, did I want a ride? They'd never seen me before, but people who know Atlantis are like that. They took me to this mansion that sits on the top of Queen's Hill like good news in her crown and we went in and met the whole pack of Tarot cards. Every one of them seemed to have felt Atlantis' touch one way or another, and they were all beautiful—beautiful but, well, sort of random. She takes all kinds of lovers. I decided to find her my own way.

Later Randy and NM were driving me out to the District along Lake Street, which passes just above where my shack used to be. I said I used to live down there, and NM said she did now. I asked if she knew my old neighbor, Walt the Fisherman. Yes . . . So we stopped to see him. He'd just built a house next door to his shack, which is next door to where my shack used to be, and he was about to move in, so he gave me his shack as long as I was in town. That's the way her lovers are.

The next day Robin dropped by with Jo and lots of welcome. Maybe half an hour later he pointed out the window and said why didn't I use that car over there. I asked him whose it was, and he said not to ask questions, just drive it. I still don't know who owns it, but it more or less runs. Maybe Atlantis owns it. In a way, I'm sure she does.

So I knew she was here—could feel her everywhere. Everything was open and easy, all my old friends seemed to know I was back and kept dropping in—coming, giving, receiving—no need to fill in whachabindoin', as though I'd never left. NM decided to adopt me and kept bringing people by. I think she'd forgotten my name—but my name was everything I did.

And still I seemed to have time to make things. I don't know if Atlantis saw to that, or made me see to it. I just know that like the mother of fine wine she's carried me through arbors of people open to the rain or sun, whichever comes down—the fenceless faces that enter my open door. Everything said Home, said Flow—and I'd truly be at home, except that she who keeps her own part of my name is not here. If we can come together again—well, either way . . . The thing for me to do is stay here with Atlantis and work on the fountain.

Chapter VII: TELEGRAM

ATLANTIS is alive and will in Seacity.

Chapter VIII: SKYROCK

BUT LET ME TELL YOU how they knew she was here. Not her full-time lovers—they'd known all along. I mean the rest, all who cared or paid any attention.

Last summer more than five thousand people came to hear Country Joe try the first piano-drop in a cow pasture maybe twenty or more miles from town. Everyone said, Do it again. So the Sky River Rock Festival and Lighter than Air Fair—a benefit for the red and black defense funds—accumulated on a hilltop halfway up in the mountains, at least fifty miles out. It started as a three-day happiness, but they say there's music up there yet.

More than forty of the heaviest names in rock music drew a city-sized crowd of paid admissions, and who could guess how many more through the woods. It started fine and kept improving, and nobody left. They stayed on in thousands of wildly improvised campsites. Dealers couldn't sell anything because everyone was giving it away, but the real high was on open and each other and flowing.

It rained the second night—poured for hours—but hardly anyone worried. They all got soaked, then began discovering it was good, though they'd never thought of it that way before. And then mud, and they loved that too—out there, away from all the plastic necessities, with no resources but each other, they dug whatever came down.

The next day mud-happy hundreds descended on the laundromat in the nearest small town, took off all their clothes and threw them in the machines, waiting bare and beautiful for them to come clean. The town's nose turned blue about this for an hour or so, but cleanliness being a virtue and everyone so lovely, it soon seemed natural, and maybe even the will of God.

The third night, about dusk, whoever was on the sound system asked everyone to light a candle or make a small flame, and as thousands of small, personal flames came on across the field and hillside, everywhere—so many that no one would have thought to count them—he said he'd heard some cat blowing a flute up in the woods today, and would he play it now? Waiting, each person shared his flame, until into the silence, the flute began. No one seems to know if he played for minutes or hours—they only remember a timeless coming, a communion, a flowing together.

And that is how they knew she was among them.

Chapter IX: DARKNESS

I GUESS I make it sound like it's all joy, but anyone who knows Atlantis won't be fooled by that. I wasn't trying to kid anybody—it's just that being back, living in this flow and openness, feels so fine. But as with all women who are beautiful inside and out, you have to live up to them. Atlantis opens to many, just because they're trying, but if you're really doing more than trying, if you want it all and know what it's worth, she isn't satisfied until you've given her everything, and then a little bit more. I think that when you have to go out and find that little bit more for her is when you really begin to learn about love. And she does some strange things to make you do it.

Let me tell you about the darkness around my shack. It's

not like any darkness I've ever experienced before—though I know a couple of people I'll bet have seen it. I was a little slow to notice it, for it was raining the first night I stayed here—the streetlight is weak and quite a ways off and the wet earth seemed to soak it up. It just felt odd though, and I couldn't tell why at first, until I noticed that the sound of the rain on the low roof was making it darker. That sounds funny, I know, but it was true.

And the light doesn't go out from the house. Oh, if you're in the street you can see that the lights are on inside, but they don't cast any light on the ground outside—none at all. But the lights inside aren't very strong anyhow, so I didn't notice this until the second night when Dave and Dounnia were coming over and I opened the door to throw some light on the back porch so they could see. But none went out—it stopped right at the doorsill. It didn't seem to bother them, but after they left I checked outside. The same with the windows—you can see the light in them, but none comes out on the ground. The dark itself has, to me anyhow, a tangible quality, and I admit it's frightening —but I think I know what it is.

I haven't been cold since I've been here. The weather's a little chilly, but that's not what I mean. Before, when I'd go down inside after some of the things I wanted to work into a big new poem I'm trying to make, and I couldn't tear them loose down there and I'd have to come back empty-handed because that part of me wasn't ready to come, I'd get so goddamned outer-space cold I didn't think I'd be able to move. It's a kind of terror, I guess. But I haven't really gone after these things since I've been here—I've been into so many other things and flowing easy and making things as they came.

I think she's just reminding me that I'm not going to get off that easy. There's a terror in that darkness, but I've been there before and I know it, and I know I can go on through it. It's only when you try to stay inside, to avoid it, that it closes in on you and takes you apart—a slow death, and inevitable. No, I know what she's telling me, and I'm going to go out into it, because I'll find what I'm after there—that little bit more. She'll know.

Chapter X: DEATH MASK

OUT OF POEMS and pieces and visceral maps and scraps and some barnacle cement I've constructed a manuscript that hopes to prove stones don't float, but I wonder about it now, for most of it looks like a death mask of past energies—the forms they took and could not break. A name on a board.

How can a death mask come alive? Should I let it try, because it's of a son who knew his own father—or a father who wanted to become the son I hope to be? I'm not sure. Though he begot me, and I am younger, I feel like *his* father, as the Gypsy Moth must feel toward its chrysalis.

It is strange to spring from your own brow, breaking the skull that bore you because it was time to break it. Now my fatherson who bore me lies rigid in such a sarcophagus, taking with him a few snapshots of the son who may yet give him birth, and who still values the mask of his younger father—the death mask his own fetus wore.

Chapter XI: HISTORICAL GEOLOGY

By Cretaceous times the evolution of most of the invertebrate tribes had been practically accomplished, and nothing but details were left for the Cenozoic Era. Only the Amonites and Belemnites gave the medieval aspect. Many species forsook their symmetrical plan of coiling, and developed bizarre shapes; some became spiral, like a snail's shell, a few straightened, many became loosely coiled, and a few lost all semblance of regularity, or symmetry. The significance of this extraordinary development in a decadent race is not fully understood. In any event, not a single species lived past the end of the Cretaceous.

—from *Historical Geology*
by Carl O. Dunbar

Chapter XII: THE MARKET

ONCE YOU'VE BEEN there you can start from anywhere and you are back in the Pike Street Market. But the first time, turn toward the seagull and descend into those ramshackle layers of boards and girders, timbers torn from the Ark, primeval iron—all angling over the waterfront, down the hill from skidroad to the sea along the lost lease between Pike Street and perdition, the land Howard Johnson forgot, a wilderness no credit card could cross.

Start at Gabriela's Special Fresh Fruit Bread Sweets, where Stewart drops into Pike Place, and turn down the street of vegetables with old ladies in aprons barking artichokes, old men with walrus eyes and big rubber boots stuffed with rutabagas, hand-truck hustlers in sheepskin coats—why isn't this a railway station?—are the tomatoes on time?—blocks of insatiable bins and cornucopian tables —where will we find enough people to eat all this?— carrels and cubbyholes, booths and barrels, Rabelaisian ruins where sausages tumble through the blind skylights, and the cheeses, *ai*—Feta, Fontina, Kasseri, Liederkranz, Gouda, Tilsit, Nokkelost, Samsoe, Gjetost, Metost, Primost, and cheeses yet unnamed radiate mouthbending messages from scrubbed cutting blocks.

Once an out-of-work scissors-grinder fell into a vat of Greek olives, and when the stevedores hauled him out he was a 5'9" pickled mackerel and never ate another olive as long as he swam the taverns at the other end of town.

Beyond, above, below—caverns and arcades, ramps and passages, and doors that might have anything behind them —genies in bottles, bottles in wicker, wicker in shapes like birds or dinosaurs, dinosaurs in clay, clay turned into bottles containing genies that look like girls selling psychedelphian baubles, dusty men in rimless eyes behind bookstalls full of Upton Sinclair, Jack London, Victorian essayists, classical historians, and esoterica like *Steamboating on the Yukon,* or three thousand pages of instructions on how to coddle a ginch; another bookstall whose windows look down on the roofs of the long wharves, shining like wet lead, and on the water, where you can watch the history of marine transportation passing on its way to China, Cape Horn, or the Battle of Waterloo.

Beyond the barber college, Sanitary Super Grocery, Pure Food Market, Liberty Malt Store Home Brew, Athenian Lunch, Fox Court, Qraz Gallery, Mug's Mish-Mash, Mr.

Myklebust's Old Time Shop—yes, and Flower Street, all tucked and folded among such places where prim ladies in glasses on spidergold chains sell the strictest laces and cloche hats full of nostalgia.

Or, behind a door you can't always find, off a ramp that often leads somewhere else, a unicorn in disguise sells no thing but things. What's that? Never saw anything like it. Well how should I hold it?—like a feather?—like a stone? Like a child. Is it beautiful? I think so—can't really tell. It may be something beyond beautiful that no one ever knew how to name. It touches me—but what is it? I don't know. But it makes me glad it is.

EPILOGUE

They're going to tear down the Pike Street Market—ancient, unsanitary . . . I try to understand this. She could stop them, but I don't think she will. I guess everything's expendable—maybe just the motion counts, the joy and terror, the flow of love, the coming . . .

The World as Brueghel Imagined It

Howard Nemerov

THE WORLD as Brueghel imagined it is riddled with the
  word:
Whatever's proverbial becomes pictorial; if people habitu-
  ally
Go crawling up a rich man's ass, they must be seen to do so
(through an orifice widened for the passage of three
  abreast;
The rich man, scattering coins from a sack, pays them no
  heed).
If people are in the habit of turning into toads without
  notice
They must be seen to do so; if the owl is said to carry
Nestlings and nest upon her back, she must be seen to
  do so.

The world as Brueghel imagined it is hardly easier to read
Than is the one we glibly refer to as The Real World:
The proverbs get forgotten, or their meaning leaches out,
And in the unmoving frame all motions are arrested
In an artful eternity—the hay runs after the horse
Forever—so that we can't always tell coming from going,
Or literal good from allegorical bad, or arsey-versey:
The Cross may be headed for Hell, the pruning-hook for
  Heaven.

But it remains, the world as Brueghel imagined it,
A plenum of meaning though we know not what the mean-
  ings are
In every place; and after having once experienced
The innocent and deep delight of understanding one
Or another emblem, acknowledging his just equation
Wedding the picture to the word, we take his word

In many matters wherein we have no further warrant
Than that his drawings draw enciphered thoughts from
    things.

So if the Ship of Fools is propped up on a pair of barrels,
Or if a man is shitting on the Beauty Shoppe's roof,
Or if Saint Anthony is somehow tempted (but to what?)
By a helmeted human jug with dagger and diarrhea,
So that he has to turn away his halo and his head,
We get the picture, as we say, although we miss
The shrewd allusion to some ancient smart remark
That would have told us what we know and never say.

The world as Brueghel imagined it is full of decaying fish
With people in their hulls, it is centered on allegorical
    dames
With funny hats, who queen it over the seven deadly sins
And as many deadly virtues—the millinery architecture of
    Pride,
And silly Hope standing on water—: it is the world we
    know
And fail to know that he has seen for us and minded too,
Where from Cockaigne it's but three steps to Heaven or
    Hell—
Hallucinating, yes, but only what is truly here.

(*Continued from page 10.*)

story of a love affair from the 40's becomes a meditation on desire and art. Frederick Tremallo's "Seven Sketches" are less story or essay than anecdotes of consciousness. Milton Klonsky's "Down in the Village" is a kind of culmination of free-style sensibility: an encounter with a panhandler on Eighth Street that circles back through various frames of reference—personal, social, philosophical, historical—before its import is dramatically revealed.

I won't comment specifically on the poetry in *NAR 13*, much less incorporate it into these ruminations. It bulks larger and, I think, more variously in this issue than it has in any previous one, and perhaps the next time around, Richard Howard will say something about the reasons for that.

TS

CORRECTION:

The following correspondence was received from A. Alvarez concerning his essay, "Sylvia Plath: A Memoir":

I originally wrote [*NAR 12*, p. 17]: "Driving on her own, Sylvia had had an accident, hurting herself and smashing up their old Morris station wagon." I later discovered that this was not quite accurate, so I changed the last part of the sentence: "apparently, she had blacked out and run off the road on to an old airfield, though mercifully without damaging herself or their old Morris station wagon."

Since the publication of the memoir, Sylvia's sister-in-law, Miss Olwyn Hughes, has pointed out a couple of minor inaccuracies. Apparently, Sylvia herself was wrong when she told me that the hillock in their garden was a burial mound; it was, in fact, an ancient fort. Miss Hughes also thinks that the "wall of old corpses" refers not to this but to the wall between the Hughes' garden and the adjoining cemetery, in which old graves were embedded. I myself can't vouch for the accuracy of either of these suggestions but I think it best to put them on record, if only to save some future doctoral researcher a journey to Devon and a footnote.

Contributors

A. R. Ammons teaches English at Cornell; his most recent collection of poems, *Briefings,* was issued by Norton last year.

James Applewhite is co-editor of *The Brown Bag* and on the editorial board of *The Greensboro Review.* He is visiting poet at Duke this year.

Gail Arkley's "Staff of Life" is her first published story. She's at work on a novel in the comparative peace and quiet of Eugene, Oregon.

Roland Barthes, the French critic, is the author of *Elements of Semiology.* "Authors and Writers" will appear in *Critical Essays,* a collection of Barthes' writings, which Northwestern University Press will issue this spring.

Michael Berryhill taught creative writing at the University of Minnesota and is now living in Hollywood. He has previously published poems in *Athanor* and *Black Flag,* a Minneapolis poetry chapbook for The Resistance.

Edward Bonetti has been a radio repairman, longshoreman, social worker, fisherman, and actor. When not writing, he "slakes off dread by rebuilding and repairing automobile engines."

Jorge Luis Borges received the 5th Biennial Jerusalem Prize for the Rights of Man last year. His most recent books include *The Aleph and Other Stories* and *The*

Book of Imaginary Beings; Dutton will publish *Doctor Brodie's Report* this month.

Robert Chatain's poems and stories have appeared in *New American Review* (7, 11), *Poetry, Bennington Review,* and *Extensions.* He has just completed a novel on Vietnam.

Alan Feldman teaches English at SUNY at Buffalo. He hasn't been to Rome since 1952 but has traveled a lot elsewhere.

Gabriel García Márquez is the author of the widely acclaimed novel *One Hundred Years of Solitude.* "A Very Old Man With Enormous Wings" will be included in a new collection of stories by García Márquez, *Leaf Storm and Other Stories,* to be published by Harper & Row early this spring.

John Haag, a former member of the Seafarers' International Union, teaches English at Penn State. His poems have appeared in various magazines.

Marilyn Hacker is co-editor of *Quark,* a quarterly review of speculative fiction. Her poems have appeared in *NAR 11* and other periodicals.

Mark Halliday is a recent graduate of Brown. He has published poems in several small magazines and is now editing an anthology of student poetry at Brown.

Richard Hugo's collections of poems include *A Run of Jacks, Death of the Kapowsin Tavern,* and *Good Luck in Cracked Italian.*

William Keens attends the University of North Carolina at Greensboro and has published in *The Greensboro Review.*

Milton Klonsky, a longtime resident of Greenwich Village, contributed "Mc²Luhan's Message" to *NAR 2.*

Thomas Lux, editor of The Barn Dream Press, is the

author of *Memory's Handgrenade,* to be published by Pym-Randall Press next month.

Leonard S. Marcus, a senior at Yale, won the 1970–71 Academy of American Poets Prize at Yale.

James McCourt's "Mawrdew Czgowchwz" is his first published story. He attended Manhattan College, NYU, Yale School of Drama, and the old Met.

Michael McMahon's poems have appeared in *Plaintiff, The Fiddlehead, Yes,* and other magazines. He teaches English at Colby Junior College.

Sandra McPherson's *Elegies for the Hot Season* was published by Indiana University Press last year.

Leonard Michaels previously appeared in *NAR* with "Crossbones" (*NAR 3*) and "Getting Lucky" (*NAR 10*). *Going Places* (Farrar, Straus & Giroux) was nominated for a National Book Award.

Sara S. Mitter lives and writes in Washington, D.C. This is her first published poem.

Robert Morgan has contributed poems to *The Nation, Sumac, Choice,* and other magazines. *Zirconia Poems,* a collection, was issued by Lillabulero Press in 1969.

Howard Nemerov's books include *The Blue Swallows, Stories, Fables & Other Diversions,* and *The Next Room of the Dream.* He is on the faculty of Washington University in St. Louis.

James Nolan was born and raised in New Orleans and has lived in Florida, New York, and San Francisco. His poems have appeared in *Florida Quarterly* and several other magazines.

Joyce Carol Oates's latest book, *Wonderland,* was recently published by Vanguard. *them* received the National Book Award for Fiction for 1970.

Grace Paley is the author of *The Little Disturbances of Man.* "Faith: In a Tree" appeared in *NAR 1.*

Donald Pearce teaches English at the University of California, Santa Barbara. He is working on a book, *Art and History.*

John Peck taught English at Princeton and has published poetry in *Hudson Review, Southern Review, Salmagundi,* and other magazines.

James Richardson is a doctoral candidate in English at Indiana. These are his first published poems.

Edward Rivera was born in Puerto Rico and now lives in New York. "Antecedentes" is part of a longer work in progress.

Richard A. Selzer, a general surgeon practicing in New Haven, began writing stories a few years ago. He is at present completing a novel.

Gilbert Sorrentino is the author of several books of poems, most recently *Corrosive Sublimate.* A novel, *Imaginative Qualities of Actual Things,* came out last year.

Terry Stokes's last collection of poems, *Natural Disasters,* was recently issued by NYU Press. He has published poems in *The Nation, Esquire, Sumac,* and elsewhere.

Dabney Stuart teaches English at Washington and Lee University and is poetry editor of *Shenandoah. The Diving Bell* (1966) and *A Particular Place* (1969), two volumes of poetry, were published by Knopf.

F. G. Tremallo is associate dean of Phillips-Exeter Academy, where he teaches creative writing and filmmaking.

Mona Van Duyn received the National Book Award for Poetry (1971) for *To See, To Take* (Atheneum).

Tom Wayman lives and writes in Vancouver. His poems have appeared in *Poetry Northwest, Atlantic, El*

Corno Emplumado, as well as in several Canadian anthologies.

C. K. *Williams'* first volume of poems, *Lies,* was put out by Houghton Mifflin; a second collection, *I Am the Bitter Name,* will be issued next month.

Complete Your Set of NAR

ISSUES 1–11 are going out of print. We have a limited supply available at $.75 each.

☐ NAR #1 William H. Gass *In the Heart of the Heart of the Country,* Philip Roth *The Jewish Blues,* William Mathes *Swan Feast,* Stanley Kauffmann *Drama on The Times,* Benjamin DeMott *"But He's a Homo-Sexual . . . ,"* Grace Paley *Faith: In a Tree* . . .

☐ NAR #2 Alan Friedman *Willy-Nilly,* John Barth *Autobiography,* Nat Hentoff *Reflections on Black Power,* Arlene Heyman *Strains of Iris,* Günter Grass *Four Poems* . . .

☐ NAR #3 George Dennison *The First Street School,* Donald Barthelme *Robert Kennedy Saved from Drowning,* Paul West *A Passion to Learn,* Philip Roth *Civilization and Its Discontents,* Albert Goldman *The Emergence of Rock* . . .

☐ NAR #4 Robert Coover *The Cat in the Hat for President,* C. C. O'Brien *Politics as Drama as Politics,* Mordecai Richler *A Sense of the Ridiculous,* Alan Lelchuk *Of Our Time,* Richard Gilman, *The True and Only Crisis of the Theatre* . . .

☐ NAR #5 Pat Watters *"Keep on A-Walkin', Children,"* Wilfrid Sheed *Eugene McCarthy,* Eric Bentley *The Unliberated University,* Jay Neugeboren *Reflections at Thirty,* Jules Siegel *The Man Who Believed in Christmas Trees* . . .

☐ NAR #6 Jane Jacobs *Why Cities Stagnate,* Ellen Willis *Lessons of Chicago,* Robert Stone *Porque No Tiene* . . . , William H. Gass *We Have Not Lived the Right Life,* Eric Salzman *The Revolution in Music* . . .

☐ NAR #7 Kate Millett *Sexual Politics*, Rosalyn Drexler *Like . . .* , Michael Herr *Illumination Rounds*, L. Woiwode *Don't You Wish You Were Dead . . .*

☐ NAR #8 John H. Schaar *Reflections on Authority*, George Dennison *On Being a Son*, Eric Bentley *Theater and Therapy*, Theodore Solotaroff *Silence, Exile, and Cunning*, Ernest Callenbach *The Death of the Movie Aesthetic . . .*

☐ NAR #9 Alfred Chester *The Foot*, Theodore Roszak *The Artificial Environment*, Samuel R. Delany *The Unicorn Tapestry*, Richard Gilman *Jerzy Grotowski*, *Symposium: The Writer's Situation I . . .*

☐ NAR #10 Philip Roth *On the Air*, William H. Gass *In Terms of the Toenail: Fiction and the Figures of Life*, Arno Karlen *The Guardian*, Jules Siegel *Family Secrets*, *Symposium: The Writer's Situation II . . .*

☐ NAR #11 M. F. Beal *Gold*, Paul West *The Season of the Single Women*, Michael Rossman *The Day We Named Our Child*, Robert Coover *The Last Quixote*, Nicholas von Hoffman *Nixon*, Norman Martien *Getting Out of Schools*, *Symposium: The Writer's Situation III . . .*

New American Review

Subscription Dept., Simon & Schuster, Inc.

1 West 39th Street, New York, N.Y. 10018

Please send me the copies of *New American Review* checked above.

Enclosed is my check for $_____$, calculated at $.75 per copy.

Name _____

Address _____

City _____ State _____ Zip Code _____

Please allow at least three weeks for delivery.

Foreign orders: add $.50 per copy for postage.